FAST BREAK FOOTBALL

Adapting the Florida State Offense to High School Football

Wayne Wilkes

ISBN: 1-58518-321-0
Library of Congress Catalog Card Number: 00-108337
Book layout: Paul Lewis
Cover design: Rebecca Gold
Diagrams: Jennifer Bokelmann
Front cover photo: Courtesy of the Florida State Archives
Back cover photo: Ron Harris, Daily Mountain Eagle

Coaches Choice
P.O. Box 1828
Monterey, CA 93942
www.coacheschoice.com

DEDICATION

This book is dedicated to my family. To my wife, Gena, who has tolerated so many years of both college football and coaching, yet has always supported my decisions about my career. To my three children, Cory, Blake, and Haley, who live the life of coach's children having moved around and wondering where Daddy is during the season. I love you all very much. Also to my parents, whose encouragement to play in the early years led to my burning desire to be a part of the game of football. I thank you all for your love and support.

– W.W.

ACKNOWLEDGMENTS

The game of football effects many lives day in and day out. The lessons it teaches about character, humility, and perseverance carry on with both players and coaches long after they step off the playing field. No other sport has that type of effect on our lives. For that reason, I would like to acknowledge a few people for having a lasting effect on not only my football career, but also my life.

I would like to thank both Tommy Bowden (Head Coach Clemson), and Jimbo Fisher (Offensive Coordinator University of Cincinnati), for spending time with me individually at coaching clinics in Auburn, as well as on other occasions. They shared incredible amounts of knowledge about the passing game to me during these times. They also made it possible for me to view numerous videos for literally hundreds of hours to gain background knowledge of the FSU attack. I realize a college coach has his job on the line every day, and I sincerely appreciate the time they took for this ordinary high school coach.

I would also like to thank Coach Bobby Bowden for granting me permission to share what I have learned about these plays with other high school coaches. The job we have often depends on learning things from other folks as we go along, so his permission for me to share this information is very much appreciated.

Finally, I would like to thank all the players and coaches I have worked with over the last few years. Without the effort players give, football coaching could not be the fulfilling job I have found it to be. I would also like to thank some specific coaches that I have both played for and worked with over the years. All of these men have had a strong impact on my coaching. Thank you gentlemen.

Doyle Parker, Texas Tech University

David Johnson, Luverne High School (AL)

Royce Young, Brilliant High School (AL)

Hassel Marlin, Curry High School (AL)

David Williams, Curry High School (AL)

Dale Seals, Curry High School (AL)

Fred Parnell, Curry High School (AL)

Aaron Williams, Curry High School (AL)

TABLE OF CONTENTS

PREFACE

Many books detailing various types of offenses have been written over the last several years. Most of them have dealt with the Wing-T, or the option-type offenses. Then came the Run & Shoot fad that lasted a short time, but it did open the door for books dealing with the passing game. Still, most of those books I have read discussed only quick passing games, or a complex drop-back passing attack.

None of those books have gone in depth to cover both running and passing attacks from multiple formations varying from under center to the four & five receiver shotgun. I believe that is because so few coaches have been willing to adjust and adapt their offenses with the changing times. One coach has done just that. Bobby Bowden at Florida State University has adjusted his offense over the last 23 seasons to turn an offense that scored at will in the 70's into a dynasty in the 90's. He has done that by utilizing a brutal I formation running attack with play action passes off of each run play. The offense also incorporates a quick passing game, roll-out passes, and a shotgun passing attack that uses three, four, and five wide receivers. These adjustments to the offense have proven that Coach Bowden's offense is one of the best at adapting to change.

While there are excellent books on offensive football available today, none of them have addressed what I truly believe to be the best offense in the country—Florida State's. I believe that because I have watched both the running and passing games evolve without losing the foundations of the offense. This book shows the reader the flexibility of the FSU offensive system. It virtually opens the play book on approximately 45 of the top running and passing plays in the FSU offense that can be easily used at the high school level. Many high school coaches are looking for a style of offense can vary according to the talent they have in a particular year. The FSU offense can give a coach that flexibility. If a coach has a weak offensive line, he could insert the quick passing game, draws, and shotgun plays. If a coach has an excellent athlete at quarterback, he could use both shotgun and option plays, as well as the bootlegs and roll-out passes included in this book. This book is designed to offer something for everyone.

INTRODUCTION

Consistency, explosiveness, flexibility: These are all words that a true offensive-minded coach is looking for in his offense. I first noticed a team with these qualities back in 1984 while watching highlights of the Florida State 42-41 loss to Auburn University. It was the first time I had witnessed an offense be able to combine a tough running game, a dangerous option attack, and a wide-open passing game, all when the game dictated it necessary.

Needless to say, after compiling a 151-26-3 record since that loss, along with a 12-2-1 bowl record during that time, the FSU offense has proven itself to be consistent. The 'Noles have finished among the top 25 in the country each year since the 1984 season including 12 straight top 4 finishes in the Associated Press Poll and an unheard of 12 straight 10-plus winning seasons. Playing in three National Championship games—winning it all in 1993—during that span has helped the Seminole offense become an icon of consistency, explosiveness, and flexibility. All of those amazing record breaking statistics have captivated the many fans of the FSU program, but also the attention of many high school coaches across the country, including myself.

Many people believe that the Florida State offensive system has only succeeded so well only because of the talent FSU has recruited over the years. However, the undefeated seasons of teams coached by Coach Bowden's sons have proven that lesser talent can be successful with the system. Terry Bowden was able to go undefeated during the 1993 season with an Auburn team that had won only five games the previous year. Tommy Bowden was able to put together an undefeated season at Tulane in only his second season after the Green Wave program had been down for years. What is even more amazing than the fact that they both used parts of the Florida State offensive system is the complete differences in the two teams. Auburn had their success with Terry Bowden using mostly an I formation run and play-action passing attack, much like the early years of his father at FSU. Tommy Bowden would gain his success at Tulane with a shotgun, no-huddle attacking scheme that closely resembled the 1993 Seminoles' offense. The coaching success of the Bowden sons dramatically demonstrates the flexibility within the FSU offense system.

I wrote this book to share what I have learned about the Florida State offense over several years of film study, clinics, conversations with coaches, and implementation of the offense into my teams' offensive attack during the last seven seasons. Every play, formation, blocking scheme, and protection that is presented in this book has been used by my teams at the high school level for several years, with the primary scheme having been employed by FSU at some point during Coach Bowden's tenure. The first part of the book includes some of the formations used in the FSU offense that are easily used at the high school level without complicated terminology.

Once these formations have been covered, the basis of the FSU offense is reviewed. The most basic running plays in the offense that have changed very little over the last 20 years are presented, including the toss sweep, belly, trap, sprint draws, and counter plays, as well as some options off of the belly and trap. The next section of the book examines the quarterback fundamentals involved in proper ball-handling techniques, as well as effectively throwing the ball. The book also covers the basic fundamentals for sound receiver play, including an overview of base routes for receivers.

Play-action passes that work off of each running play from the sprint draw to the bootleg off the counter play are the next topics addressed in the book. The importance of nakeds and boots to control the backside defensive end from making plays on the sweep and the weakside sprint draw is reviewed. After play-action passes have been discussed, shotgun running plays are examined.

From the shotgun formation, several of the most effective passing plays in the FSU offense—from the Smash route to the shallow cross series—are covered, including shotgun play-action passes, rollout passes, and screens. The final section of the book presents several trick plays, the three-step passing game, and the goalline and short-yardage offense.

One critical issue that should be addressed is whether these plays can be adapted to the high school level? Yes. I have been using most of them during my coaching career at the high school level since 1993. I should stress, however, that I have made some modifications in both blocking schemes and route adjustments to make this success possible. These modifications will be pointed out, as appropriate, throughout the book.

Not only can these plays be used at the high school level, but the up-tempo, no-huddle style Florida State made famous in the early 90's can also be used in high school competition. To be honest, the no huddle can be very difficult for an opponent at the high school level. Because a team's scout coach cannot teach all of the plays to his scout team to be run from the line of scrimmage without a huddle, an opposing coach has no opportunity to adequately prepare his team to get aligned and ready for a play as it will be seen on game night. As a result, the offense has a substantial advantage. Accordingly, a chapter on the no-huddle offense in high school is included at the end of the book.

CHAPTER 1

Basis of the FSU Offense

While the Florida State offense seems to be an extremely complicated offensive system that no high school team could ever dream of adapting, I have found that to be nothing more than a myth. Yes, there are some items, such as blocking schemes that have to be "watered down" a little due to the talent level in high school relative to big time college football, but not nearly as much as you might otherwise think.

While Florida State has a tremendously large offensive package, if you look at it as a whole, you discover it is really just a series of small packages that are built one atop another to develop an exceptionally large package. That factor is what convinced me that proper installation is the key to success with the FSU offense. Not necessarily the amount of the FSU offense that you install, but rather the order in which you install it will have a significant impact with your team's success with the FSU offense.

Florida State's offense should be installed in a series rather than just saying you are going to put in their style of offense. For example, if you install the toss sweep play, the complimenting run play to put in with it on the same day is the fullback belly. You should also consider installing play-action passes at the same time off of these two run-action plays — e.g. the 46 or 34 naked or the 46 bootleg.

If you are installing the shotgun passing attack, you should work your vertical stretch routes in together, such as the 560 vertical or 560 smash, and then work some horizontal stretch plays together, such as the 560 choice or 560 bench. Following that, you might build in the shallow cross series the Seminoles have had so much success with from the shotgun formation.

All of the aforementioned plays are covered in great detail later in the book. However, to build up the offense, you need to install the offense in a way that the plays compliment each other in order to prevent any unnecessary confusion for your players. As a point of fact, the FSU offense is very easy for your players to understand if you install it properly.

Another important factor to consider when installing the offense in series is exactly what plays you want to incorporate. This book presents a number of different options of plays you could install. However, because each coach has a little different offensive philosophy, each coach might take different things from this book.

On one hand, you may be a coach who is looking for a better play-action game. If so, if you install some of the runs that are presented in this book with the complimenting pass plays, your team's play-action game should improve. If you are a coach who is looking for ways to improve your two-minute or third-down passing game, the shotgun plays included in this book can provide your team with the basis for a great two-minute and third-down attack. On the other hand, your team may occasionally employ the bunch-formation offense. As such, you may be looking to expand your offensive package from that formation. The near formation discussed in this book can easily be compressed to use with the bunch routes to give your team an even more potent offense. The point to be emphasized is that his book is designed for coaches who are looking to improve any aspect of their offense, not just for those individual coaches who want to install the whole FSU offensive package.

The formations presented in this book, like the plays, should also be installed carefully. The FSU offensive system involves a wide variety of formations that can be employed. Primarily, these formations entail four different personnel groups. The "Base" group includes two backs, a tight end, and two wide receivers. The "Panther" group includes two backs, no tight end, and three wide receivers. The "Rifle" group includes one back, no tight end, and four wide receivers; and the "Pistol" group includes one back, one tight end, and three wide receivers. All of these groups could employ motion or different splits by the receivers, as well as be used under center or in the shotgun formation.

Diagrams of each of the formations that could be used with the four personnel groups are provided in the next section. You should notice, however, that the offensive line flip-flops with a strongside and quickside. The right or left in each formation call dictates that the strongside will line up to the call side, while the quickside will be lined-up opposite of the call.

BASE PERSONNEL

Formation: Right

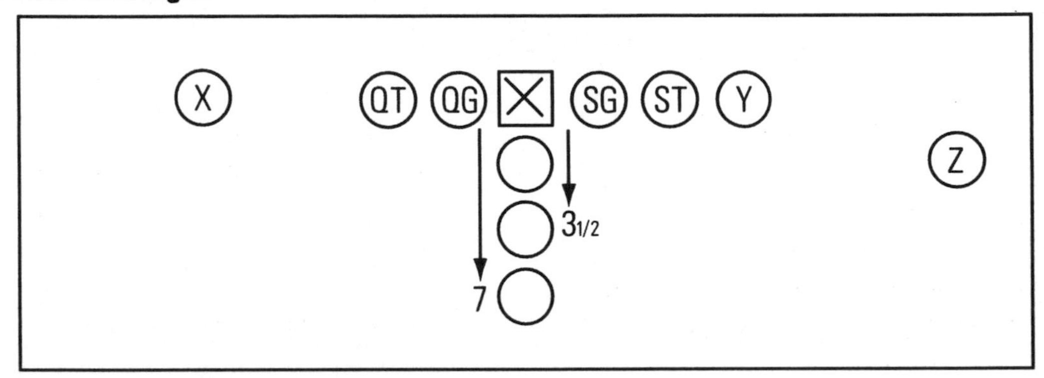

Primary coverage faced: 3-deep zone
Primary fronts faced: 5-2, 4-3, 4-4
Top run plays: Toss sweep, belly, trap, sprint draw
Top plays: 3-step drop, sprint draw action passes, boots & waggles.

Formation: Right Over

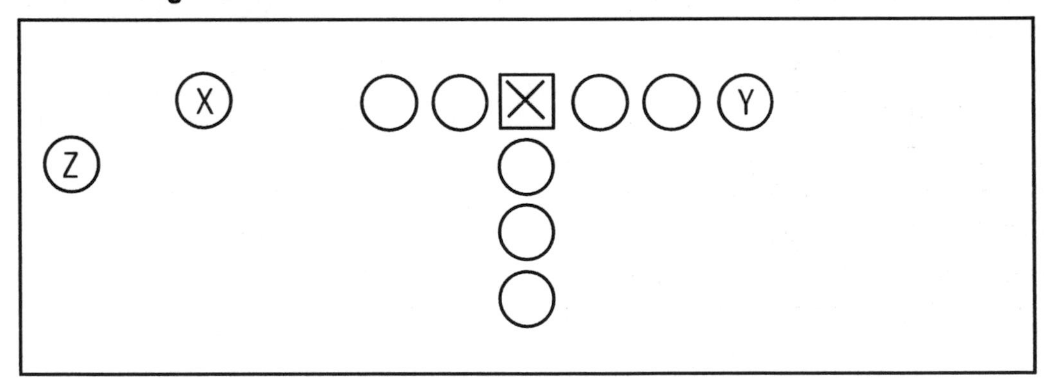

Primary coverage: 3-deep zone, banjo (corners)
Primary fronts: 5-2, 4-3
Top run plays: Strong and weak sprint draw, counter, toss sweep, trap
Top pass plays: 3-step passes, choice & bench route
Special: Can motion back to the regular pro set.

Formation: Right Gun

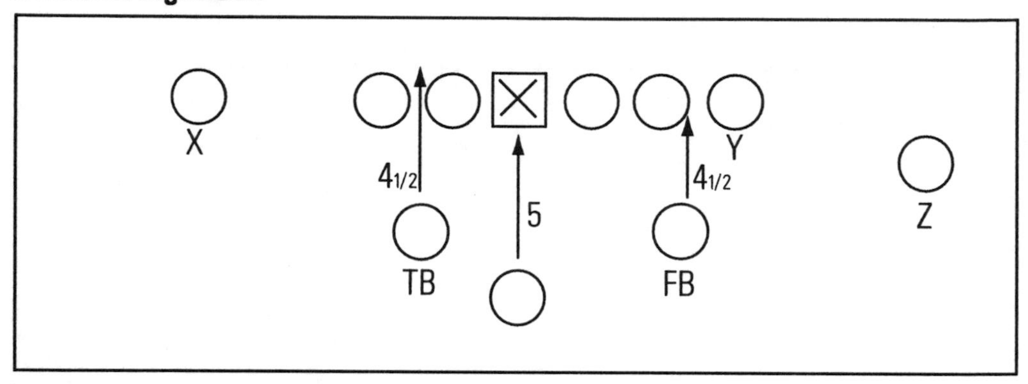

Primary coverage faced: 3-deep zone, roll strong/weak
Primary fronts faced: 5-2, 4-3
Top run plays: Lead draws, counter, quarterback draw (refer to Chapter 12)
Top pass plays: Horizontal stretch routes (refer to Chapters 15-18), screens, play-action passes, roll-out passes
Specials: This formation is excellent for the roll-out trick plays covered in Chapter 28.

PANTHER PERSONNEL

Formation: Right Panther

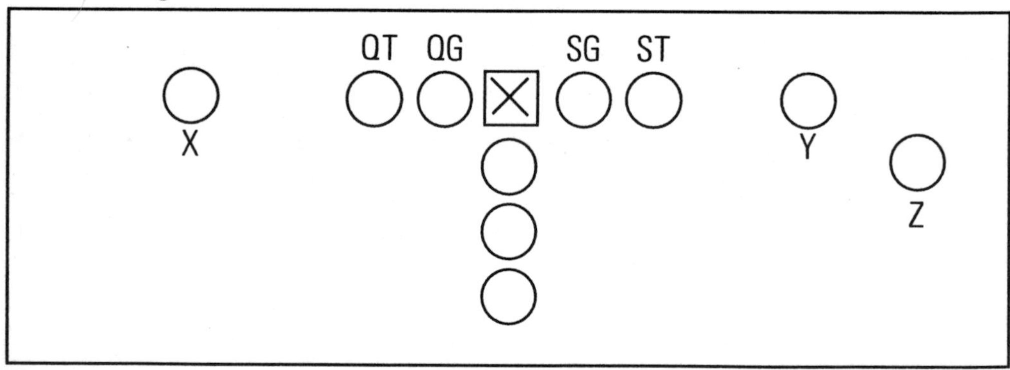

Primary coverage: 3-deep zone, roll strong/weak, 92 (man strong/ 2-deep weak)
Primary fronts faced: 5-2 double eagle, 4-3
Top run plays: Sprint draw strong & weak, trap, toss sweep
Top pass plays: 3-step passes, sprint draw action passes, bootleg, bench & choice routes

Formation: Right Panther Gun

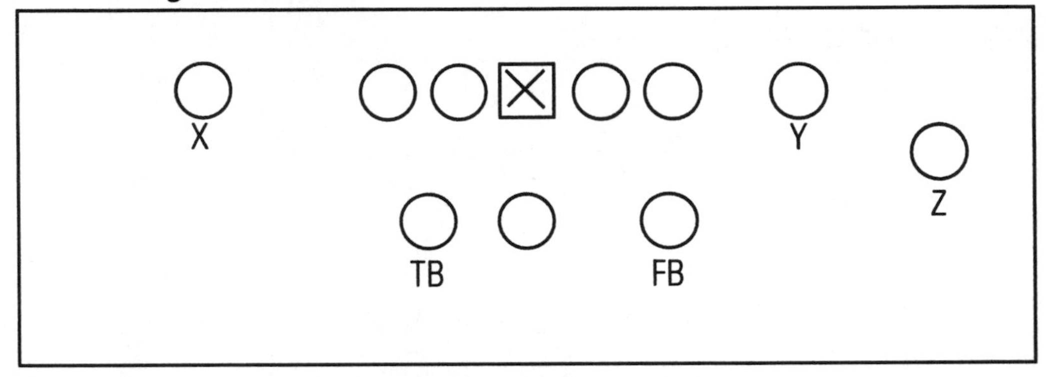

Primary coverage faced: 3-deep zone, roll, 92
Primary front faced: 5-2 double eagle, 4-3
Top run plays: Lead draws, (refer to Chapter 12—shotgun draws)
Top pass plays: Horizontal stretch routes, shallow cross (Y & Z)

PISTOL PERSONNEL

Formation: Right Pistol

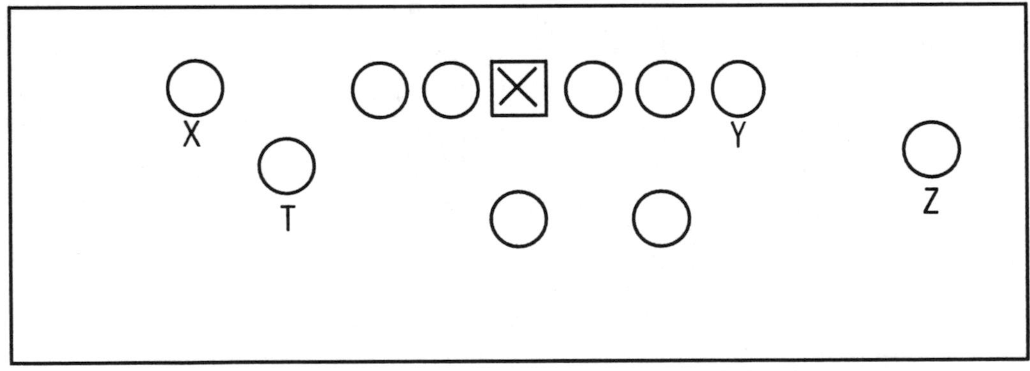

Primary coverage faced: Cover 2, man under 2, cover 4
Primary fronts faced: 4-3, 5-2
Top run plays: Counter, draw trap, quarterback lead draw
Top pass plays: Verticals, choice route, shallow cross series, smash route, roll out passes

RIFLE PERSONNEL

Formation: Right Rifle

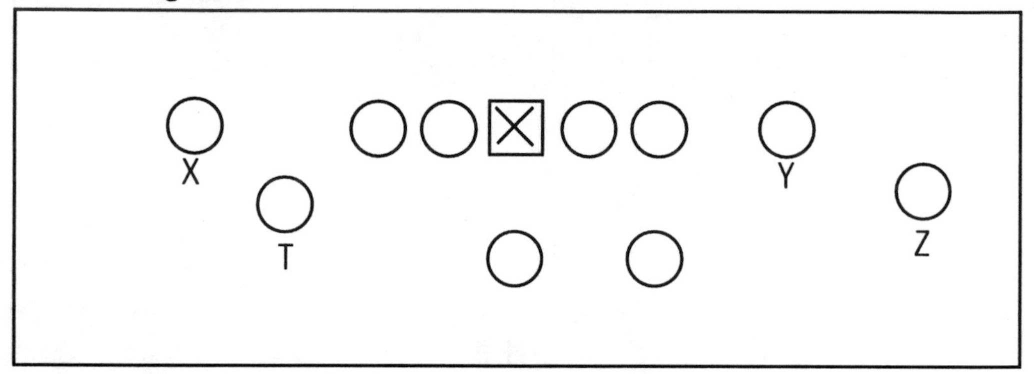

Primary coverage faced: 2 deep, cover 4, man under
Primary front faced: 3-4, 4-3
Top run plays: Direct snap, draws (refer to Chapter 12—shotgun draws)
Top pass plays: Smash route, verticals, choice route, shallow cross series

While the Rifle personnel group is a four-wide receiver group, it does not always have to line up with two receivers to each side. The "T" receiver can be moved to the same side of the formation as "Y" and "Z" to get the benefits of a trips formation to one side. However, the "T" receiver can be placed inside of "Y" or outside of "Z", depending on what you want him to do. One reason I like to place him inside of "Y" is to get the benefits of the bunch-type formation. Adjustments have been made for him so that he can be moved over on certain plays without changing the route he was assigned in the regular Rifle formation. This step decreases the amount of information that the "T" receiver has to learn, yet still gives a coach the ability to move the "T" receiver around. In the Near formation, the "T" receiver is lined up inside of "Y"; in the Far formation, the "T" receiver is lined up outside of "Z."

Formation: Right Near Rifle

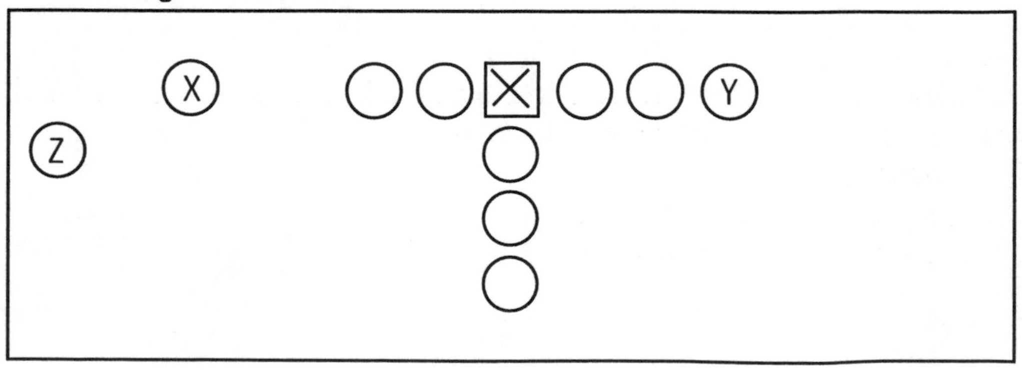

Formation: Right Far Rifle

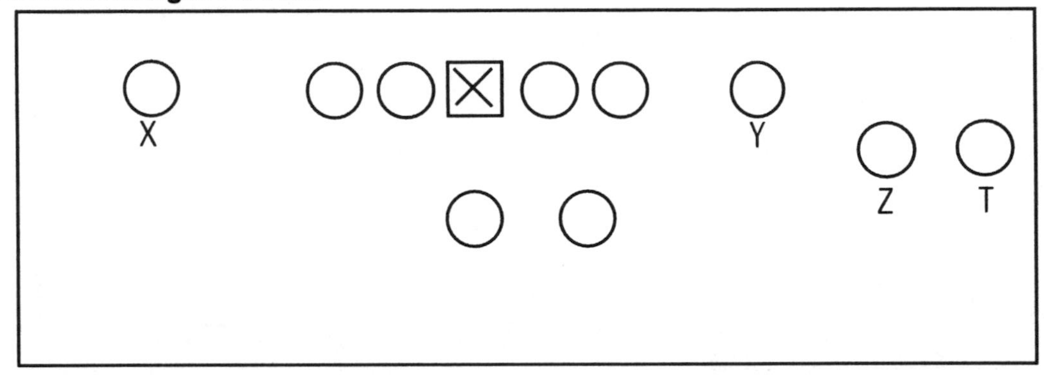

Several other adjustments can be made to the Rifle personnel group, including "emptying" the running back out of the backfield by motion or placing him in a position much like that of "T" when he lines up in the Near formation, thereby creating an Open, or no-back formation. My teams have had particular success with using motion to empty the back out of the backfield because we see so much of the 4-3 defense against the Rifle personnel group. On numerous occasions when the running back has motioned out of the backfield, the middle linebacker has gone with him. In that instance, we either hit an easy completion to a shallow cross receiver for a big play, or check off to a quarterback draw, creating an opportunity for a big-yardage rushing play. Refer to the Empty and Open sets with Rifle.

Formation: Right Rifle Empty

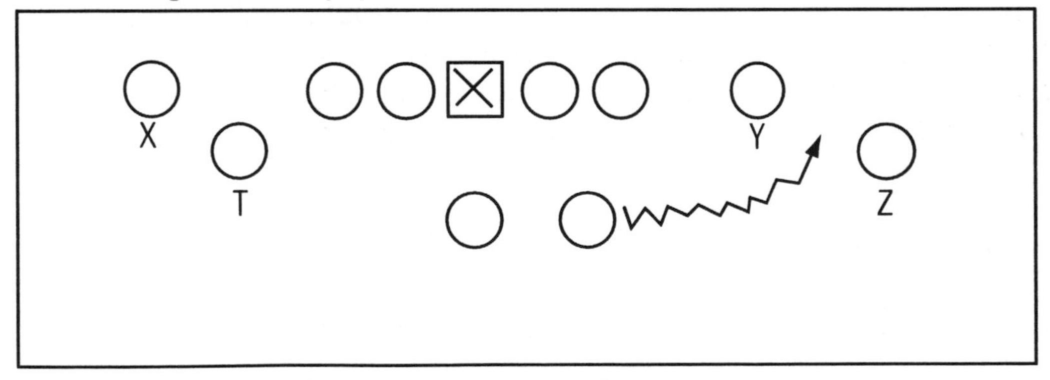

Primary coverage faced: 2-deep zone, man under
Primary front faced: 4-3
Top run plays: Quarterback draw, draw trap
Top pass plays: Shallow cross series

Formation: Rifle Right Open

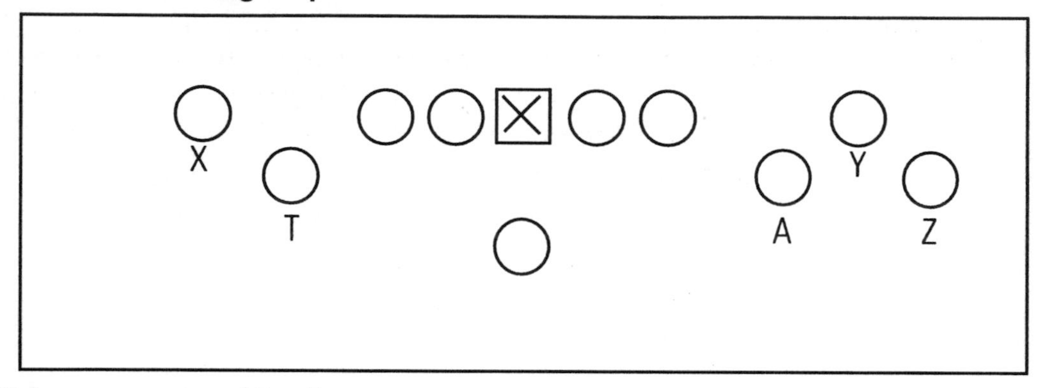

Primary coverage: Man free
Primary front: 3-4
Top run plays: Quarterback draw
Top pass plays: Shallow cross series, verticals, smash route

As can be seen, a variety of ways exist to line up a team's personnel in the FSU style of offense. Some coaches may feel that they do not have enough receivers to run a four-receiver set. The point to remember is that a team doesn't need four receivers on the field all of the time.

The feasibility of a team employing a four-receiver set may be enhanced if coaches were to ask themselves the following question: What is always the longest line of position personnel a team has when practice starts? It has been receivers everywhere I have coached. Coaches should keep in mind that in this regard, all they need to do is to develop four to six of those athletes sufficiently enough to get them on the field, playing at an acceptable level. As a rule, lots of throwing and catching over the summer can make that a reasonable objective. Another advantage of the four-receiver set involves situations similar to mine where my team is usually thin on offense. More often than not, we have a pretty good tailback and fullback that can block and catch the ball out of the backfield. On the other hand, there is usually a pretty good drop off from the number one backs to the number two players on the depth chart in the backfield. Occasionally using a four-receiver set allows a coach to get the fullback or the tailback out of the game for a few plays to keep him fresh.

Keep in mind that the order of installation is the key. The following order for installing the offense is recommended. First, install the base set for the sake of the running game. If you can't run, you can't win. Then work on some shotgun run and pass plays from the Base personnel group. Once your players are comfortable with Base, drop the tight end out and add a wide receiver in his spot to install Panther. Again, work your I formation plays in first, and then work from the shotgun. Finally, begin to install the basic Rifle formation. Make sure that all of your plays are mastered before adding Pistol, Near, or Far. You will already have more than enough offense to keep opponents off balance early in the year. Work the other formations in as the season progresses. For special situations, such as a 2-point play, execute repetitions on the Empty formation from Rifle, because of the possibility of picking up an easy conversion the first time you show it.

CHAPTER 2

I Formation Runs: The Toss Sweep

While Florida State is best known for a wide-open passing attack, they regularly out-rush their opponents. In fact, their offense has gradually evolved from running a lot of options in the late 70's and early 80's to the current offense that utilizes a lot of shotgun, drop-back passing, without changing the base offense itself. That means that even an option package is available to use from this offense for those teams that have always had it as a staple of their offense.

Florida State's basic philosophy with regards to the running game is relatively straightforward: quality beats quantity. Similar to high schools, colleges have a limited amount of practice time. As a consequence, in order to have a truly effective running game, you need to have fewer plays, and get more reps on the ones you decide to utilize. To make those runs more effective, you should develop a play-action passing package off of those run plays and make the package look as similar close to the runs as possible.

Whenever I think of the Florida State offense and Bobby Bowden, the first play that comes to mind is the toss sweep—before I ever think of trick plays or wide-open offense. However, I don't think of a toss sweep to the sideline like most teams run, but, rather, a bone-crushing, smash-mouth, "downhill" toss sweep. In fact, the first year I coached, we named the play "downhill" to run the strongside toss sweep. When we man our offense, the quarterback would call "Brown I Downhill" to communicate the play to the offensive line, backs and receivers. In our frame of reference, the term "downhill" does not refer to stretching the play out to the sideline, but rather to looking to square our pads and cut up the field as soon as possible. Our blocking scheme allows us to do just that.

While the 46 can be blocked in several ways, what we look for first is a reach block from our tight end. If he can make that block, we will get either a kick-out or a wrap block on the force player by our pulling strong guard. The fullback will block the playside linebacker. Everyone else is scoop blocking. That is our bread and butter play. It is also the play that Florida State has used to set the tone in many of its victories over the last 12 seasons.

Sometimes our tight end can tell by the defensive alignment that the defensive end is too wide to reach block. If that situation occurs, we make a call at the line that tells the tight end to block down, and directs the pulling guard to block the defensive end (usually kicking him out). However, if the defensive end squeezes down, the pulling guard will proceed to wrap him. The fullback and tailback must hear the call by the tight end. The fullback then blocks the force player because the tight end and the offensive tackle are now both blocking down. That step takes care of the strongside linebacker.

The tailback then knows that he has to make a quicker cut because the tight end is going down on either the five-technique tackle or the playside linebacker. The tailback follows the block of the strongside guard. He should watch the hips of the guard to see which way to make his cut. The hips of the strongside guard signal to the tailback if the guard is going to wrap the defensive end or kick him

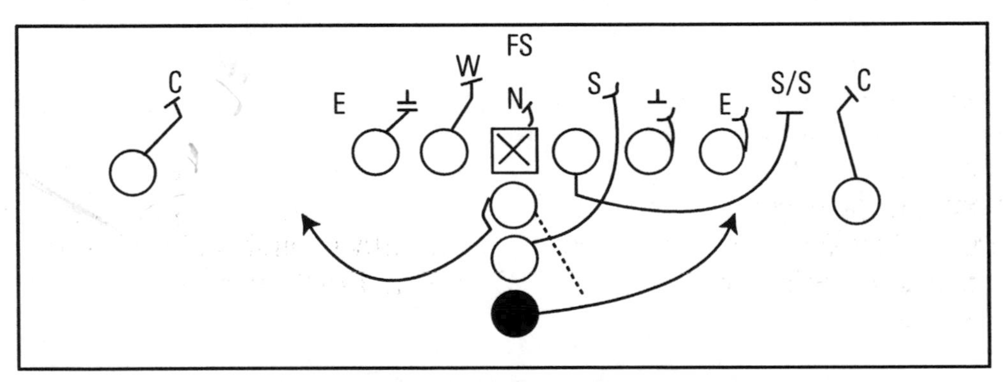

Figure 2.1—The base way to block the 46 versus a 50 defense. The tight end reach blocks, while the strongside guard pulls and either kick-out blocks or wraps.

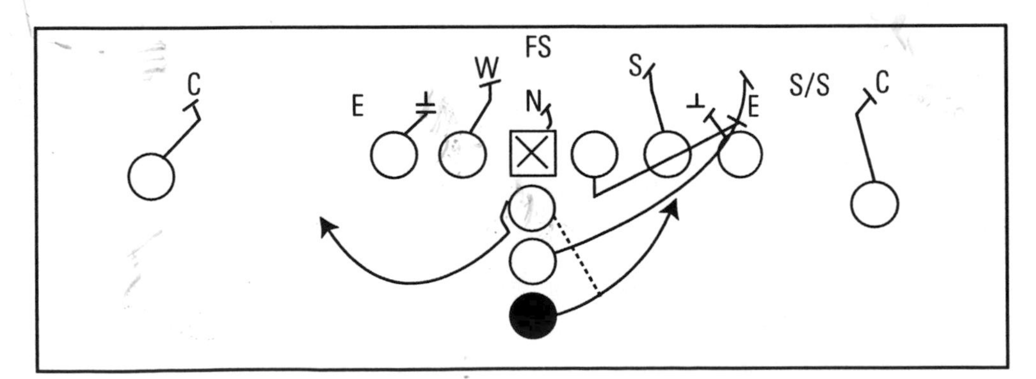

Figure 2.2—Blocking the 46 when the tight end is unable to make the reach block. The tight end blocks down, while the strongside guard kicks out or wraps the end.

out. A kick-out block tells the tailback to cut off the guard's inside hip, while a wrap signals him to cut off of the guard's outside hip. Both wide receivers stalk block the cornerbacks. Figure 2.1 and 2.2 illustrate both of these blocking schemes versus a 50 defense.

The numbering system that we employ for the running game is no different than the numbering systems that almost all teams use for the same purpose. For example, the tailback is the "4" back so "40 anything" goes to the tailback. The fullback is the "3" back so "30 anything" goes to the fullback. The running "holes" are numbered 0, #2, #4, #6, and #8 to the strongside, (i.e. tight end) side. The quickside holes are numbered #1, #3, #5, and #7. The offensive line flip-flops. As a result, the tight end side always involves the even-numbered holes, while the quickside always includes the odd-numbered holes.

The center, quickside guard, and quickside tackle all scoop block to the strongside on 46, leaving the weakside contain player unblocked. The contain player is controlled by the threat of a naked or a reverse. Whenever 46 is called, someone in the press box should have the responsibility of watching the back-side contain player. The first time he comes close to running the back down from behind on the sweep is a signal that he is not honoring his responsibility. As such, it is probably time for you to run either 46 naked or 46 reverse to get him back to doing his assigned job properly.

Several blocking schemes exist for 46 versus various fronts. The ones presented in this chapter (Figure 2.3) have been modified for the high school level. No one can reasonably expect their players to be able to fully handle the complicated schemes of collegiate-level blocking assignments. The runs I have been discussing are basic, as are the blocking assignments for those runs that are covered in this chapter. Keep in mind, however, that if you have better personnel, you can get a little more advanced with your team's blocking assignments. No one, however, ever seems to short change themselves if they stick with the KISS theory of "keep it simple stupid."

COACHING POINTS: 46

Fullback

Blocking assignment: Block the Sam linebacker with low pads.

Technique: Go on a direct path to the inside hip of the strongside tackle with your eyes on the linebacker; always be aware of the linebacker blitzing and meet him in the hole; attack his outside hip to seal him away from the tailback.

Figure 2.3—Blocking Assignments: 46

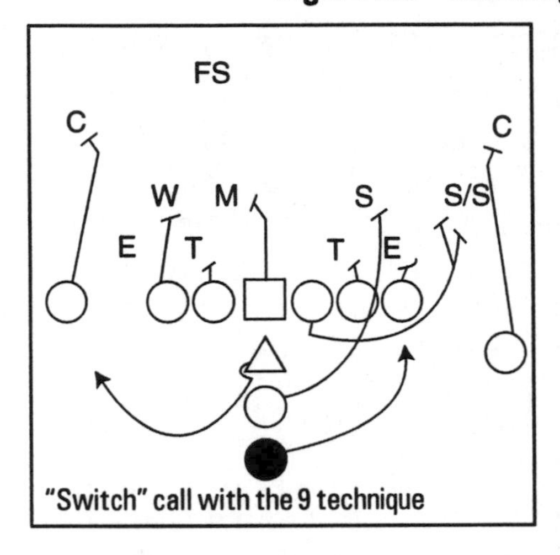

"Switch" call with the 9 technique

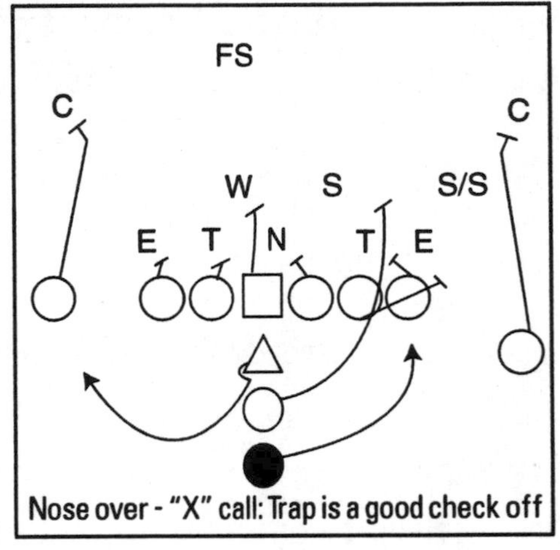

Nose over - "X" call: Trap is a good check off

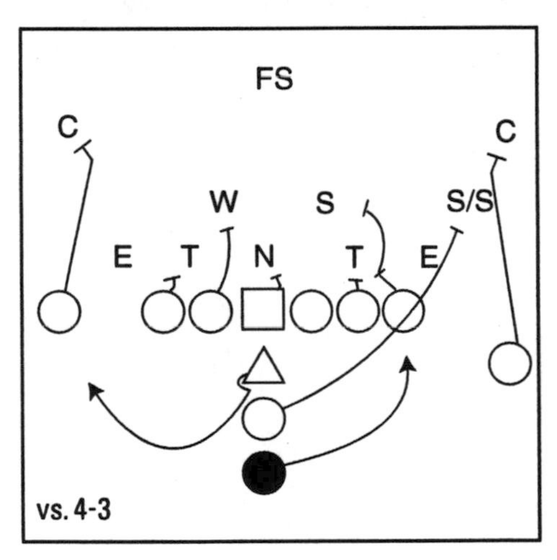

vs. 4-3

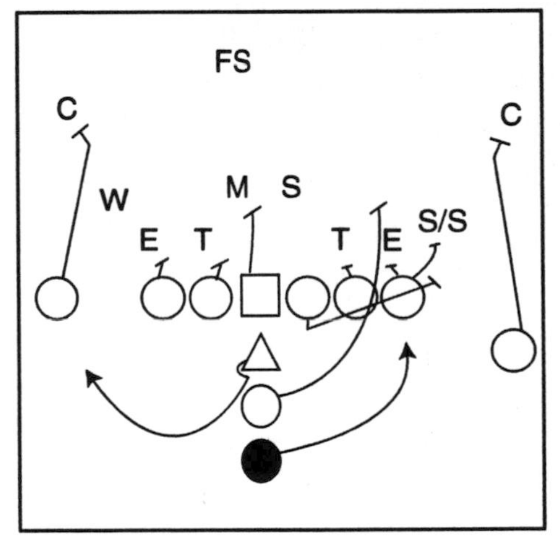

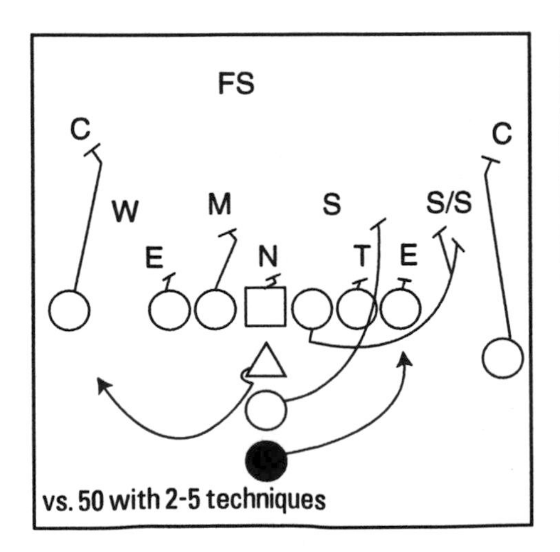

vs. 50 with 2-5 techniques

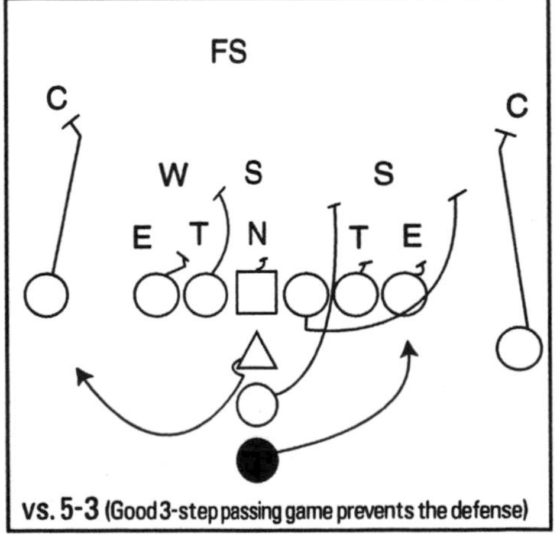

vs. 5-3 (Good 3-step passing game prevents the defense)

Tailback

Assignment: Read the block of the strongside guard; follow a downhill path.

Technique: Take a drag step (i.e., step with your right foot and drag your toe to keep from flying out too fast) with your back foot at the snap. Look the ball into your hands and put it in your outside arm. Take a flat step after the drag step as you read the block of the strongside guard. If he wraps, run off his outside hip. If he kicks the force player, be ready to slow step and cut off his inside hip. If the tight end makes a call, the strongside guard will attempt to kick out the defensive end. As a result, be ready to make a quicker downhill cut.

Quarterback

Technique: Reverse out to 7 o'clock. Pitch the ball softly to the tailback's numbers, using a knuckle ball with no spin. After eyeing the pitch to make sure it is caught, fake the bootleg with your hands in your stomach. Do not watch the tailback after he has received the ball. Sprint and carry out the fake past the line of scrimmage.

CHAPTER 3

I Formation Runs: The Fullback Belly

The next running play—the fullback belly or 34—is a simple one, but is a vital part of the offense, especially when its is set up by a sweep. We run it very much like FSU does, giving it the same action look as 46. Successfully running the sweep can greatly enhance the effectiveness of the belly play. Often, the backside linebacker will run right by the fullback on this play if everyone does his job.

The belly is run according to the specific technique employed by the defensive front, especially the strongside defensive tackle. For example, we might run the play tight, closer to the 2 hole, or we might hit it slightly wider than the 4 hole. In fact, we even make a "killer" call at times to have the guard trap the end, in which case, the play goes almost to the 6 hole. Figure 3.1 illustrates our base-blocking assignments, versus a 50eagle-weak defense.

The tight end will step as if to reach the defensive end on the play. Keep in mind that we want the play to appear to be a sweep. If the defensive end is good, he will try to fight across the reach block. In response the tight end will stretch him to create separation at the line of scrimmage. The strongside tackle will turn out a five-technique defensive tackle, while the strongside guard will climb to the linebacker. If the defensive tackle is in a 4i, the offensive guard and tackle will execute a combo block, with the guard chipping off to the linebacker. Either of these situations should cause the fullback to hit the hole tighter than usual. The fullback should hit the hole wider against a 3-technique tackle, a defensive alignment that is common in a four-man front.

It should be noted that on 34, the backside of the offensive line will still scoop block, just as on 46. At this point, the tailback now makes what we refer to as a "10-digit" fake, by extending his hands as if he caught the toss. He then tucks away the phantom ball and runs just like 46. This step is his way of paying back the fullback for all the bone-crushing blocks he is asked to deliver on the toss sweep. The quarterback can do one of two things at this point, depending on the ability of the quarterback or your team's style of offense.

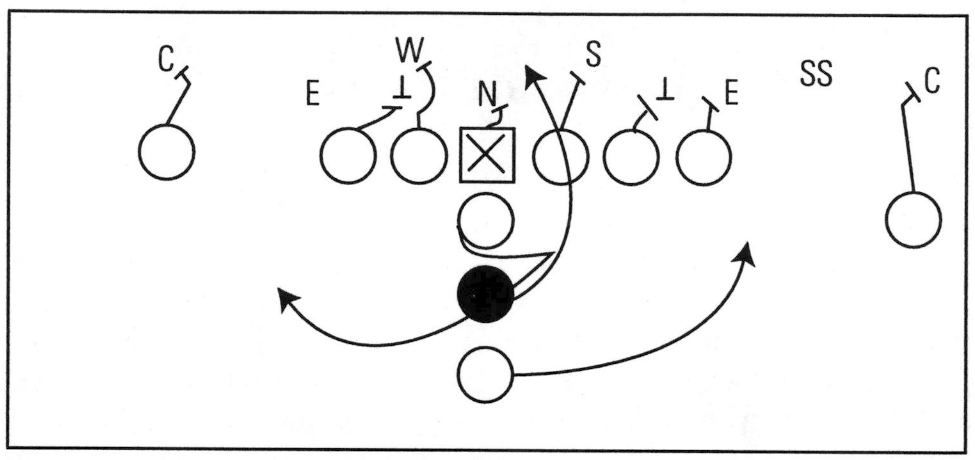

Figure 3.1—34 versus a 50 eagle-weak defense. Note the natural running lane that opens up when the backside pursuit gets used to chasing the sweep.

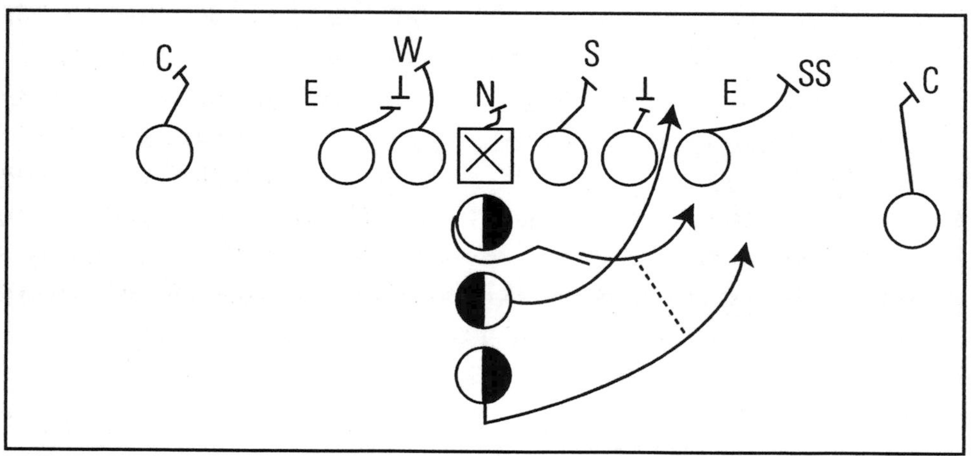

Figure 3.2—The blocking scheme for the belly option, a play that can be run off of the belly play.

If the quarterback is a pure drop-back passer, he should handoff to the full-back, and then carry out a naked fake around the quickside contain player. On the other hand, if he is very athletic, or if you emphasize the option, then he can come directly down the line after the handoff so you can eventually use him to run a belly option as well.

To set up the belly option, the quarterback should sprint down the line of scrimmage following the handoff. If the defensive end is crashing down and tackling the fullback, you should run the belly option with the quarterback. As such, it can be seen how the FSU I formation runs can easily adapt to the option game. Figure 3.2 illustrates the blocking scheme on the belly option.

On the belly option, the tight end should not touch the defensive end at all. We want to read the defensive end to decide if we should give, keep, or pitch. The strongside tackle will block the defensive tackle, while the strongside guard will block the playside linebacker. The backside will continue to scoop block. The fullback will hit the hole wide. The tailback should keep a good pitch relationship.

Another adjustment that can be made with the belly play is the "killer" call. If your quarterback is not real athletic and the defensive end is crashing down on the dive, block the play with a kick-out block on that crashing end. That step can spring the fullback into the second level of the defense. The tight end and strongside tackle will both block down. The strong side guard will pull and kick out the end.

Figure 3.3 illustrates an example of the blocking scheme on a "killer" call. This adjustment can be an important addition to the offense. In fact, it could turn into a big play for your offense if the fullback has a little bit of speed. If the force player is getting involved in the play, have the "Z" receiver spread the cornerback to the sideline. The threat of a slant should force the strong safety (i.e., the force player) to slide out with him. If the force player does not adjust to the stretch of the receiver, coach your quarterback to check off to the quick-passing game and take advantage of this "gift". Figure 3.4 shows the blocking assignments for 34 by the offensive backs against various defensive fronts.

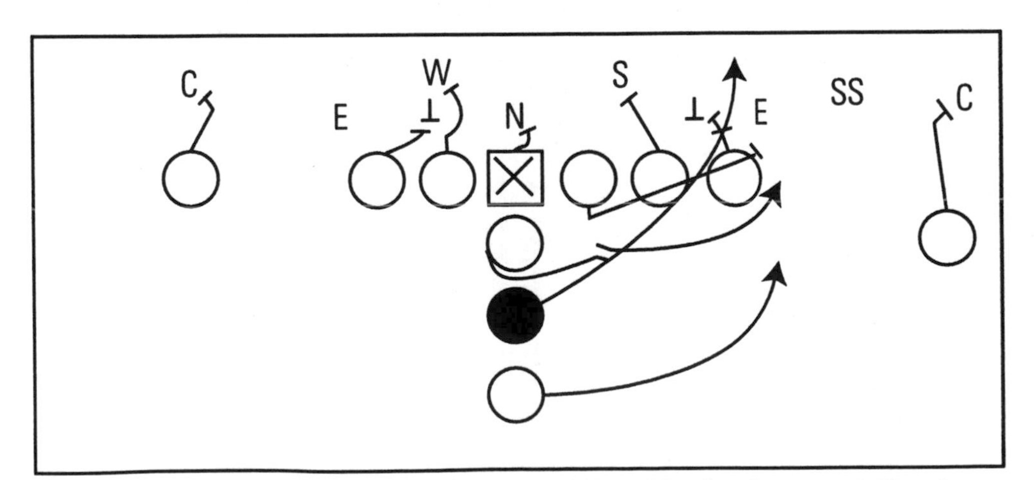

Figure 3-3. The "killer" blocking scheme could be a big play for your fullback.

Figure 3.4—Blocking Assignments: 34

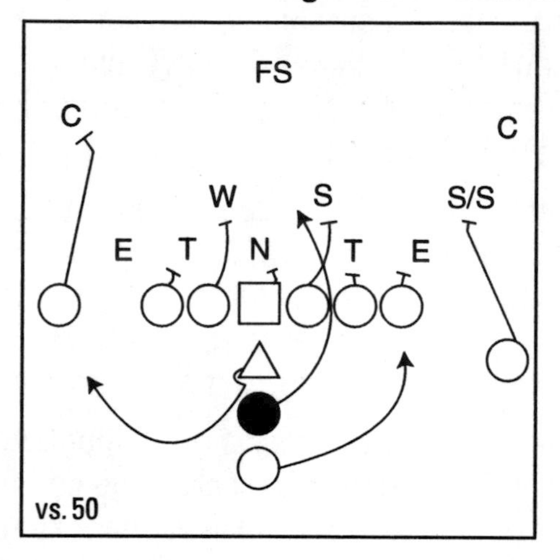

vs. 50

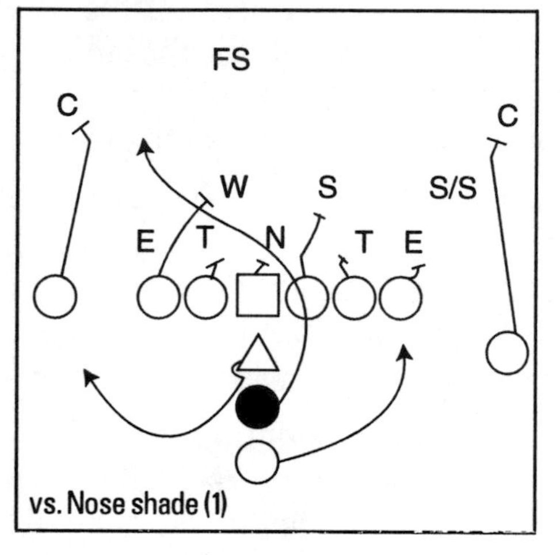

vs. Nose shade (1)

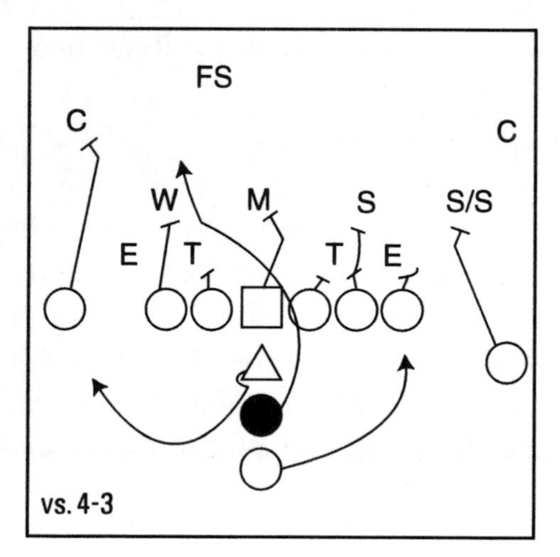

vs. 4-3

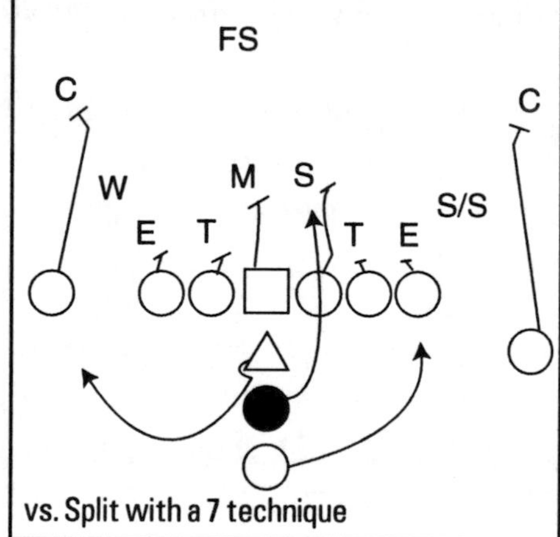

vs. Split with a 7 technique

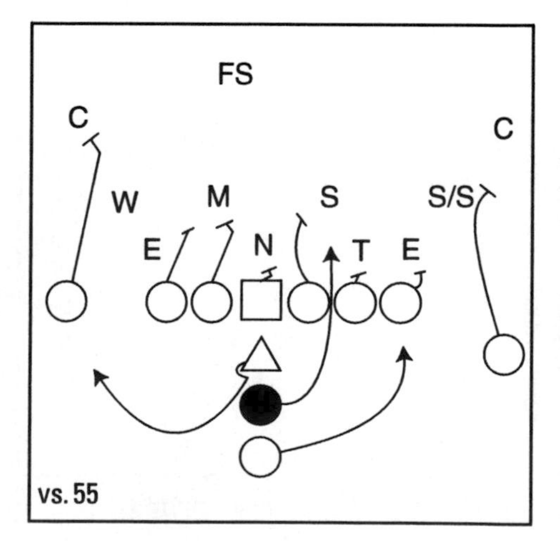

vs. 55

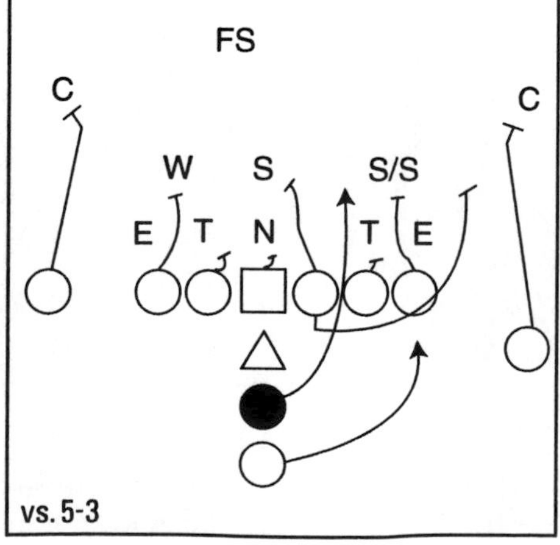

vs. 5-3

COACHING POINT: 34

Fullback

Assignment: Read the technique of the first-down lineman from the nose.

Technique: Take an open step and crossover, gaining ground and square up your pads to the line of scrimmage. Aim for the outside hip of the stronside guard if the defensive tackle is in a 5-technique. If he is in a 3-technique, aim for the inside hip of the guard. Make shallow cuts along the line of scrimmage and look for a possible running lane, bending back toward the weakside of the defense. Hug the offensive linemen and cover the ball with two hands in traffic.

Tailback

Assignment: Make a great 46 fake.

Technique: Make a 10-digit fake with your hands open at knee level and tuck away the imaginary football. Hunch over the upper body and accelerate seven yards outside the last man on the line of scrimmage. Then, cut back inside, looking to throw a block if the fullback breaks the line of scrimmage.

Quarterback

Technique: Reverse out to 7 o'clock just like on 46. The step must be as deep as possible to get the ball to the fullback quickly. Really exaggerate the pitch fake with both your head and shoulders. Your momentum will take you around to the fullback to give him a handoff deep. After the handoff, either carry out the bootleg fake like 46, or sprint down the line like an option at the inside-shoulder pad of the defensive end.

CHAPTER 4

I FORMATION RUNS: THE FULLBACK TRAP

When your team runs a lot of belly and sweep plays, or drop-back passes a lot, defensive tackles will begin getting up field, and linebackers will over-pursue. That situation is a good time to run the fullback trap, or 31. While Florida State has gotten away from the trap play since the mid 1990s, it should still be a staple of the base fast break offense. It certainly has been a staple of our team over the years.

We have made a slight modification in the way we run the play at the high school level. At FSU, on the fullback trap, they have the quarterback face out directly to the fullback to hit it quickly. We still hit the play quickly, but have achieved much better results by reversing out to give the play the same appearance as the sweep or the belly play. That step helps facilitate an easy washdown block on the backside linebacker because the linebacker usually begins his steps as if he is pursuing the sweep because of the action in the backfield. By the time he reacts, our quickside tackle is in his ear hole.

If the weakside defensive tackle is in a 3-technique, we will always trap him. However, if he is in a 1-technique (and he usually is in a 4-3 defensive alignment), we may or may not trap him. If he is quick to get up the field, we will trap him. Also, if we do not feel our quickside guard can block him down, we will trap him. Those decisions are usually made week-to-week, as we break down our opponent's game film. If neither option looks very promising, then we simply run 30 trap to go back at the 3-technique on the other side. The center then blocks back on the 1-technique that is giving us trouble.

If we do not trap the 1-technique tackle, we block him down and the strongside guard pulls all the way out to the weakside end to trap him instead. Figure 4.1 illustrates the trap of the weakside 3-technique in a 50 defense, while Figure 4.2 shows the blocking of a 1-technique tackle in a 4-3 front.

Against a 3-technique tackle, the quickside tackle will wash down on the weakside linebacker. The quickside guard will chip from the nose to the backside linebacker. The center gets help from the quickside guard with a chip, and must seal the nose to the strongside. The strongside guard pulls to the quickside "B" gap and kicks out that defensive tackle. The strongside tackle scoops to pinch or choke off the strongside defensive tackle. The tight end turns out the defensive end, and then advances to level two as the play develops.

If the defensive tackle is a 1-technique, and we decide not to trap him, the quickside tackle still washes down. The quickside guard now blocks down on the 1-technique. The center blocks the middle linebacker, while the strongside tackle pinches off the strongside 3-technique. The strongside tackle must move his feet quickly to execute this block properly. The tight end punches the defensive end, and then progresses to the second level, preferably to the linebacker.

We control the weakside defensive end with the threat of the option. If you have only one option play in your offense, this play should be it. The tailback takes a counter step giving a 10-digit fake, just like 46. However, he then plants, cuts back, and keeps a pitch relationship with the quarterback to the weakside. The fullback receives the fake exactly like 31 trap, cutting back and running right at the weakside linebacker, forcing him to honor the fake.

The quarterback reverses out and rides the fullback, who pulls him all the way back to 360 degrees, facing down the line at the defensive end. The quarterback pressures the defensive end, forcing him to take either the quarterback or the pitch. Often, though, the defensive end has seen the trap so many times he will squeeze down and tackle the fullback. If that situation occurs, the quarterback should be looking to pitch to the pitch-support man. The reason the defensive end develops a tendency to squeeze down and tackle the fullback is the success of the sweep, belly, and the trap plays.

As such, you can see how plays within the FSU scheme compliment on another. Furthermore we haven't even begun to cover the passing game yet. Figure 4.3 illustrates the trap option with the defensive end taking the quarterback, while Figure 4.4 shows the defensive end tackling the fullback and allowing the quarterback to continue the pitch threat to the corner.

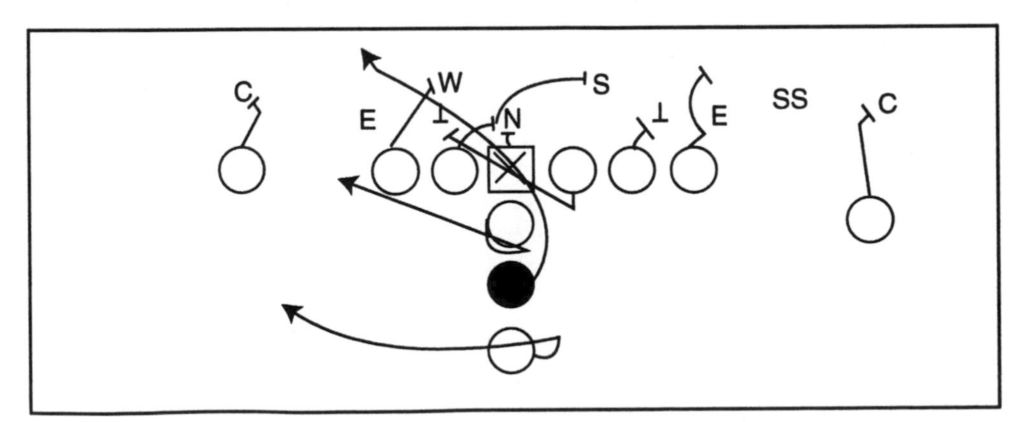

Figure 4.1—The 31 trap versus a 3-technique tackle.

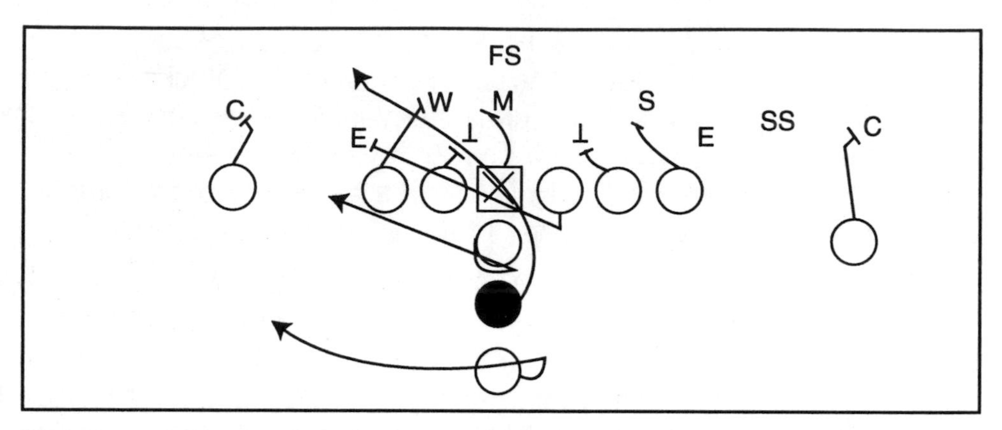

Figure 4.2—The 31 trap versus a 1-technique tackle in a 4-3 defense.

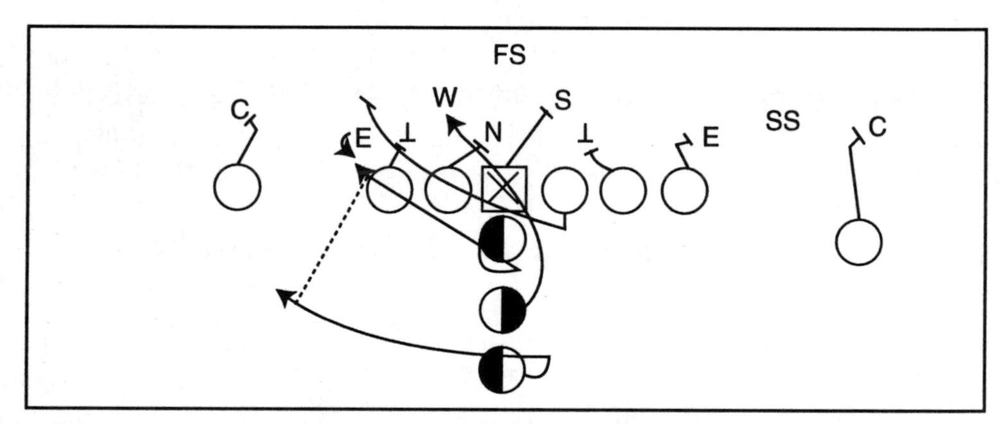

Figure 4.3—The 31 option with the defensive end taking the quarterback.

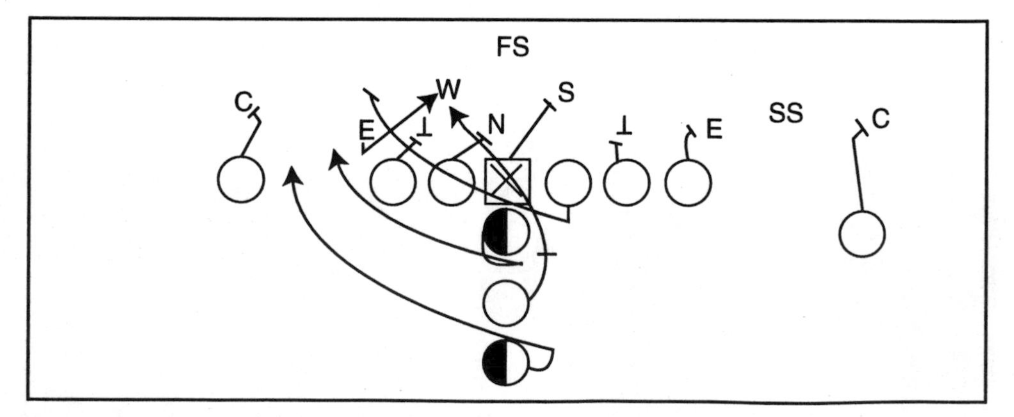

Figure 4.4—The 31 option with the quarterback pressuring the corner.

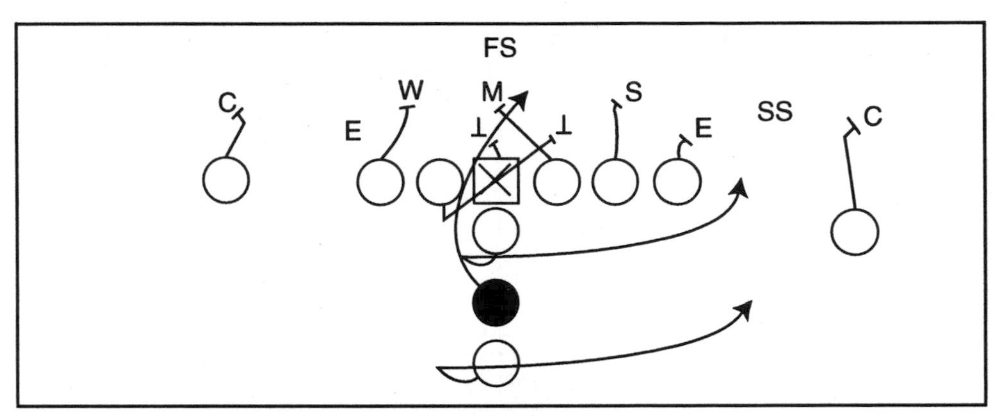

Figure 4-5. The 30 trap versus a 4-3 defense.

One final adjustment on the 31 that we can make is to run the trap back to the strongside if the 1-technique is giving us trouble. In this scenario, the center blocks back on the 1-technique tackle. The quickside tackle proceeds to the second level, while the quickside guard pulls and traps the 3-technique tackle on the strongside. The strongside guard and tackle wash down on the linebacker, while the tight end turns out on the defensive end.

The fullback steps to the weakside of the formation, like he is getting a handoff for 35, and then cuts back to the strongside on the bend trap. The tailback does a 10-digit fake to the weakside, like he is getting 27 toss sweep. He then goes back to the strongside, faking a pitch relationship with the quarterback around the strongside end. Figure 4.5 shows the 30 trap versus a 4-3 defense. Figure 4.6 illustrates the blocking assignments for a 30/31 trap.

COACHING POINT: 31 TRAP

Fullback

Assignment: Read the block of the pulling guard on the trap play.

Technique: Open step and square pads to the line of scrimmage. Push off of your outside foot back toward the weakside "A" gap. Follow the block of the strongside pulling guard. The trap will be tight versus a 3-technique tackle and wide versus a 1-technique tackle if he must be blocked down.

Tailback

Assignment: Make a great 46 fake; keep a pitch relationship.

Technique: Make the 10-digit fake taking a drag step to the strongside. Plant on your outside foot and push back to the weakside of the formation; keep a pitch relationship with the quarterback (i.e. five-and-five).

Figure 4.6—Blocking Assignments: 30/31 Trap

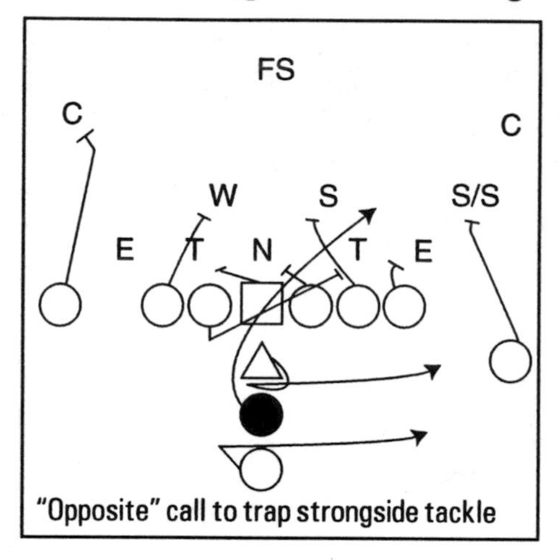

"Opposite" call to trap strongside tackle

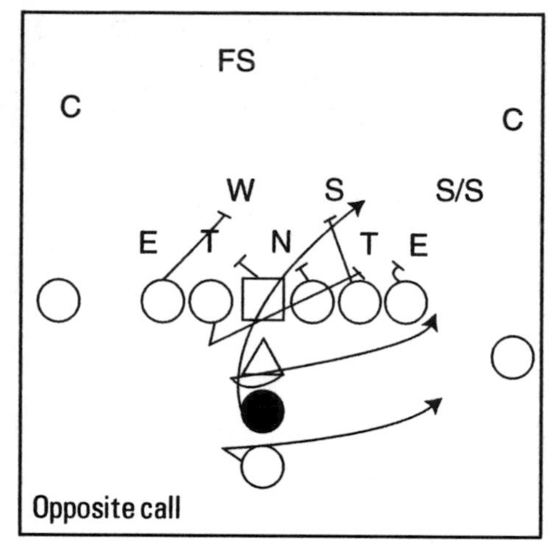

Opposite call

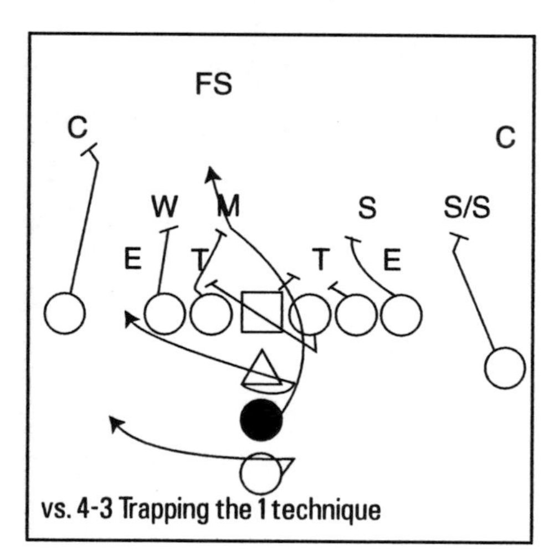

vs. 4-3 Trapping the 1 technique

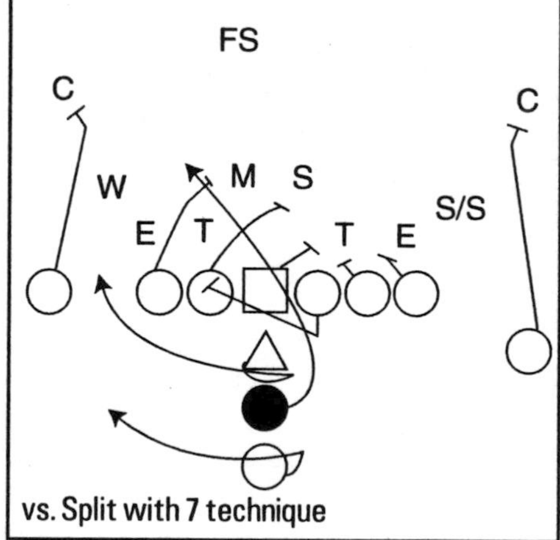

vs. Split with 7 technique

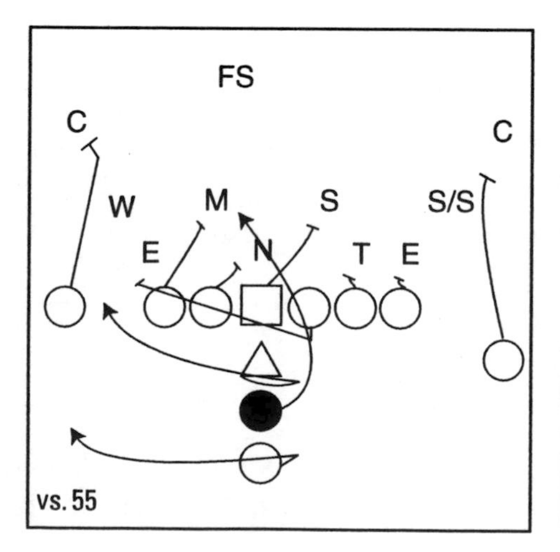

vs. 55

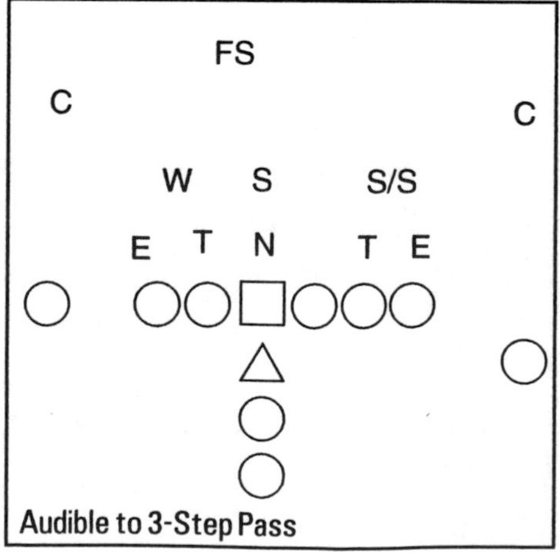

Audible to 3-Step Pass

Quarterback

Technique: Reverse pivot to 7 o'clock and exaggerate the pitch fake to the tailback while taking a deep step to allow the pulling guard to move through. Place the ball in the fullback's stomach as deeply as possible and ride him all the way through the hole. Pivot all the way around to face the weakside defensive end. Attack his inside shoulder pad and force him to honor the pitch option.

CHAPTER 5

I Formation Runs: The Strongside Sprint Draw

One of the basic foundations of a good passing team is a solid sprint draw and sprint draw passing series. All of the teams that utilize or have utilized the FSU style of offense have had exceptional sprint draw and sprint draw action passes. For example, Florida State, Tulane (under Tommy Bowden), Auburn (under Terry Bowden), and South Carolina, when Brad Scott was the Gamecock's coach, employed a combination of draw and play action to keep teams off balance. In all likelihood, that approach to offense will become a strength at Clemson now that Tommy Bowden is the Tiger's head coach.

While the strongside sprint draw, or ISO, is called 44, there are cutback lanes possible as far back as the weakside end. The way we block it depends upon the alignment of the defense with regard to who is covered. Against a 50 defense, a weak eagle for example with a 5-technique tackle and a head-up nose, the tight end will turn out the defensive end as he sets up, much like as on a pass play. The strongside tackle will gate and force the 5-technique up the field, not letting him cross his face. The tight guard chips the nose, helping the center, and then progresses to block the backside linebacker. The fullback blocks the playside linebacker, taking him on with low pads to drive him out of the hole. The quickside guard and quickside tackle invite the weakside defensive tackle and defensive end up the field, but do not let them cross their face to get inside position. If that factor becomes a problem, then the quickside guard and quickside tackle should be allowed to scoop block instead. The tailback takes a lateral shuffle step to the strongside, and then begins to attack the line of scrimmage. He should not look for the ball. He should be coached to read the blocking to determine if he should take an inside or outside cut on the play. In this instance, the hips of the fullback and the strongside guard should help him make that read. (Refer to Figure 5.1).

If the 50 defense has a shaded nose, the tailback should read the block of the center. The strongside guard will give the center help with an aggressive shot to combo the nose, and then chip off to the backside linebacker. However, the nose might still get across the center's face, and in between the A and B gap. If the nose crosses the center's face the center should simply keep driving him toward the strongside C gap. The tailback then cuts back inside this block off the center's inside hip. All of the other blocking assignments stay the same. Occasionally, the weakside tackle will move to a 2-technique when the nose shades. As a result, the quickside guard is then forced to scoop him rather than invite him up the field. (Refer to Figure 5.2).

Against the popular 4-3 alignment with a 3-technique tackle on the strongside and a 1-technique on the weakside, the tight end will still turn out the defensive end. The strongside tackle will come down to combo the 3-technique tackle. The strong guard will chip the 3-technique, and then progress to the middle linebacker. The center blocks back on the 1-technique tackle, while the quickside guard sets to pass block and then climbs to the Will linebacker. The quickside tackle gates and blocks the backside end. The fullback is responsible for the Sam linebacker, attacking him with low pads to get him out of the hole. It is important that the tailback is aware of the fact that the strongside tackle is down blocking on the 3-technique, thereby allowing him to hit the hole off the outside hip of the tackle. (Refer to Figure 5.3).

Another important coaching point on this play involves the quarterback and the wide receivers. Both should be trying to make the play look like a pass. The quarterback should always continue back and set up after the handoff, and then look down the field as if to locate an open receiver. The wide receivers should explode off the football just like a pass route. However, as they break down the cushion of the defensive back, they should settle down and stalk block him.

Another way for the wide receiver to block the play on the backside is the circle block. This block is a vicious one for a defensive back to take if it is executed properly. Keep in mind that executing this block the "right way" does not involve a cheap shot. Rather, the wide receiver sprints past the defensive back, who recognizes that it is a run play after a few seconds. A well-coached corner will begin to move to the middle of the field as the flow goes away from him. The wide receiver then circles around him just out of sight. If the running back were to cut back to the opposite side of the field, the corner would think he is in good position to make a play on him. However, the receiver has circled around and is in a position for a block very similar to a crackback block on a linebacker or force player.

The wide receiver's running start typically generates a pretty good impact on the defensive back. You might want to try this particular block on the sprint draw play because there often is a cutback lane. Figure 5.4 illustrates the blocking schemes for the sprint draw against various fronts. Keep in mind that the 44 is a great I formation run play.

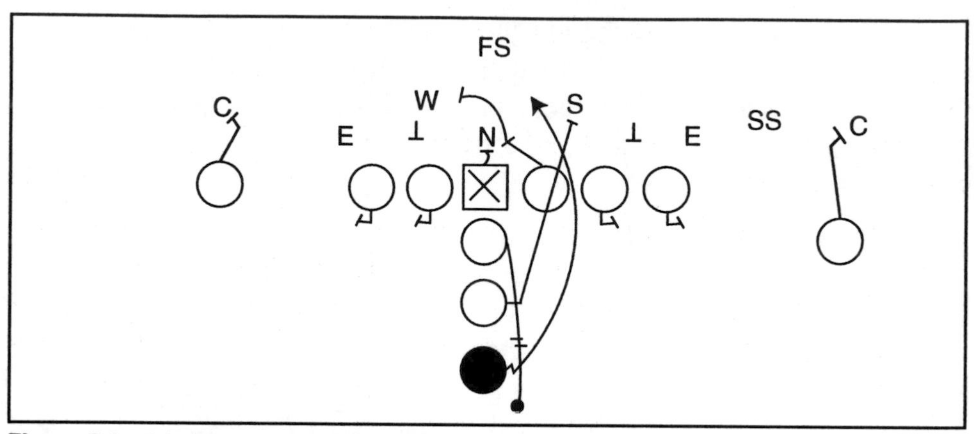

Figure 5.1—44 versus a 50 defense.

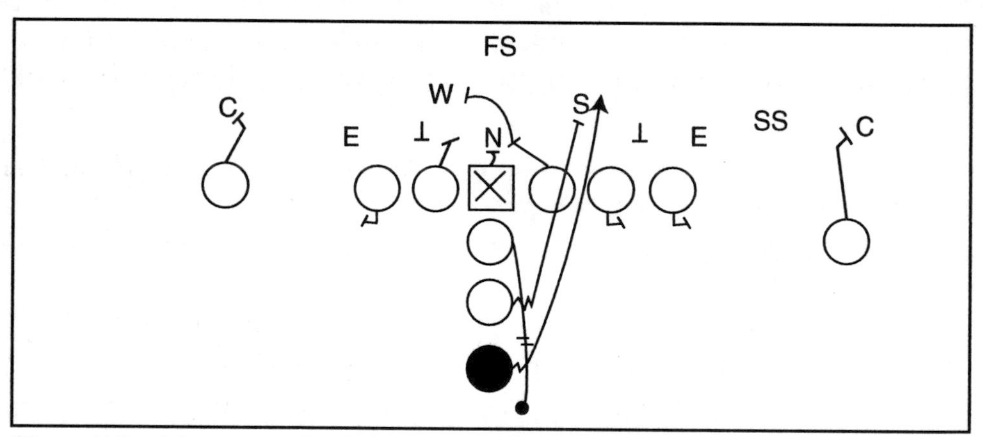

Figure 5.2—44 versus a 50 defense with a shaded nose.

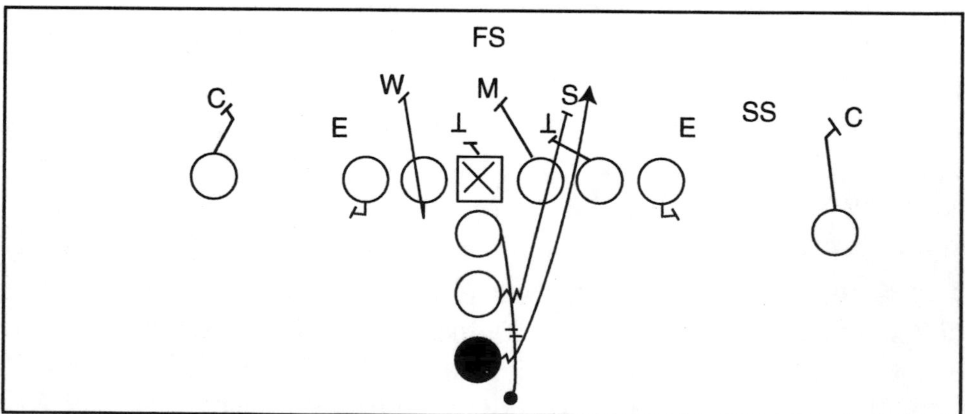

Figure 5.3—44 versus a 4-3 defense.

COACHING POINT: 44

Fullback

Assignment: Block the strongside linebacker.

Technique: Take a lateral, open step to square up to the line of scrimmage. Go inside a 5-technique tackle. If there is a 3-technique tackle, we will combo him. You should go outside that block. Against a split defense, go inside the block of the 2- or 3-technique to get to the inside linebacker. Attack the strongside linebacker with low pads to create separation for the tailback within the line of scrimmage.

Tailback

Assignment: Read the block on the defensive tackle.

Technique: Take a lateral step; stay square to the line of scrimmage; and then take a shuffle over the strongside guard. When your outside foot lands, attack the line of scrimmage. Do not look at the quarterback. Trust him to deal the ball. If the tackle comes down to combo on a 3-technique, work off his outside hip. If he turns out on a 5-technique, cut off his inside hip. If there is a shaded nose, and he crosses the center's face, cut back inside the block of the center.

Quarterback

Technique: Open at 5 o'clock to the strongside. Adjust to the path of the tailback. Start extending the ball to the tailback on the second step. Hand the ball off to the tailback behind the guard at a depth of five yards. (This should occur on your fifth step). Then get your hands back into your stomach and set up to show pass on your seventh step. Keep your hands in your belly and your eyes downfield.

Figure 5.4—Blocking Assignments: 44

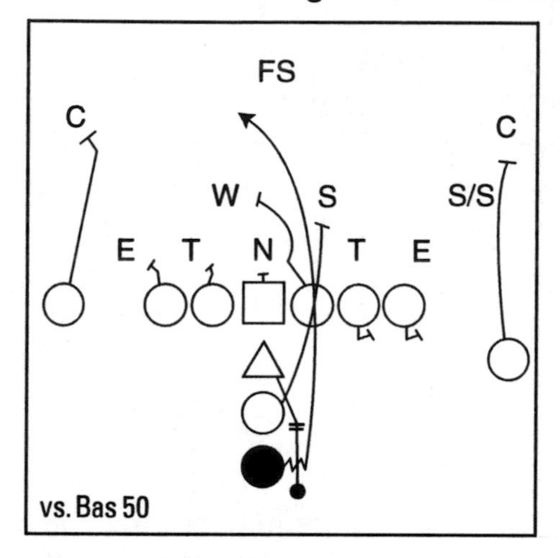

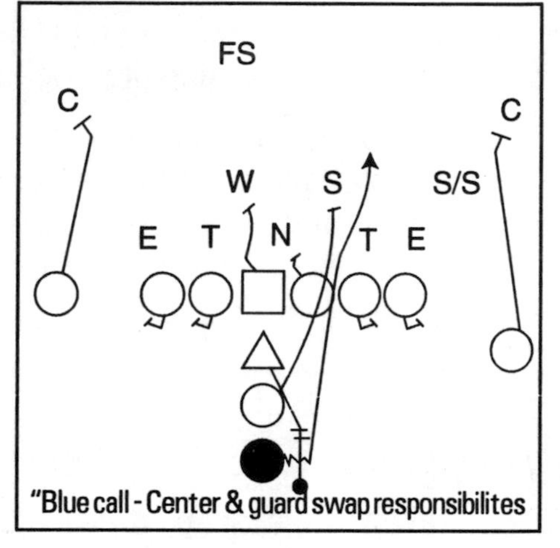

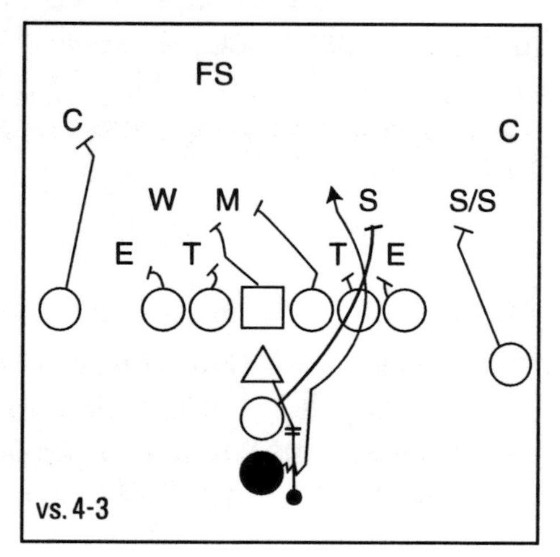

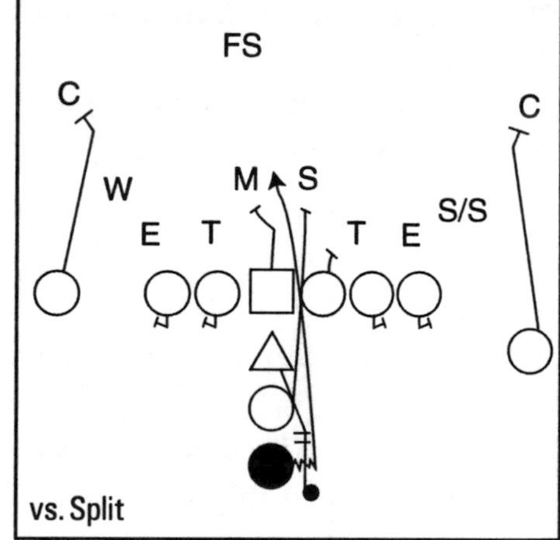

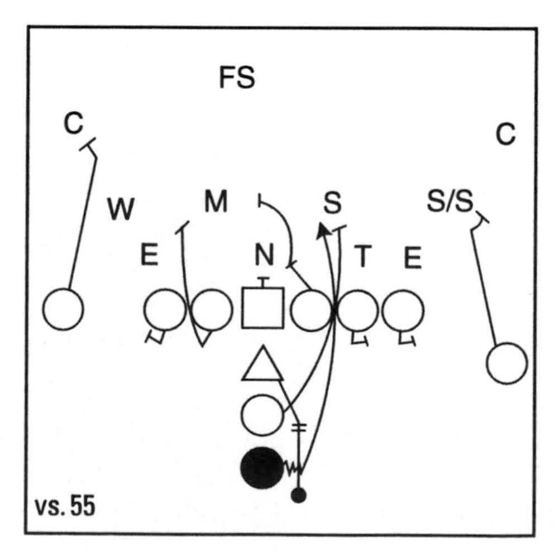

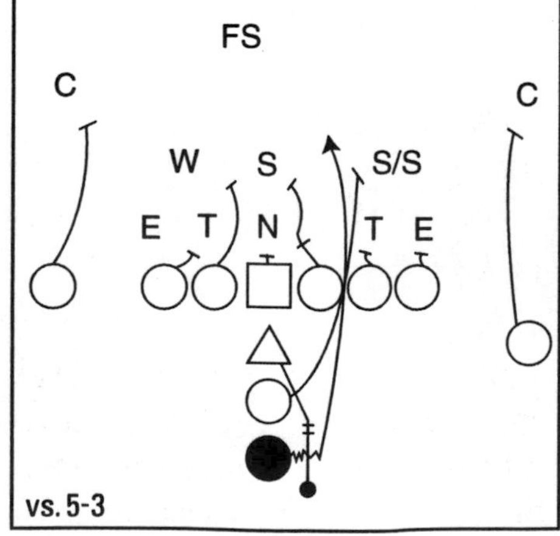

CHAPTER 6

I Formation Runs: The Weakside Sprint Draw

When the sprint draw is run to the quickside of the formation, the play is called 43. This particular play sets up a wonderful play-action pass called 43 dash that is covered in Chapter 8. However, for any play action to work, the run play must be made to look as much like it as possible.

On 43, the fullback and tailback have virtually the same responsibilities as 44, but now they go to the quickside, away from the tight end. Against a 50 defense, eagled down (i.e., the defensive tackle slides down; instead of being in a 5-technique, he slides down to a 3-technique) on the weakside, we are facing a 3-technique defensive tackle. The quickside guard will turn him out, allowing him to cross his face. The guard can set pass to invite the 3-technique up field, but must keep him out of the A gap. The quickside tackle turns out the defensive end as well, and can also set pass to invite up-field movement. An alternate way of blocking the 3- and 5-techniques at this point would be to "X" block (i.e., also referred to as a combination block) with a kick out by the guard.

We most frequently use that option with a 2-technique defensive tackle. The center seals the nose to the strongside with a good scoop step. The strongside guard climbs to the Sam linebacker, while the strongside tackle turns the defensive tackle on him to the outside, inviting him up the field. The tight end progresses up the backside, where the defensive end is controlled with the dash pass (i.e., a play-action pass that is covered in detail in Chapter 12). The fullback blocks the Will linebacker with low pads to get him out of the hole. (Refer to Figure 6.1).

If the nose were to shade to the strongside, which is a common occurrence, the center should chip off of him and climb to the Sam linebacker. The strongside guard then scoops to the shaded nose, sealing him from any pursuit into the quickside of the formation. All other blocking assignments stay the same. (Refer to Figure 6.2).

The quarterback can help the backside blocking on the play with an excellent fake. He should place the ball in the belly of the tailback as the tailback passes him, using the arm closest to the line of scrimmage. The arm of the quarterback nearest the tailback should then be pulled back into the quarterback's own stomach, while the quarterback shows an empty palm extended toward the tailback

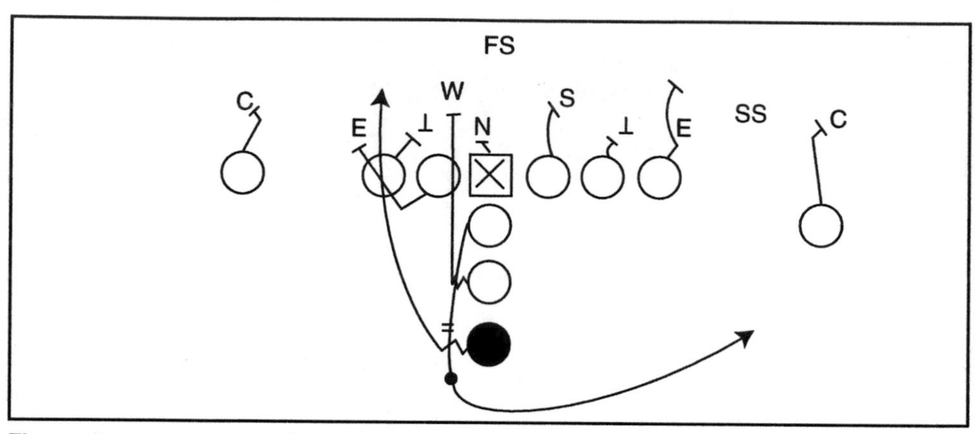

Figure 6.1—43 versus a 50 defense.

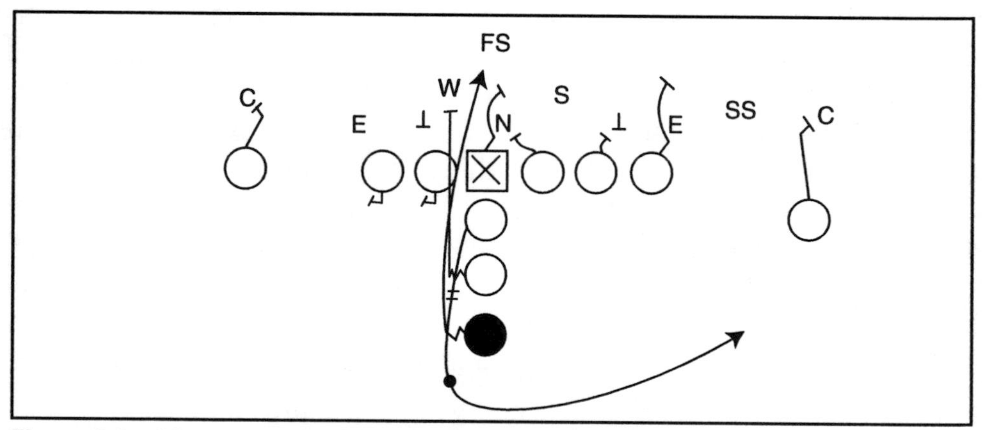

Figure 6.2—43 versus a 50 defense with a shaded nose.

as he runs. The quarterback then sets up, freezes, and sprints back to break contain without the ball to force backside containment to honor the threat of a bootleg or naked.

Another common adjustment we often have to make on this play occurs when the defensive tackle on the weakside plays a 2-technique, and we can't force him up the field. The adjustment that I have found easiest to make at the high school level is to simply cross block the quickside. The quickside tackle should come down first, and then the guard should kick the end out. All other blocking assignments should stay the same on the play.

If a cross block is needed, a line call must be made that lets the tailback know that the quickside tackle will be coming down on the 2-technique tackle. As a result, the hole will be slightly wider than when the 3 technique is invited up the field with our base block. The slightly wider path by the tailback should be noted (refer to Figure 6-3). The fullback must also hear the call to adjust his path. Normally, he will go through the cross block to the linebacker, and the tailback will

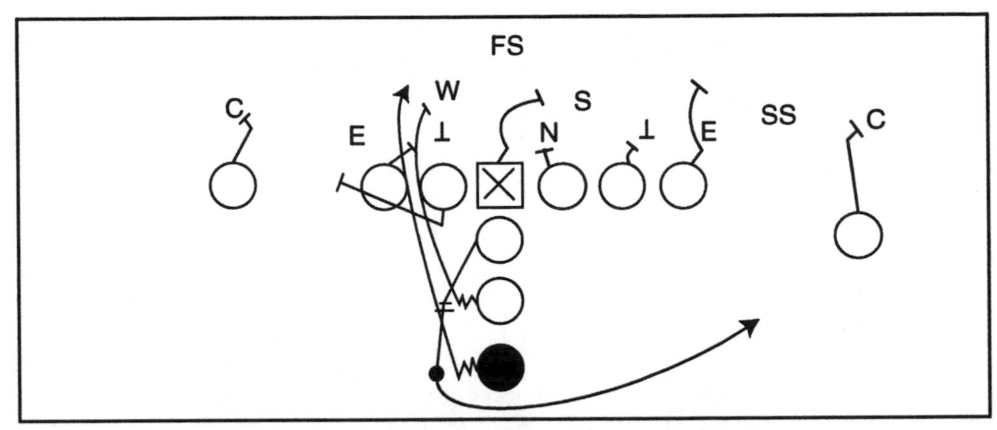

Figure 6.3—43 versus a 2-technique tackle with a cross block.

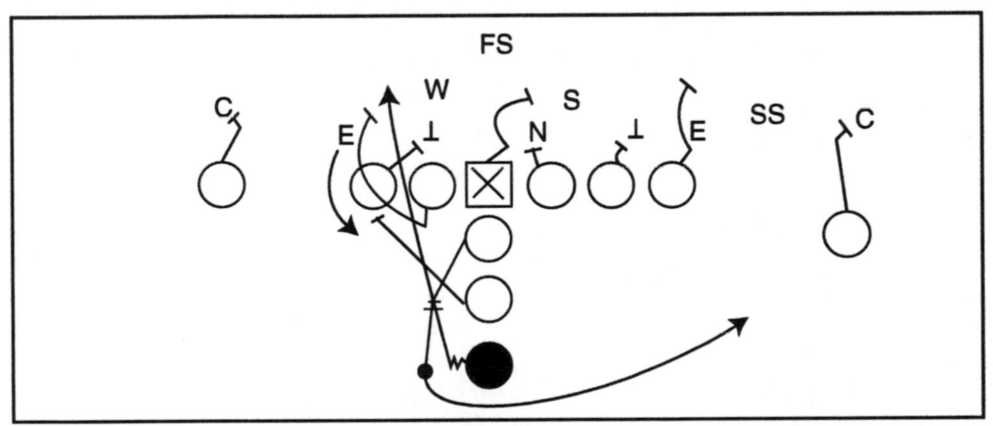

Figure 6.4—43 versus a 2-technique with a fold block by the quickside guard and quickside tackle.

follow. However, if the Will linebacker were to blitz through the A gap, the fullback's path would be different from that of the tailback, since he must meet the backer in the gap and prevent penetration.

Finally, if there is a 2-technique tackle, and the defensive end is coming on a hard rush (thereby causing difficulty for the guard to get to him), I suggest you fold block the play. The quickside tackle comes down just as on the cross block. However, the quickside guard now folds, blocks around to the Will linebacker to seal a running lane. The fullback now kicks out the on-rushing end. This step forces the tailback to get the ball tight, (i.e. inside the fullback), and requires him to angle off the hip of the tackle once he has the football. (Refer to Figure 6.4).

The blocking schemes for 43 versus various fronts are illustrated in Figure 6.5.

Figure 6.5—Blocking Assignments: 43

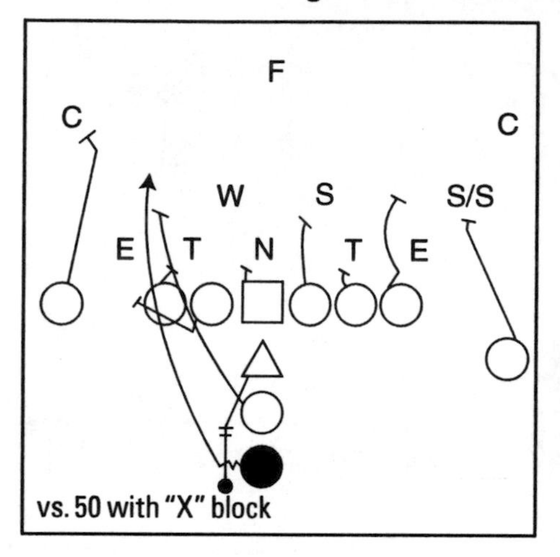

vs. 50 with "X" block

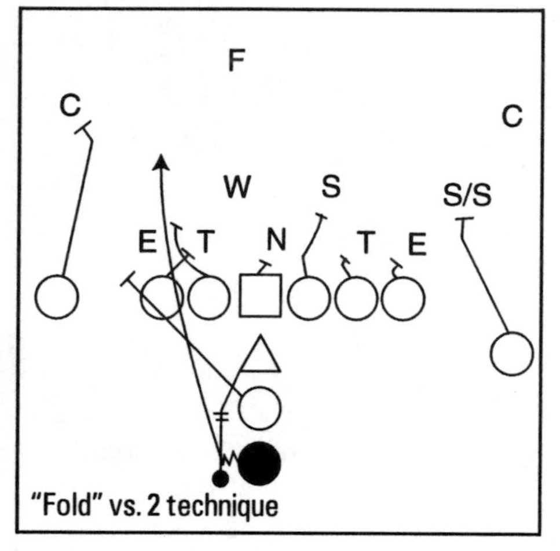

"Fold" vs. 2 technique

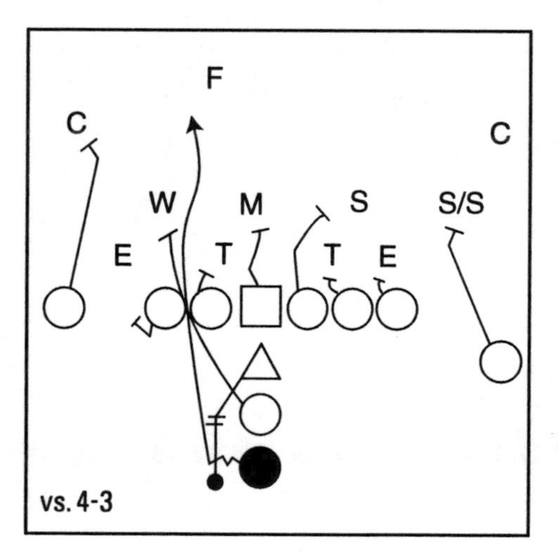

vs. 4-3

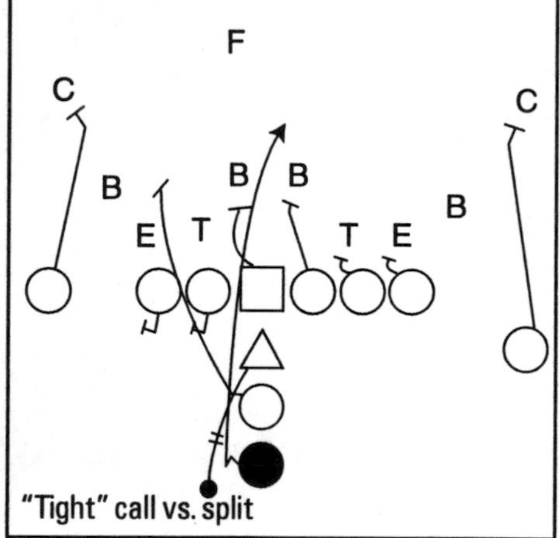

"Tight" call vs. split

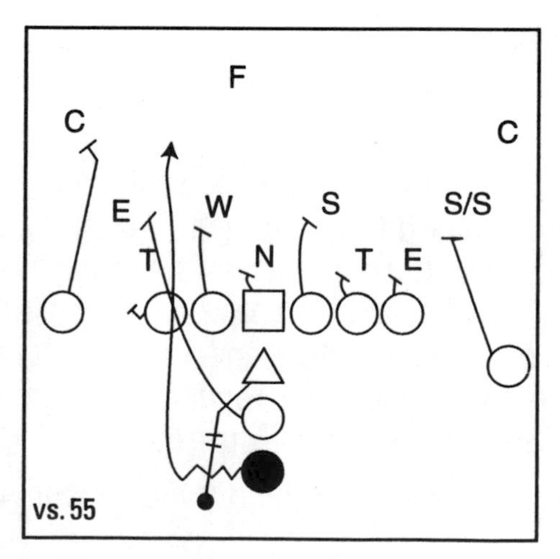

vs. 55

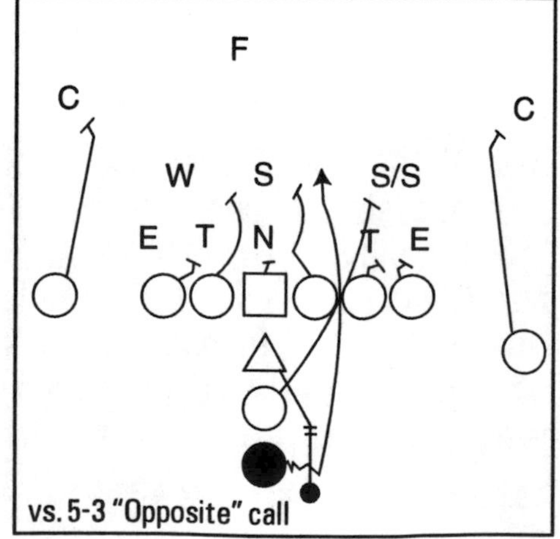

vs. 5-3 "Opposite" call

COACHING POINTS: 43

Fullback

Assignment: Opposite of 44

Tailback

Assignment: Opposite of 44

Quarterback

Technique: Same action as 44 to the weakside of the formation. However, once you place the ball in the tailback's stomach, place your hand nearest the tailback back in your own stomach. Allow your hand closest to the line of scrimmage to complete the handoff, and then extend your arm and show an empty palm with your back turned slightly to the backside contain player. This step should force the contain player to honor a possible naked.

CHAPTER 7

I Formation Runs: The Counter

If you run the sprint draw enough, you can really set up the counter. FSU still uses this play often in its offense, but not as often as they did in the late 80's and early 90's. The counter sets up a bootleg pass that is the number one pass play in our offense.

While the counter can be run to both the strongside and the weakside, most of this chapter deals with the strongside counter, because the strongside counter sets up the weakside bootleg, and it counteracts a shaded nose. On the strongside counter, the strongside of the offensive line blocks down one man. The strongside guard can either pull or block down as well. Both ways are discussed in this chapter. You should decide how best to use him within your scheme.

If the nose is shaded, the strong guard can chip off of him and to the backside linebacker unless the guard is assigned to pull. The center takes over the block on the nose. The quickside guard pulls to either kick or wrap. If the strongside guard is designated to pull, then the quickside guard turns up inside, looking to seal off the backside linebacker from pursuing. If the defensive end is coached to close down the gap on the down block, it is likely we will wrap (log) him rather than kick out. The quickside tackle pinches down on the 3-technique tackle, and the fullback fills for the pulling guard. The backside end is controlled with the bootleg.

The tailback should take a lateral shuffle step, just like on the sprint draw. Then he should plant his outside foot and push back to the strongside, receiving the ball behind the retreating quarterback, and following the block of the quickside guard. If the guard kicks out, he cuts inside of the block. However, if the guard wraps, the tailback should come off the guard's outside hip.

The quarterback reverses out to about 5 o'clock. His next two steps should be gathering steps that place him at the tailback. While moving, he should have the ball extended to the tailback. On his third step, he should set his feet, have his knees bent, and show an empty palm as he rides the tailback past his own hip. The quarterback should then place his hands back in his own belly and carry out the bootleg fake around the weakside end. Figure 7.1 diagrams 48 versus a 50 defense with the strongside guard pulling, while 7.2 depicts the play without the strongside guard pulling. Figure 7.3 illustrates how to block the play with a nose over the center and with the strongside guard pulling versus a 50 defense.

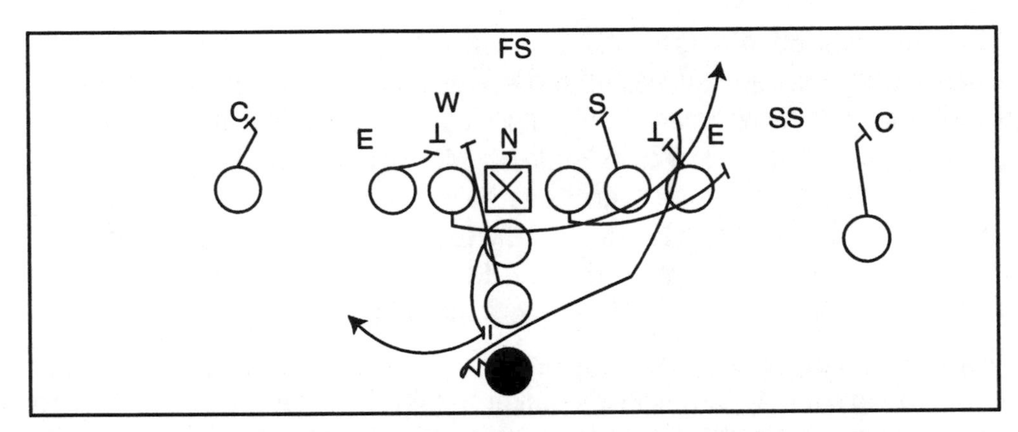

Figure 7.1—48 versus a 50 defense with the strongside guard pulling.

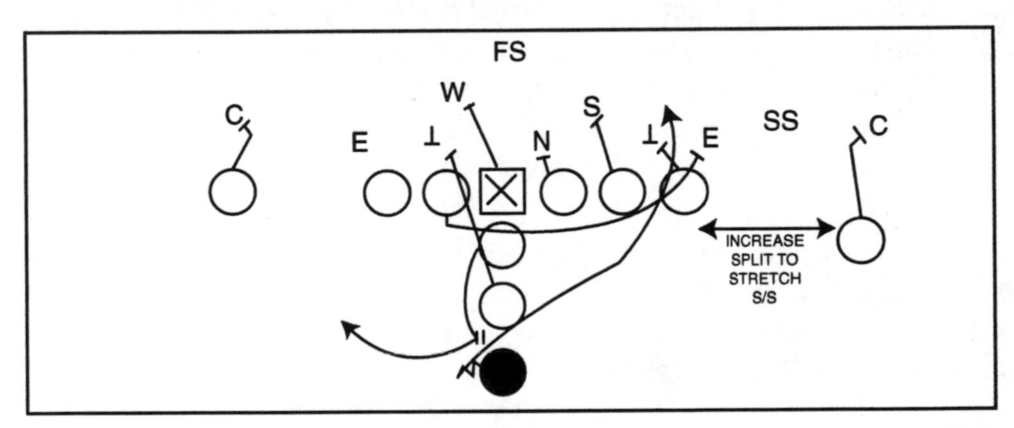

Figure 7.2—48 versus a 50 defense with a shaded nose without the guard pulling.

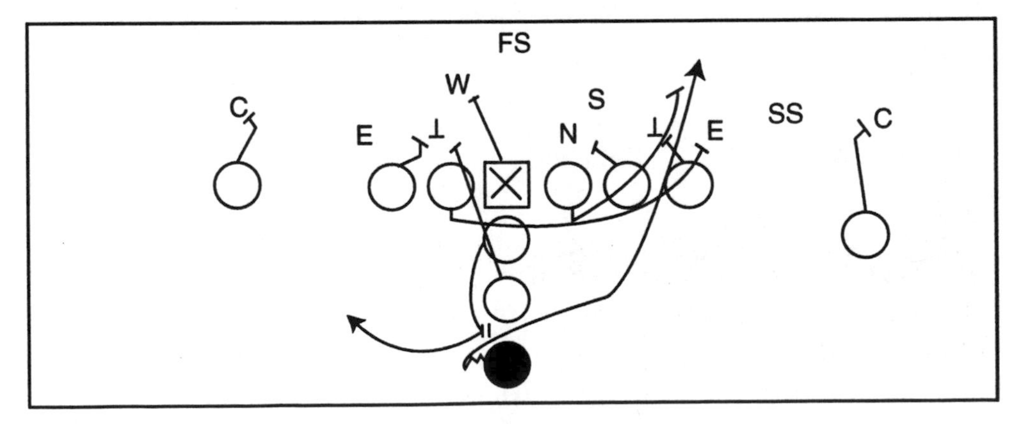

Figure 7.3—48 versus a 50 defense with a nose over the guard.

The weakside counter is much the same as the strongside, but in this instance the strongside guard and tackle pull. If the nose is not shaded, the quickside tackle and guard block down one man. The center blocks to the backside linebacker, while the strongside guard pulls to kick out the weakside defensive end. The strongside tackle is at the guard's hip, pulling to wrap the Will linebacker. The tight end pinches to the strongside defensive tackle, and the fullback fills for the pulling guard. The defensive end is controlled with the bootleg threat. The weakside counter can also be effectively run from an "Over" formation (Refer to Figure 7.4).

If you don't have a strongside tackle who moves very well, both guards can be pulled. In this instance, the quickside tackle should block down on the 3- or 2-technique. The center should block the nose, scooping if the nose is head up or blocking back if he is shaded. The strongside tackle then climbs to the backside linebacker, and the tight end scoops the 5-technique defensive tackle. The fullback fills for the pulling guard. The quickside guard pulls and kicks out the weakside defensive end. The strongside guard pulls and either kicks out or wraps the first man to show after turning underneath the block of the quickside guard. The tailback follows the block of the strongside guard (Refer to Figure 7.5).

If the nose shades to the strongside and the tackle moves to a 2-technique, the center blocks back on the shaded nose. The quickside tackle blocks down on the 2-technique, while the quickside guard pulls and kicks out or wraps the end. The strongside tackle climbs to the backside linebacker, and the tight end scoops the 5-technique with fill help from the fullback. The strongside guard pulls to the weakside and turns inside towards what will likely be a kick out block by the quickside guard. He should be looking behind him to the inside to pick up the playside linebacker, who can cause this play trouble from his position (Refer to Figure 7.6).

Additional blocking schemes for 48 and 45 against various fronts as illustrated in Figure 7.7.

Coaching Points: 48

Fullback

Assignment : Block the quickside "B" gap.

Technique: Go on a path at the inside hip of the quickside guard (adjust as needed according to the block); fill for the guard as he pulls. If the center easily blocks the defensive tackle, proceed to the second level.

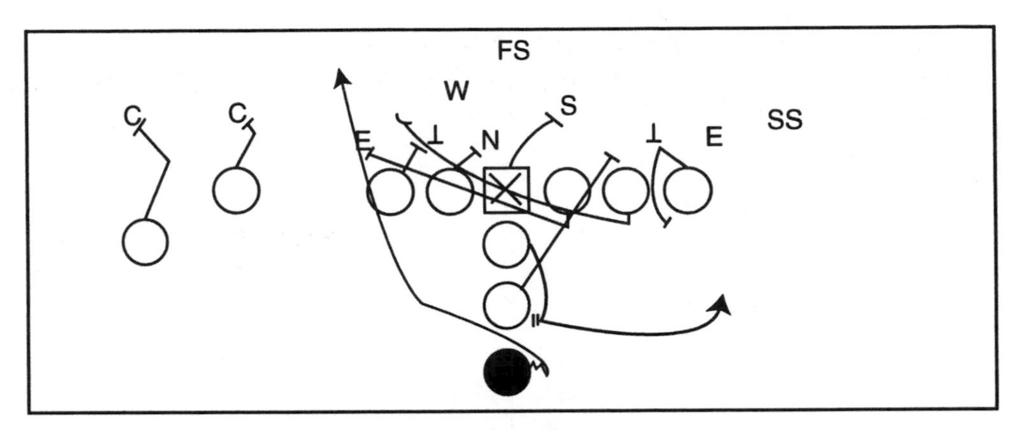

Figure 7.4—45 weakside counter versus a 50 defense.

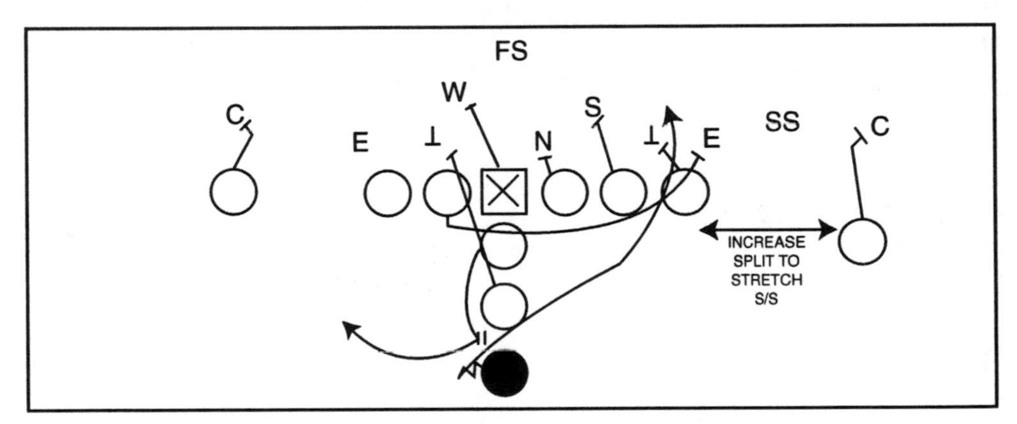

Figure 7.5—45 versus a 50 defense with both guards pulling.

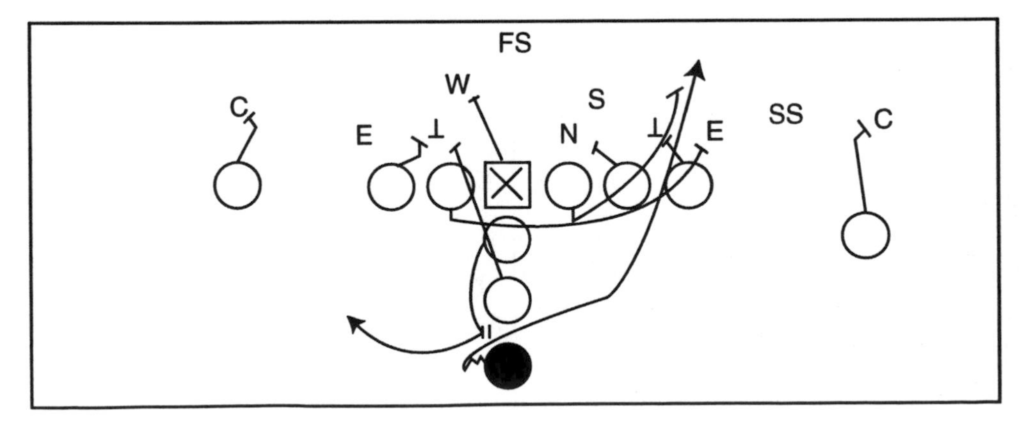

Figure 7.6—45 versus a 50 defense with a shaded nose and a 2-technique tackle.

Figure 7.7—Blocking Assignments: 48/45

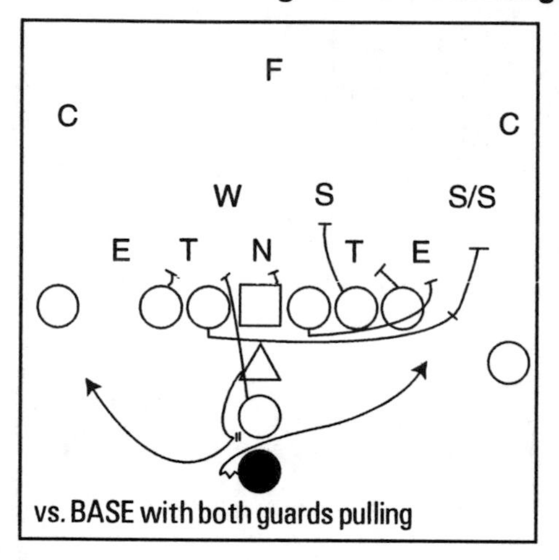

vs. BASE with both guards pulling

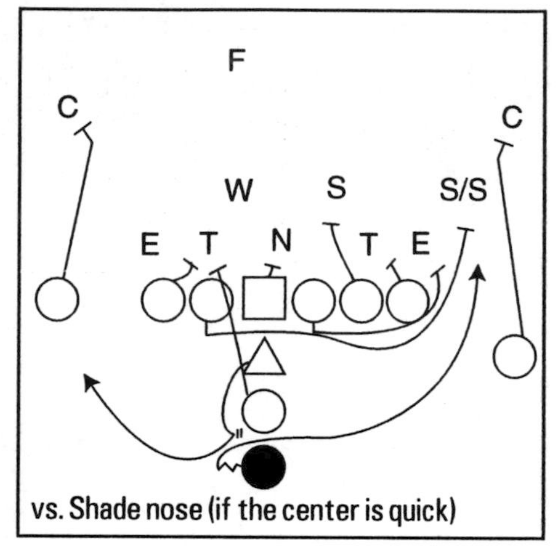

vs. Shade nose (if the center is quick)

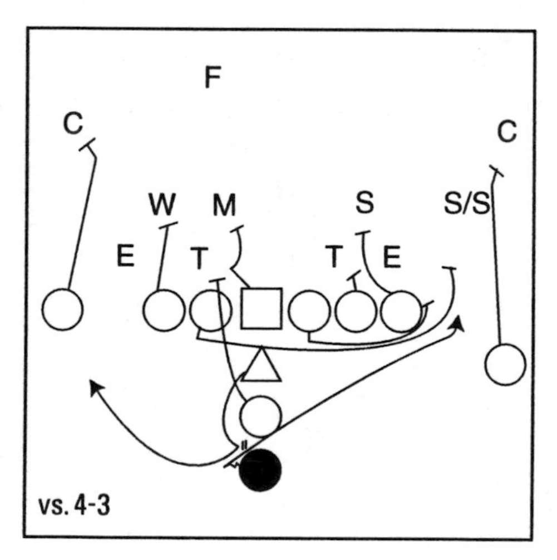

vs. 4-3

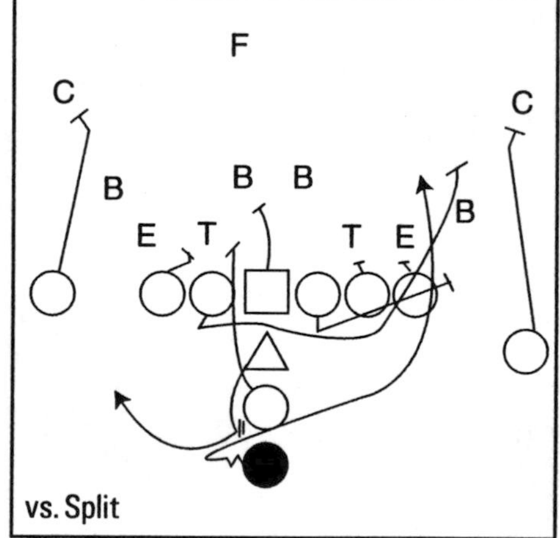

vs. Split

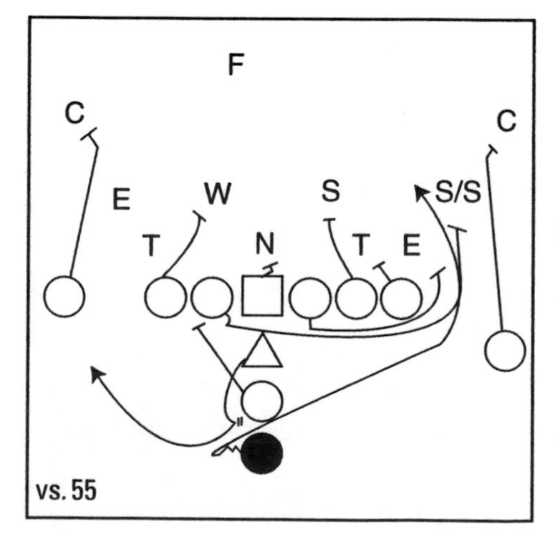

vs. 55

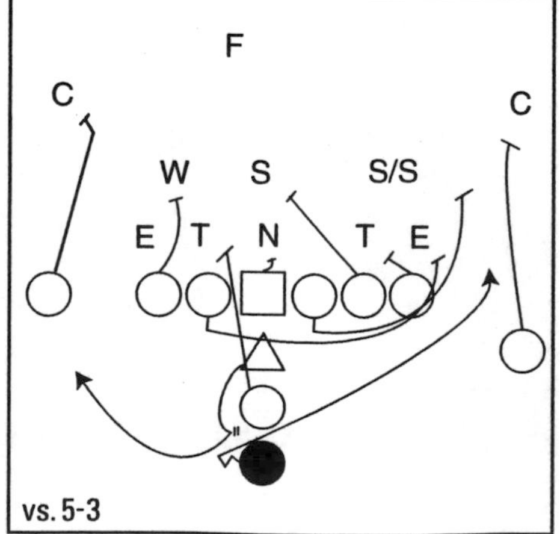

vs. 5-3

Tailback

Assignment: Read the block of the pulling guards.

Technique: Take one lateral step while staying square and then one shuffle step behind the quickside guard. Once you've completed the shuffle step, plant on your outside foot and go on a path at the hip of the strongside tackle. Stick the ball inside the kick-out block of the pulling guard. If the guard wraps the defensive end, cut off the guard's outside hip.

Quarterback

Technique: Open to 5 o'clock to the quickside. Your next two steps should be gathering steps, but you should gain ground while taking them. Reach the ball out to the tailback. Set your feet on your third step and hand off to the tailback with your knees and upper body slightly bent. Place the ball in the tailback's stomach and pull the hand closest to him back into your stomach. Allow the hand completing the handoff to extend toward the tailback as he passes you and show an empty palm. Then, place both of your hands into own stomach and sprint past the line of scrimmage.

CHAPTER 8

Quarterback Ball-Handling Techniques for Play-Action Passes

This chapter was written to provide a mental image of the quarterback's responsibilities for play-action passes. While these responsiblities are relatively easy to show in person or on videotape, they are much more difficult to put into words. As such, a little imagination on your part is essential. Hopefully, you will find the coaching points presented in this chapter (all staples for running the play-action plays of the FSU offense) helpful.

344 Action: The sprint-draw action pass.

The quarterback should open to the strongside at about 5 o'clock. He should begin extending his arms with the ball on his second step toward the tailback. He should not stand straight up. Rather, he should stay low as he continues to drop back. His shoulder nearest the tailback should be in a direct line with the tailback's inside shoulder. As he approaches the tailback, he should place the ball in the tailback's stomach with both of his hands. He should then pull the football back into his own belly with his arm nearest the tailback. He should allow the arm nearest the line of scrimmage to stay in the tailback's belly as he drops and the tailback comes by him—showing an empty palm as the tailback passes. He should snap his head around, watch the tailback, bring the ball back into the throwing position, and begin to look down field through the tailback. His setup should place him directly behind the strongside guard, while standing tall, approximately 9-10 yards deep.

43 Dash: Sprint-draw bootleg pass.

This play is executed the same as 344, except in this instance, the quarterback opens to the quickside. When he reaches the fifth step, he should release the ball from his hand closest to the tailback. The quarterback should give the tailback an empty palm and ride him as his shoulder opens up with him. He should make sure that his back is turned to the backside-rush defensive end. On this particular play, as the quarterback's head follows the defensive end, the quarterback should place the ball in his own stomach, take his final three steps, set, and freeze with a hand extended toward the tailback. The quarterback should stay on his toes, reverse out, and break contain back to the strongside with a pass/run option.

6 Bootleg: Counter play-action pass.

The quarterback's steps are just like 48. His weight should be on the balls of his feet as the tailback comes by him. The quarterback should ride the tailback as he comes by, with an empty palm, and then prepare to roll. After the quarterback passes the tailback, he should get his head around quickly to find the fullback, and get the ball to him if he is not covered. If the fullback is covered, the quarterback should gain depth and break contain if the quickside guard has wrapped the contain player. If the guard has to run the contain player up the field, the quaterback should pull up underneath the block and set up behind that guard. The quarterback should then look for the tight end dragging at 10 yards or X on a takeoff route. The backside receiver is running a post.

P 46: Toss sweep play-action pass.

The quarterback should reverse out to 7 o'clock and give a good toss fake, making sure to show the toss action of the ball. The quarterback's pivot step from under center should be larger than his pivot step on the sweep in order to gain depth from the line of scrimmage. On his second step back the quarterback should continue to gain ground, while his third step is a set-up step without hitching. He should get the ball into a throwing position and be ready to hit X on the slant.

46 Boot: Bootleg off toss-sweep action.

The quarterback should reverse out to 7 o'clock and show the ball to give a good toss fake. After the fake, he should get the ball to his stomach, and then get his head around to find the defensive end. He should follow the pulling guard and gain depth and should break containment. If the pulling guard kicks out, the quarterback should pull up under him and deliver the ball to the receiver. If the guard wraps, the quarterback should continue rolling out, looking to throw the pass first and run second, since high school-level quarterbacks tend to be better passers than runners.

Shotgun play-action rollouts.

The quarterback is aligned five yards from the line of scrimmage. He should heel kick to receive the snap. He should not move until he receives the football. He should then place the ball in the running back's stomach, according to whatever bootleg is called. Then, he should pull the ball out and place it on his hip furthest from the line of scrimmage. He should break contain by gaining depth to seven yards from the line of scrimmage as he rolls out. Then, he should attack downhill directly toward the primary route. He should look to pass first and run second. If the initial receiver is covered, he should adjust the angle of his attack to the path of the secondary receiver.

All of the aforementioned play-action plays can be applied to play-action passes that are described in detail later in the book. However, before you can throw play-action passes, your quarterbacks and receivers must develop certain fundamentals. The next two chapters address some of the most important of those fundamentals.

CHAPTER 9

Fundamentals of Quarterback Play

In the FSU style of offense, the quarterback is the most important player on the field. He must be an individual who can get it done. He must be a student of the game. When you select a quarterback, you should consider arm strength, mental toughness, and heart. If there is not an obvious candidate for the position, you should consider taking one of your better athletes on the field and develop his skills. Keep in mind that the quarterback must be a player who will take control of the situation and have the respect of his teammates. If he doesn't have it at practice, he won't have it on game days.

FSU quarterback coach Mark Richt has produced an excellent video on fundamentals for quarterbacks titled Quarterback Fundamentals: Florida State Style. I have viewed the tape several times and use many of Coach Richt's techniques with my own quarterbacks. In fact, I have our quarterbacks review it every year when we begin 3-a-days. I highly recommend this video for not only you as a coach, but also for your quarterbacks, right down to the junior high level.

While an entire book could be written on quarterback fundamentals, among the most important factors that are involved in adapting the FSU offense to your team are the grip, stance, throwing the football, throwing on the run, throwing touch passes, footwork, and doing the "extras."

The Grip:

When throwing the football, the initial factor that should be addressed is the grip. Because the size of a quarterback's hands tends to vary from individual to individual, the way each one grips the football can also vary. Some individuals put their fingers on the laces, while others have their fingers across the laces. Concerning the grip, however, the most important thing to teach is to have the quarterback grip as much of the back of ball as possible. If you don't, you may eventually see a wet football slip right out of the quarterback's hand.

One of the best tips I ever received on throwing a wet football, other than gripping as much of the back of the ball as possible, was to grip it lightly. If you squeeze a wet football, it will just squirt right out of your hand when you try to throw with any velocity. Therefore, you should coach your quarterback to grip the ball lightly, and to keep some of his weight back as he throws the ball, similar to a touch pass. His arm speed should remain the same as for passing a dry ball. As a result, the rotation on the ball should increase, making the pass easier to catch.

Stance

When in the pocket, the quarterback should be on the balls of his feet, with a slight bend in his knees and back. If an imaginary nail were to be driven from the sky, it should go through his shoulders, kneecaps, and toes. Over the years, I have found that one of the best ways for me to communicate to my quarterback regarding where to seat the ball is to tell him to hold it about where he would hold a baseball bat in his batting stance. That step usually puts him in a pretty good throwing position without much more explaining. His head should be cocked slightly over his front shoulder to help him scan his blind side during his drop back.

Throwing the Football

In order to improve your quarterback's awareness of the proper footwork when passing, you should paint a straight line for him to stand on when he throws. When the quarterback steps, his stride foot should land directly on that painted line. If his stride foot lands to either side of the line, he is either throwing across his body or opening up his torso too quickly. The ball should be brought back and up as he cocks to throw, never down or in a circular motion. Otherwise, the delivery of the ball would be slowed down. As he steps to the target, the quarterback should rotate his trunk and shoulder in a way that the receiver goes from seeing the back of his front shoulder to the back of his back shoulder. His elbow should be extended in his motion, not at or below shoulder level during the throw. At the end of the throw, his throwing hand should be in his opposite "hip pocket", with his thumb pointed down.

For incorporating variety in the distance and velocity of his passes, the quarterback should adjust (i.e., increase or decrease) the length of his stride when throwing. One of the best ways to accomplish this objective is for him to get a lot of reps throwing following each type of drop back. He should practice 3-step, 5-step, and play-action drops as he works on his distance and velocity. Over time, as the drops become more natural to him, his throwing accuracy should improve.

Throwing on the Run

The best way for a quarterback to improve his ability to throw on the run is to work on gaining ground from five to seven yards, and then to practice attacking the line of scrimmage directly at the primary receiver. In this regard, the quarterback should square his shoulders to the receiver, giving the receiver the back of his non-throwing shoulder. The quarterback should then rotate his trunk around as he continues to run toward the receiver. At the end of the motion, the back of the quarterback's throwing shoulder should face the receiver. If the quarterback throws while either fading away from the receiver or drifting toward the sideline, his pass will flutter and will be inaccurate. He should work the ball across his chest, back and forth as he rolls out, and then push the ball back into a good throwing position before throwing it to the receiver.

Throwing Touch Passes

To throw a touch pass, such as a fade, the quarterback should keep his weight "loaded" on his back foot. A quarterback should shift all of his weight to throw a bullet pass. Throwing touch passes, however, does not require that he transfer his weight entirely. By keeping his weight back, the quarterback can still throw a touch pass with the same arm speed as a frozen-rope sideline or an out route. To throw a touch pass, the quarterback should slightly tilt his shoulders upward and keep his weight loaded on his back foot. He should then throw the ball, using the same upper body motion as with more forceful throws. He should shift his weight proportionately in relation to the amount of touch he wants on the pass. Keep in mind that as a rule, the more of his weight held back equates to more touch he can put on the football.

Footwork

The best prescription for improving a quarterback's footwork is to practice a lot of drop backs. I recommend at least five drops looking to each side of the field on the 3-step drop, the 5-step drop, and the 344-play-action each day during individual work. Jumping rope several hundred times or for a preset time period (e.g., continuously for 20 minutes) per day can also enhance a quarterback's ability to exhibit quick feet. Furthermore, performing agility drills, such as a dot drill, can also be very effective.

Doing the Extras

Almost every good quarterback will commit the time and energy to performing those extra tasks that can enhance his performance without being asked to do them. For example, strength training, throwing practice, and film watching are essential undertakings in the summer and off-season for the quarterback who wants to make a positive difference on game day.

CHAPTER 10

FUNDAMENTALS OF RECEIVER PLAY

Receivers in the FSU-style of offense must be fundamentally sound and consistent in their performance. At the high-school level, it is not critical that they have super speed, nor do they all have to have perfect hands. It is essential, however, that you develop receivers who run consistent routes and who are able to catch the relatively easy throws. In the process, you should get enough exceptional catches just off the momentum that receivers tend to achieve by just doing the fundamental things properly. As a rule, you should have your receivers perform drills that are specifically designed to get your receivers out of any bad habits they might have learned previously.

You should begin with a simple stance-and-start drill. Some receivers develop a false step, (i.e., stepping back before stepping forward), in junior high that they continue to exhibit. You should get them out of that habit as early as possible. The drill starts by having the receivers place their inside foot forward and bend slightly at the knee. Their weight should be loaded on the ball of their inside foot, while their outside foot should be back. They should bend slightly at the waist, with both of their hands up in front of their chest to fight off a press corner's hands. All receivers should look in at the football. The drill consists of simply putting each receiver in this stance, and having him look in at the ball being snapped. Each receiver should then practice taking off without using a false step. This practice should be done over and over to improve a receiver's ability to get a good start off the line of scrimmage.

When conducting the stance-and-start drill, both a shotgun and an under-center snap should be employed to enable the receiver to practice seeing the snap of the ball. Also, receivers should work on both inside and outside releases against a defensive back who is positioned in front of them. The defensive back should press the receiver and play bump and run with him. While receivers are working on their stance and start in the drill, they are also practicing how to get a good release to get off of press coverage. In the FSU-style of offense, they will face press coverage. As a rule, if they do not practice getting off press coverage, they will probably struggle on game days.

Another effective receivers' drill is the exaggerated catch. In this drill, the receiver focuses on a point on the ball into his hands and then watches the ball all the way down as it is tucked under his arm. While this drill might seem trivial, the habit of catching the football and putting it away can be invaluable in an offense that regularly throws the ball around. This drill can help prevent all of those dropped balls that are caused by receivers who turn their heads before they catch and put away the ball.

Once you find out who can catch the ball, and who can run well enough to get on the field, you should teach them how to block. A number of big plays are "spoiled" in high school-level competition because a wide receiver casually trots off the line of scrimmage on a running play, only to have a cornerback make a touchdown-saving tackle. Tommy Bowden had what I think was the most aggressive, vicious groups of receivers I have ever seen when he coached at Auburn, but they weren't very big. In fact, his nicknames for them were "Sticks" and "Bones". The point to keep in mind is that any size receiver can be an effective blocker if he is instilled with a little aggressiveness. In fact, too many corners are worried about getting beat deep. As a result, a receiver just coming off the line hard gets them to retreat. Accordingly, receivers need to use that initial burst of speed to either get into the defensive back's pads, or to break down and shield him off with good footwork. The circle block that was discussed in the chapter on the sprint draw can also be very effective on plays where the ball goes away.

The next section covers a few of the fundamental routes employed in the FSU-style of offense that receivers should master, including the slant, hitch, quick out, shallow cross, corner post, choice, broken arrow, and hot adjustments.

Slant Route

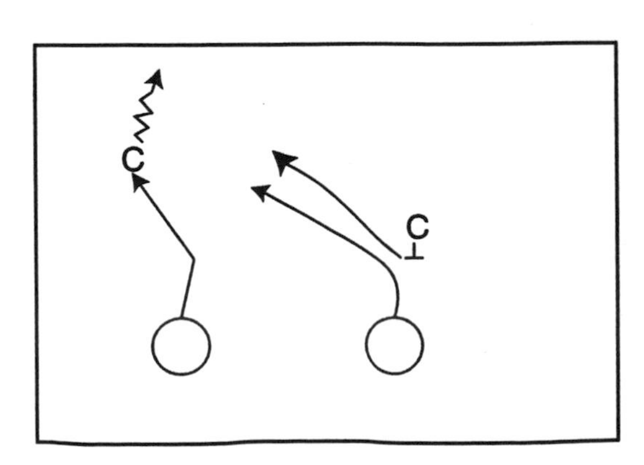

Against a soft-zone coverage, the receiver should take three steps at the defensive back's outside shoulder, and then break at a 45-degree angle to the inside, looking for the football. Against a press coverage, he should get inside position and make an inside break. If the corner aligns with an inside technique, he should fight across his face on the snap of the ball due to the blitz threat.

Hitch Route

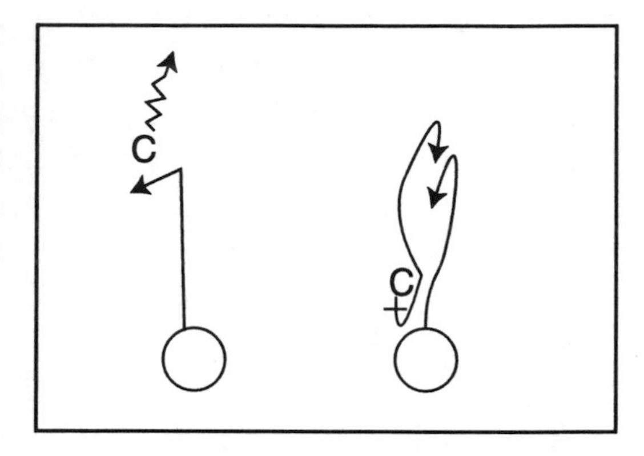

Against soft-zone coverage, the receiver should take five steps at the defensive back's outside shoulder, and then break back down the stem. This route is an effective way to control the blitz and a logical option for taking advantage of the opportunity to gain 5-7 yards against soft coverages. If the receiver is confronted by press coverage, he should collide with the outside shoulder of the defender, and then execute a swim move back to the inside to force the defender to come through his hips to make a play on the ball.

Quick-Out Route

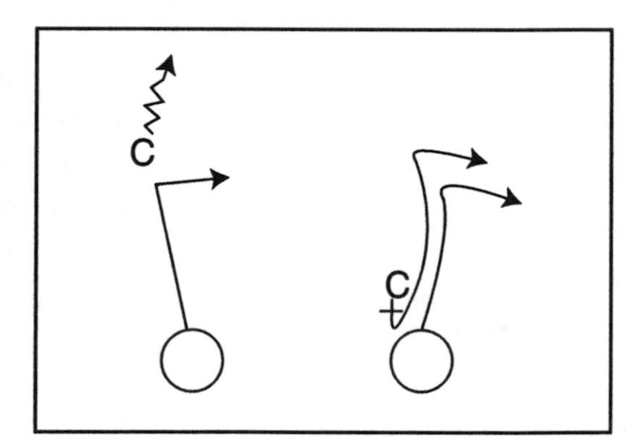

Against a soft-zone, the receiver should take four steps at the outside shoulder of the defender, and then make a speed cut, throwing both his outside elbow and head back to the quarterback. Against press coverage, the receiver should execute an outside release and lean against the defender just before making the break at five yards to the sideline. This action can create needed separation.

Shallow-Cross Route

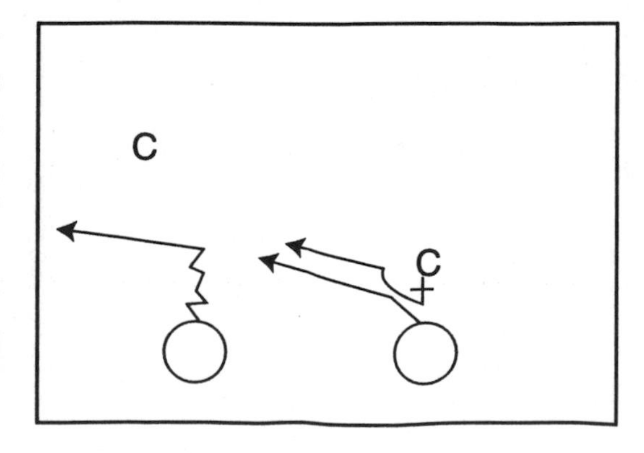

Against soft-zone coverage, the receiver should take slow choppy steps to three yards up field, and then cross underneath the linebackers at a depth of five yards. When the receiver is ready for the ball, he should make eye contact with the quarterback. He should get separation immediately against press or man coverage and accelerate across the field.

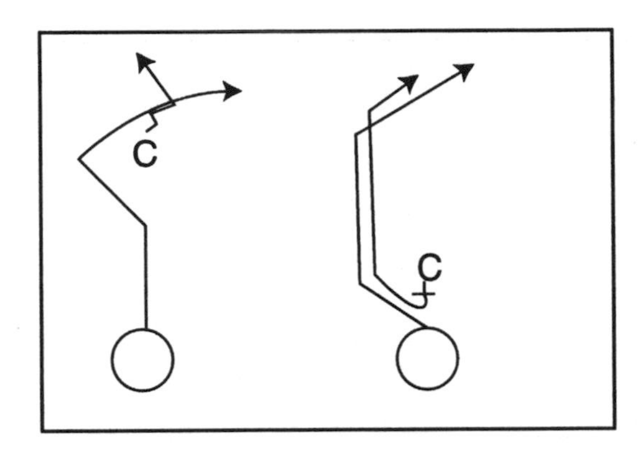

Corner Route

Against soft-zone coverage, the receiver should attack the inside shoulder of the defender and break to the post on his fifth step. He should drive toward the post through his eighth step, and then break hard back to the corner of the field. Against press coverage, he should stem inside of the defender, straighten up through 10 yards, and then break out to the corner.

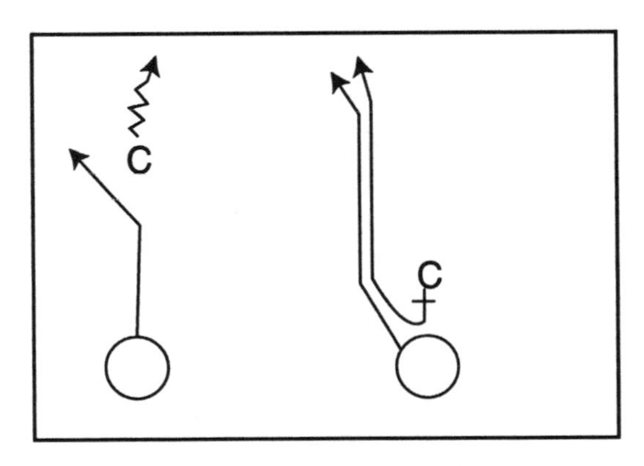

Post Route

Against soft-zone coverage, the receiver should attack the outside shoulder of the defender to gain leverage through his seventh step. He should then break to the near upright if the safety is in the middle of the field. If the safety rolls over to his hash mark, the receiver should break to the middle of the goal post. When the defender presses, the receiver should stem inside and accelerate to seven yards, and then break to the post.

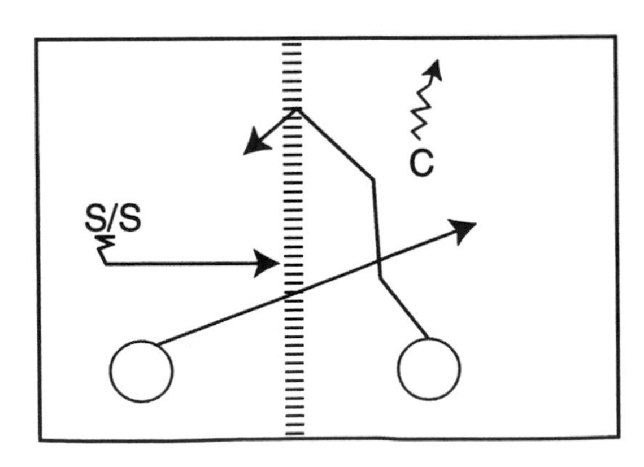

Choice Route

On this route, the receiver should stem inside the corner and work up the field 10 yards. He should settle one yard inside the curl/flat player and take one step back down the stem. The receiver should glance at the flat player on the release to see how far to work inside. The receiver should be inside the player responsible for the flat area, thereby forcing the defender to decide who to cover.

Broken-Arrow Route

This route is thrown to an inside receiver from a 3- or 4-receiver formation. The route is designed to stretch the middle of the field. The receiver should release off the linebacker to 8-10 yards, looking at the safety. If the safety is on or near the hash mark, the receiver should execute an outside move (like a corner) and then break inside the safety. If the safety is not near the hash mark, the receiver should continue on a vertical route.

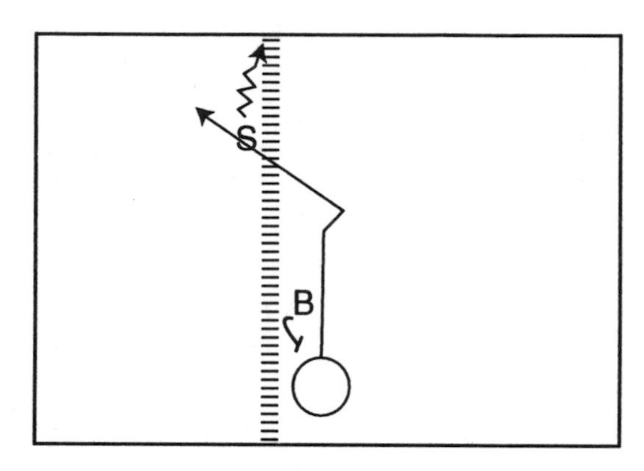

Hot Adjustments

All receivers should be able to recognize and perform hot-route adjustments. For example, if the T or Y receiver has a stick route called on a given play, and the outside linebacker over that receiver blitzes, that receiver must get his head around quickly because he is the hot receiver in that situation. In that instance, the ball will be half way to the receiver out of his break on the stick route.

If either of those receivers has a route other than a stick route called, and the linebacker blitzes, the receiver can break off on one of two hot-route adjustments. The one selected depends on which one you and your players feel the most comfortable. I have always taken the quarterback and receivers during individual periods early in the year and worked hot routes. The players then give me feedback on which hot route they feel will be the easiest for them to recognize and execute.

The first possible hot adjustment is the hitch break-off. The primary advantage of the hitch break-off is its quickness. The quarterback can shortstop-pivot and make the short throw immediately. The pass must be thrown on a line. Because the safety is replacing the linebacker in man coverage on the hot receiver, if the ball is lofted, the receiver may get his head knocked off. The disadvantage of this route involves the fact that a tall linebacker can get his hands up and obstruct the path of this particular hot adjustment. Figure 10-1 illustrates the hitch break-off.

The other hot adjustment is a pass to the quick out. On this route, the receiver breaks straight to the sideline. While this route can help prevent a deflection from being a factor, it requires is a slightly longer throw by the quarterback. This route is a wonderful adjustment to make if the quarterback is a decent passer (Refer to Figure 10-2).

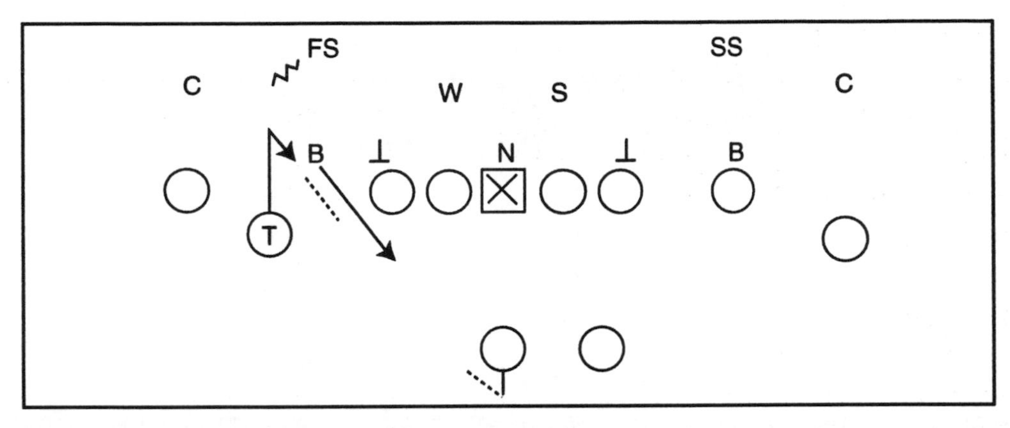

Figure 10-1. Hitch hot route by "T" versus a blitz.

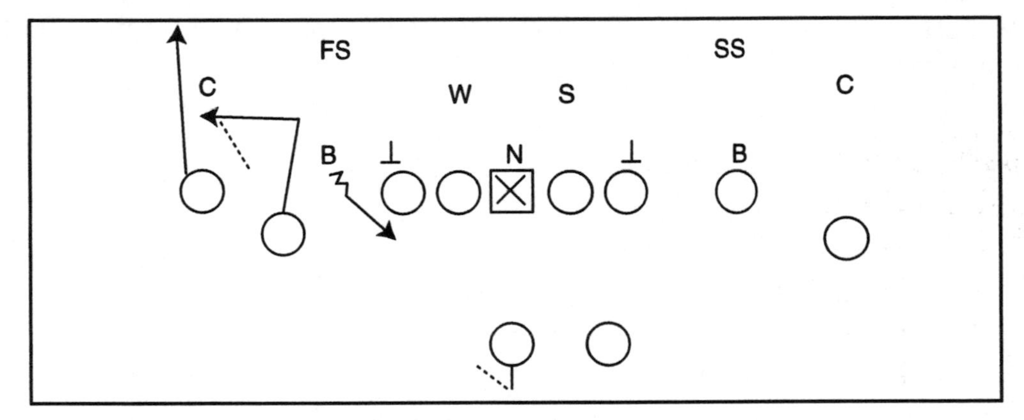

Figure 10-2. Quick-out hot adjustment versus a linebacker blitz.

CHAPTER 11

Running Back Fundamentals

The success of a FSU-style of offense is affected by the ability of running backs to adhere to several basic fundamentals. Perhaps none of these fundamentals is more important than protecting the football. Every coach spends part of the first day of practice showing running backs exactly how to carry and protect the football against their body. While it may seem trivial to go over, it could be the most important factor you cover the entire season. A simple drill daily can help remind your running back to protect the ball. The drill involves two lines of backs, usually 4-5 in each line, with four tackling dummies placed flat on the ground between them. A designated back receives a handoff and explodes between the two lines of players. The players in each line attempt to strip the football as the back is trying to get through the "hole", while stepping over the dummies on the ground that make him keep his legs pumping high.

Another essential fundamental for running backs to master is blocking. A running back has to make several different types of blocks during the course of a football game, ranging from lead blocks to pass protection. Each of the various types of blocks should be emphasized during the week of preparation for a game. During individual periods, you should have your running backs practice one or two of those blocks against a hand-held blocking dummy on a daily basis. This approach doesn't involve a tremendous amount of time and enables your backs to receive individual attention to their personal needs.

The first block that should be covered is a straight-lead block, simulating a situation involving a sprint draw or isolation play. The fullback and the tailback should perform the block. While the tailback will rarely if ever be required to execute the block in a game, practicing the block can make him appreciate the efforts of the fullback. Keep in mind that respect for teammates is an important part of the game. The drill involves having the backs explode out of their stance and attack the dummy with low pads to simulate blowing a backer out of the hole. This block should be performed once to each side of the formation.

The next block that should be covered is the lead block for the toss sweep. Fullbacks often have trouble judging where the linebacker will be on the toss sweep. Many backs want to run where the linebacker was before the ball was snapped, rather than where he will be when he is keying the flow of the football. The lead block is crucial to making the sweep go. The player holding the blocking dummy should move as if he is chasing down the tailback on the sweep. That step will give the fullbacks a good look at exactly where the line backer will be. You should also have the linebacker blitz occasionally. As a result, you can see if the fullback is picking up the movement of the linebacker so he can cut him off in the gap where the linebacker blitzes.

Pass protection is also a vital skill for running backs to master. You should cover three primary factors with running backs concerning pass protection. First, on the quick-passing game, the running backs should sprint to protect the outside hip of the tackles. The quick-passing game will involve a 3-step drop by the quarterback that must be blocked aggressively to keep defenders' hands down. Our backs are told to attack the defender at his belly button. This step will force the defender to either keep his hands down or be flipped completely over.

One way to give the running backs the opportunity to practice pass protection blocks is to roll out a "snake" with alignment spots on it and place a blocking dummy at the quickside tackle's hip and the strongside tackle's hip. The backs should attack this dummy at full speed with low pads and explode into it, landing on their belly to simulate accelerating all the way through the block. It is a good idea to perform this drill with the quarterback involved so that the backs can make sure they come in low enough not to have the short pass hit them in the ear-hole as they go by the quarterback.

The next block that should be addressed is the 5-step pass with maximum protection. This skill is essential if the running back is to be able to effectively perform his blocking responsibilities. The running back should check the linebacker on his assigned side to see if he blitzes. If the linebacker blitzes, the back should meet him in the hole. If the linebacker does not blitz, the back should protect the hip of the tackle. Defenses frequently align their defensive ends wide on passing downs to try and beat the offensive tackle off the block. This step forces the running back to step up and block.

The final block that is involved in the straight drop-back passing series is the free-release block. The running back usually has a flat or swing pass route assigned to him. He must still check his assigned linebacker, however. If the linebacker drops into coverage when the football is snapped, the back should run his assigned route. If the linebacker blitzes, the back should abandon his route and meet the backer in the hole. This step maximizes our pass protection as much as possible. One of the most effective ways to work on this technique is to assign the backs a route, and then have a linebacker either drop or blitz at the snap. Simultaneously, a quarterback should be working on his drops. If the linebacker stunts, the back should attack him. If the linebacker doesn't blitz, the quarterback should practice passing to the running back so that the back can work on his receiving skills out of the backfield.

Running backs should also be able to contribute to the play-action passing game. This contribution can involve several areas. For example, perhaps the most important aspect of a play-action pass is the fake by the running back. While the footwork of the quarterback has previously been reviewed, the footwork and the fake of the running backs are what make the play work. As such, the value of the fake should be emphasized daily in practice. A good fake should be praised, while a bad one should be quickly corrected. The next section discusses several of the play-action responsibilities of the running backs.

344 Action

The fullback should attack the defensive end off of the offensive tackle's hip on the snap of the football. Because the tight end will be releasing into his route, the defensive end will likely be aligned outside or head up on him. The critical need is to protect against the first man. If the defense were to bring a strong safety blitz, the quarterback should recognize it and deliver the ball to a hot receiver. The fullback cannot release his man to pick up the strong safety.

The tailback must first shuffle behind the strongside guard. He should stay square to the line of scrimmage. When he hits his outside foot, he should start toward the line of scrimmage. His eyes should be on the strong linebacker. If the linebacker were to blitz, the tailback should abandon his fake and meet him in the hole. If the linebacker does not blitz, the tailback should take the empty hand fake of the quarterback and lean over the imaginary football as he runs through the line of scrimmage. If the tailback is not tackled, he should fight through traffic and run his assigned route for the play.

6 Boot: Counter Play Action

The fullback releases just as if he were going to fill for the quickside guard. In a best-case scenario, he should ease through the "B" gap traffic and work his way into the flats at a depth of 3-5 yards. He should get his head around as soon as he clears traffic and expect a quick throw.

The tailback should take a lateral shuffle step to the weakside guard. He should stay square, just like the sprint draw, until he hits on his outside foot. He should then go back on a path toward the outside hip of the strongside tackle. He should then take the empty-hand fake of the quarterback and sell the illusion that he has the football, before blocking the backside contain player.

P 46 & 46 Boot

The fullback should attack the strongside "B" gap to protect. He should go in low to help sell the run action. If the playside linebacker steps up, he should meet him at the line of scrimmage.

The tailback should make a great 46 fake. He uses a ten-digit fake—palms open, knees high to receive an imaginary pitch. He should tuck away the imaginary ball and roll over his upper body. He should then sprint seven yards past the last man on the line of scrimmage, carrying out the fake. He should then get his head back around to the quarterback to receive a possible outlet pass.

Shotgun Play Action

On shotgun play- action passes, the back receiving the fake should shuffle over to the center-guard gap, staying square to the line of scrimmage. He should show pass for a split second during the shuffle, and then plant his outside foot and come across the quarterback's face to receive an empty-palm fake. He should take the fake with two hands and lean over the imaginary ball as he either fills for a pulling guard or blocks the backside contain player, depending on the play call.

All of these fundamentals are vital to make the offense successful. While there are literally hundreds of different drills possible to practice the fundamentals of the FSU-style offense, I suggest that for time-efficiency reasons, you choose only a select few that will best accomplish what you want to do with this offense.

CHAPTER 12

I Formation Play-Action Passes

Play-action passing can help make the running game go. Without it, a running game can have great difficulty reaching its full potential. With it, you have a multiple offense that can cause considerable problems for the defense.

When putting together a play-action passing game, you should make sure the plays come off of runs that you use regularly. That step will increase the effectiveness of both. While Florida State's play-action package is not talked about that much due to their use of the shotgun, they have one of the best play-action passing games in the country. In fact, when the streak of 10-win seasons and top-four finishes began, it was play-action passing that helped the 'Noles dominate games. At that time, FSU did not employ the shotgun formation. In fact, their top running plays—the sweep, sprint draw, and counter—helped them set up a deadly play-action passing game.

The play-action passes FSU uses are very easy to adapt to the high school level. However, the first thing an offense must have with the play-action passing game is a simple pass-protection scheme that allows the quarterback sufficient time to get the ball off. In this chapter, each play action that is introduced from the FSU offense is accompanied by a simplified protection scheme that goes with it. Keep in mind that you might need to modify a particular play-action according to your personnel.

P 46

The first play action examined is the P 46—a short-range pass off the toss-sweep action. Accordingly, the offensive line needs to get the hands of the defensive front down, because the ball will be delivered quickly, from about 4-5 yards behind the line of scrimmage. The tight end should stay solid for added protection on the route. The split end (X) is the primary receiver, so the ball will most likely be delivered to the quickside of the field. The offensive line should use inside-zone protection, engaging each defender low to keep his hands down. Against a 50 defense, the tight end aggressively blocks the defensive end. The strongside tackle aggressively blocks the 4i or 5-technique. The strongside guard steps down to help on the nose, while the center blocks on the nose. The quickside tackle aggressively blocks the weakside end, making sure that the end keeps his hands low. The quickside guard is on the weakside tackle, who is in either a 3-technique or a 2-technique.

If a blitz occurs to the weakside, the center steps to the weakside "A" gap to zone protect, allowing the strongside guard to take over the block on the nose. The quickside guard becomes responsible for the weakside "B" gap, while the quickside tackle takes the "C" gap. In this instance, they have inside responsibility first in a blitz situation. To the strongside, the fullback, who is attacking the line just as if he were going to block on 46, takes on the Sam linebacker if he blitzes. Figure 12.1 and Figure 12.2 illustrate the pass protection for P46 against a 50 and a blitz, respectively.

P 46 stands for Pass 46. On this play, X runs a 5-yard slant route. Z runs a 7-step post. Y stays solid to solidify the protection. While the aforementioned are the primary routes, the tailback carries out the 46 fake by making a 10-digit fake with his hands, and then sprinting toward the sideline as if he has the football. About halfway toward the sideline, the tailback's emphasis changes from a fake to the flare route. He is an outlet receiver along the sideline.

I personally have seen the ball thrown to the tailback on this play. In 1989, FSU quarterback Peter Tom Willis hit the tailback on this play in a crucial victory over LSU. While such a toss to the tailback is rare, the quarterback should know that the tailback is out there. If nothing else, the quarterback can throw the ball over the tailback's head and out of bounds if everyone is covered. As such, this type of flare route gives the quarterback a place to throw the ball away without being called for grounding. The quarterback's footwork on this play, is discussed in at the chapter on quarterback play-action techniques (Chapter 3). P46 is diagramed in Figure 12.3.

P 46 Takeoff

Another play that can be run off the 46 action is the P 46 takeoff. On the P46 takeoff, X and Z simply run a takeoff route. They each aim for a landmark 25 yards down the field, five yards from the sideline. The only other difference in the play is the depth of the quarterback's drop. On the P46 takeoff, he should take a fourth and fifth step before setting up to deliver the ball. On this play, the quarterback should really exaggerate the toss action with his head and shoulders, and then hunch over his upper body as he continues into his drop. This action could bait the free safety into stepping up, thereby possibly preventing him from giving any help to the two corners who are covering the vertical routes. Figure 12.4.

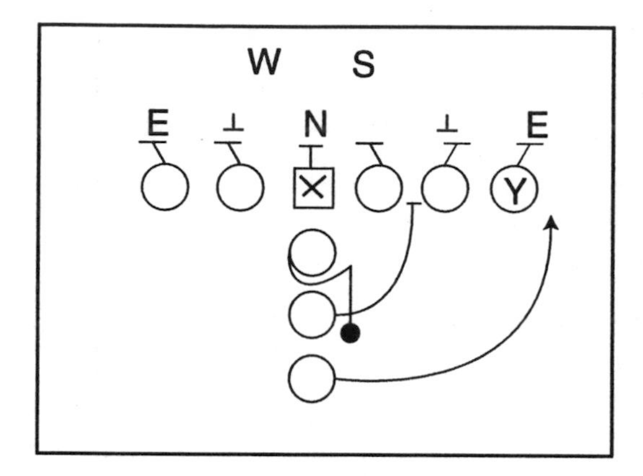

Figure 12.1—P46 protection vs. 50.

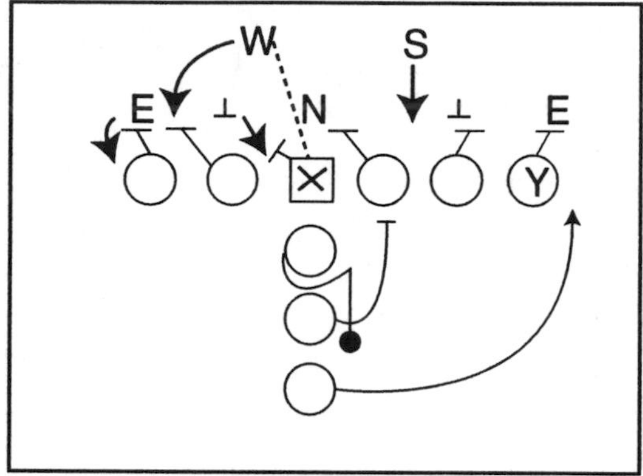

Figure 12.2—P46 protection vs. blitz.

Bootleg

The next play action off the sweep that is reviewed is the bootleg. In this instance, we try not to complicate the protection. Against a 50 defense, the quickside tackle blocks down on the 3 or 4i technique tackle. The quickside guard blocks back on the nose, and the center blocks back to the strongside defensive tackle. The strongside guard pulls to the boot on the weakside. The strongside tackle "chokes" the defensive tackle to give the center time to take him on, and then checks the back door for the defensive end pursuing. The tight end releases into his route (Refer to Figure 12.5).

To help adapt to the FSU system, you might want to follow what we have done successfully in the past with bootlegs. To the extent feasible, we "water down" things for the kids so they have less to learn. Instead of having a different route combination for every bootleg pass, we have one route combination for boots that goes to the strongside, and one route combination for bootleg passes that go to the weakside. That approach cuts down on confusion for both the quarterbacks and the receivers. While this step takes some of the various combinations that FSU uses away, it has been the most effective way I have found to adapt the offense to high school football. In fact, because 46 boot and 48 boot (off the counter play) have the same routes by the receivers, you can have just a "weak boot" signal for the wide receivers to give them the play call from the line of scrimmage in a no-huddle situation. Because their routes are the same on both plays, both plays should be signaled the same way to the wideouts.

On 46 boot, the fullback fills for the pulling guard in order to maximize protection on the backside. The tailback, after making a 10-digit fake, sprints toward the sideline as if he has the football (just like P 46). The quarterback makes the toss fake and rolls back to the quickside following the block of the strongside guard,

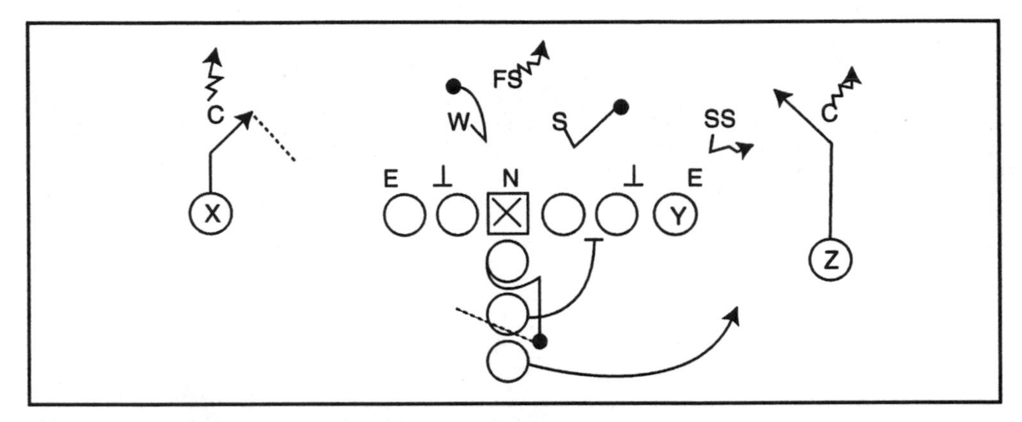

Figure 12.3—P 46 versus a 50 defense with a cover 3.

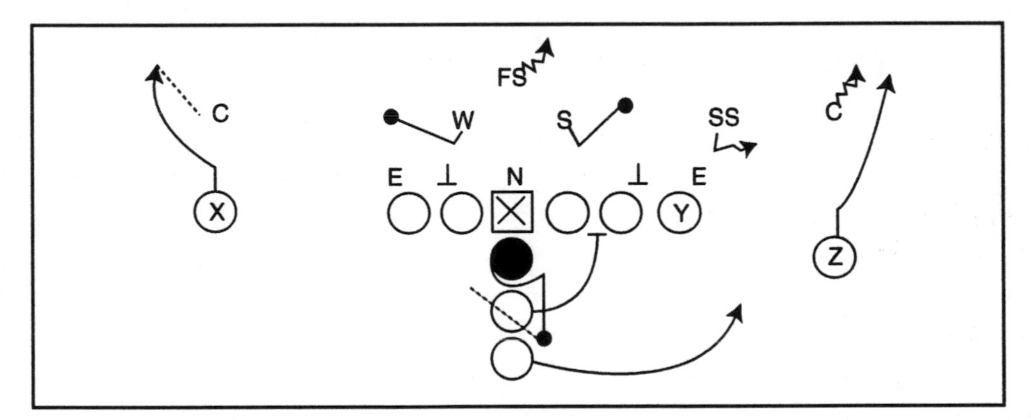

Figure 12.4—P 46 Takeoff.

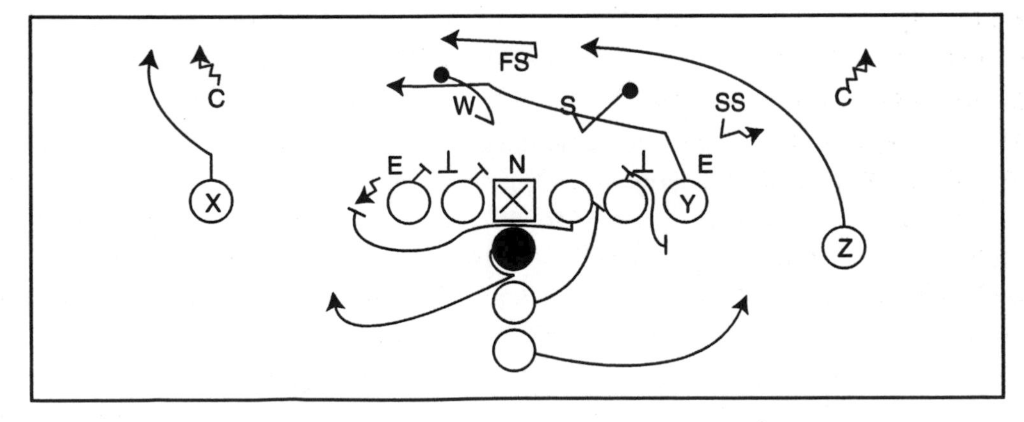

Figure 12-5. 46 boot versus 50 defense.

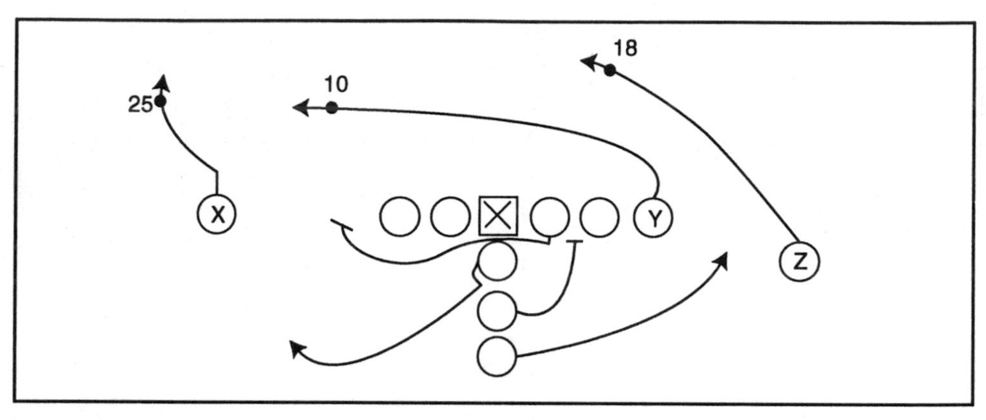

Figure 12.6—46 boot routes versus a 3-deep zone.

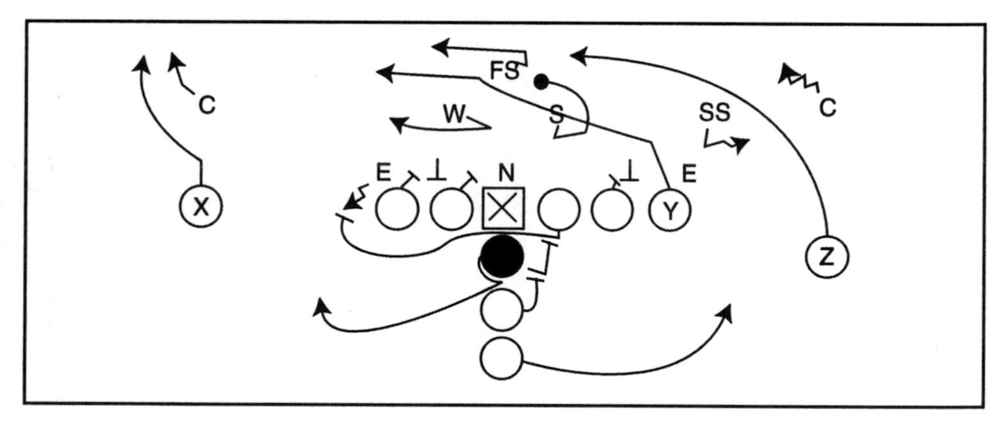

Figure 12.7—34 boot versus a 3-deep zone.

who either kicks out or wraps the contain man. A more detailed description of the quarterback's fake, is presented in the chapter that discussed quarterback ball-handling techniques (Chapter 8).

The routes on the 46 boot play involve the following actions. X runs a takeoff and has a landmark of 25 yards down the field, five yards from the sideline. The tight end has a 10-yard drag. Z has a deep 18-yard angle route, right where the free safety vacates to help over the top of X. One possible route adjustment on the play is to have X run a 10-yard out route on a speed cut. This adjustment gives the quarterback a quick outlet to deal the ball out of the fake.

The quarterback's read progresses from a quick glance at X first, and then checking Y on the drag route. If the free safety has obviously gotten out of position, the deep angle can be thrown. Running is also an option for a mobile quarterback. If the guard has kicked out the contain player, there is a small possibility of hitting the tailback on the strongside. In fact, an Auburn tailback scored a touchdown off that pass in a 1995 game against Alabama. Figure 12.6 illustrates 46 boot.

If the linebackers seem to really be keying the fullback and are stuffing him quickly, the 34 bootleg is an excellent alternative to the 46 boot. Compared to the 46 boot, absolutely everything stays the same except for the responsibilities of the fullback. The fullback still fills for the guard, but fakes 34 as he does it. The blocking and the routes remain the same (Refer to Figure 12.7).

48 Boot Counter

Another action is off the counter play. We fake the counter play to the strongside and run the old FSU 6 boot. This play is called 48 boot, because the counter goes closer to the 8 hole off of the tight end's hip. The routes on 48 boot are the same as on 46 boot. On occasion, FSU has employed the bench route with their nakeds off the sweep action. On the other hand, using a takeoff seems to work better at the high school level to get the cornerback out of the play and force the free safety to help.

Because the routes for the wide receivers and the tight end are the same on 48 boot as 46 boot, this is an easy play for them. The fullback and tailback, however, have different responsibilities. In 48 boot, the fullback is in the pattern as the number one receiver. He takes a path to the quickside that allows him to run as close to full speed as possible. He should be ready for the ball because the quarterback wants to get it to him quickly. The tailback takes a lateral shuffle step behind the quickside tackle. He then pushes back toward the strongside, taking the fake from the quarterback as he goes by him. The tailback then blocks the backside contain player. The quarterback makes the counter fake with an empty palm, and then rolls and progresses through his reads from the fullback first, then to the tight end, and finally to the deep angle. Running is also an option. Additional details on the fundamentals involved in the quarterback's fake are provided in Chapter 8. Figure 12.8 presents a diagram of 48 boot versus cover 3.

Two possible blocking schemes can be used on the 48 boot. The first option is to use the same scheme as 46 boot, letting the center and the strongside tackle know that the fullback will not be helping on pass protection, and deciding not to add another pass protection. However, there is another effective way to block for 48 boot, as long as you do not have a 1-technique defensive tackle on the quickside.

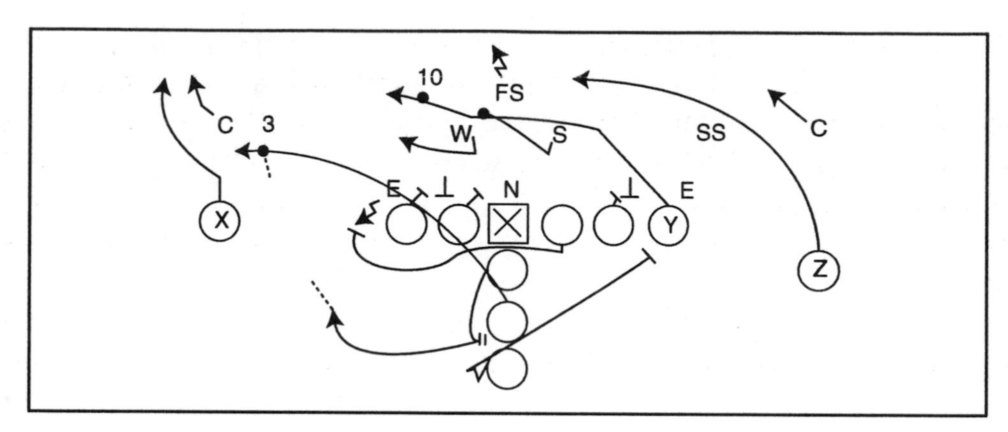

Figure 12.8—48 boot versus cover 3.

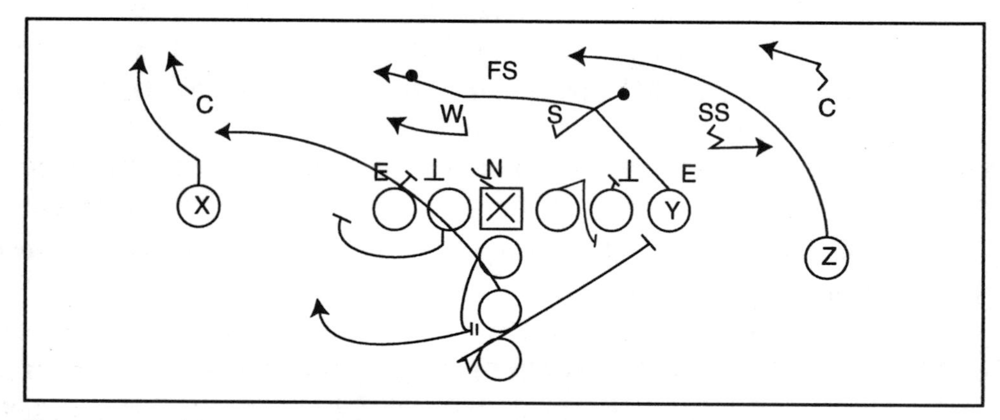

Figure 12.9—Alternate pass protection for 48 boot.

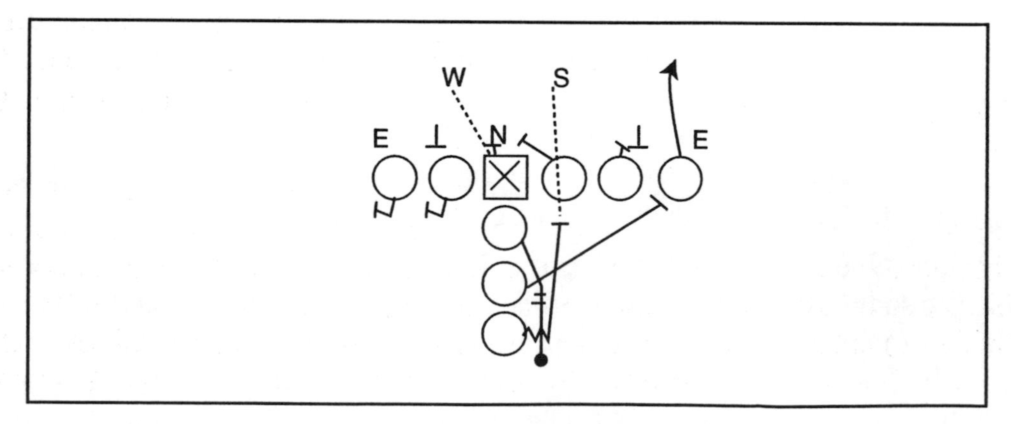

Figure 12.10—344 protection versus a 50 defense.

To employ this blocking scheme, the quickside tackle should block down on the 3- or 2-technique tackle. The quickside guard should pull out and attempt to wrap the defensive end. If the defensive end fights up the field, the quickside guard will have to kick him out instead. The center blocks back on the nose, while the strongside guard helps him. The strongside tackle scoops the defensive tackle, and the tailback blocks the rush end. This protection is diagrammed in Figure 12.9. This play has been one of our top play-action passes over the last five years.

The other FSU run-action passes that are easily adapted to the high school level come off the sprint draw, or ISO series. On all 344's, as these play actions are called, the fullback is attacking the playside rush end. The tailback takes a lateral shuffle step to the strongside, and then runs at the guard's outside hip as if running 44. If he is not tackled on the 44 fake, he should spot up at a point six yards deep, directly over the strongside guard in order to hold the linebacker inside. He then serves as an outlet receiver.

The "3" in 344 tells the offensive line that this play is a sprint draw-action pass. It also lets the quarterback know that he has three steps left after he makes the fake, except on 344 bench, where the quarterback pulls out of the fake early, plants, and drills the bench route to the receiver on timing. Before the basics of 344 bench are examined, it is first necessary to review the protection for the 344 package.

As was previously discussed, the fullback is attacking the strongside end. The tailback is faking and running his spot route unless the Sam linebacker blitzes. If Sam blitzes, the tailback takes him on in the hole. The strongside tackle blocks solid against the defensive tackle, shaded to the strongside or not. The tailback, however, helps the strongside tackle, while checking the middleline backer against a 4-3 defense. The center helps on the nose against a 50 defense unless the nose shades strong. In that instance, the center sets, pass checking the backside backer, and protects the weakside "A" gap. Against a 4-3 defense, the center blocks the backside 1-technique tackle all the way.

The quickside guard sets pass and blocks the 2, 3, or 4i-technique tackle in a 50 defense. Against a 4-3 defense, the quickside guard sets pass and checks the Will backer. The quickside tackle always sets pass and turns his man out and up field against a 50 or a 4-3. The 4-3 is covered in more detail than usual in this instance because it seems we see more 4-3 defenses on those situations when the sprint draw or sprint-draw pass might be called. Figures 12.10 and 12.11 illustrate the protections for the 344 package.

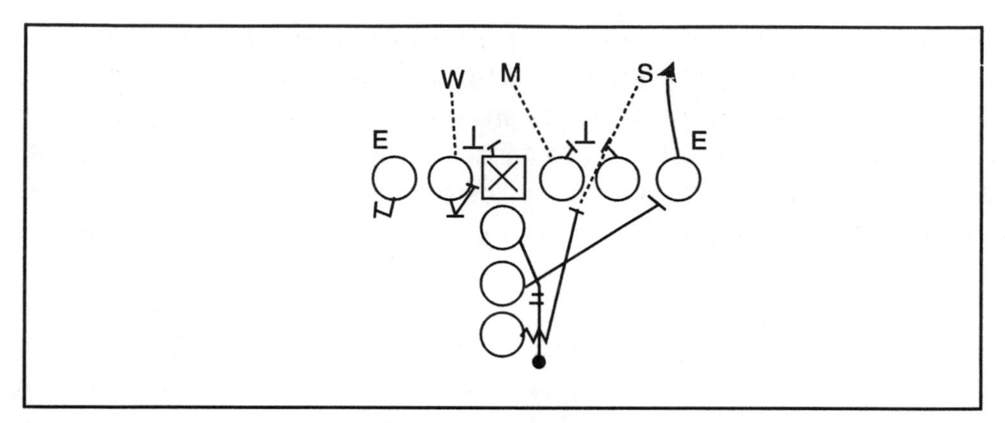

Figure 12.11—344 protection versus a 4-3 defense.

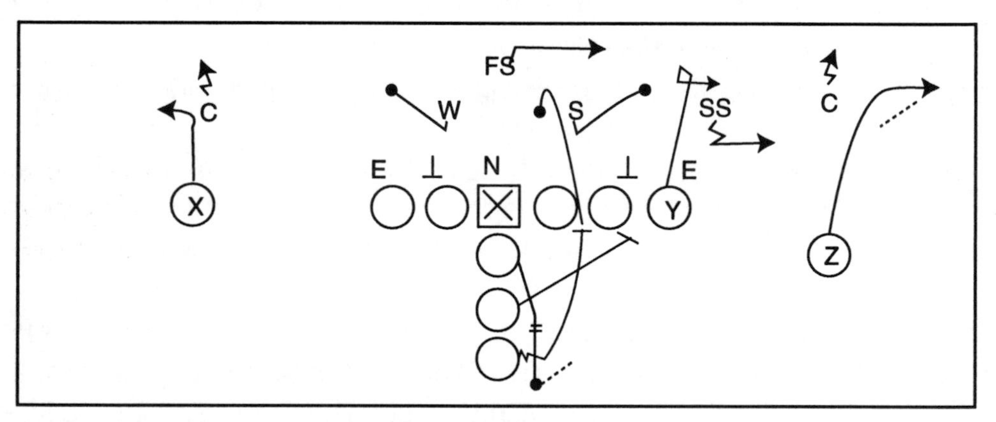

Figure 12.12—344 Bench versus a cover 3.

344 Bench

Having reviewed the protection for the 344 package, the next step is to examine the 344 bench route. The bench route tells the two outside receivers, X and Z, to run a 6-step out on a speed cut. The bench is best coached by telling the receiver to outside release at the corner's outside shoulder, much the same as on a vertical route. On the receiver's sixth step, he should throw his outside shoulder back around toward the quarterback, while simultaneously snapping his head around. In reality, this action creates a perfect pocket in which the ball can land.

The bench route, one of the most effective routes at FSU, is also run from the shotgun drop-back set as well. In this situation, the play is called either 60 bench, or 560 bench. The routes are the same on FSU's 560 bench as they are on 344 bench for us. FSU makes some slight changes from the way we run the play at the high school level. They use a broken-arrow by Y, while we like to run the "choice" route with Y, so that Y will be running the same route on both 344 bench and 560 bench. Doing this helps us with the no huddle that is discussed later in this book.

Having discussed what X and Z do on the bench play, as well as the responsibilities of the fullback, tailback, and the offensive line, the next step is to look at Y's route. The route Y is running is called a choice route. While the choice route is discussed in greater depth in Chapter 18, an overview of the route is presented at this point.

Many individuals see the tail end of the Y route and think it is a curl. In reality, it is not. It is a route designed to get the receiver one yard inside the curl/flat player. If a tight end runs the route, he will have to take an outside release to get to one yard inside the curl/flat player. He should drive up field 8-10 yards and then drive back one step toward the quarterback. If you were in the Panther or Rifle formation, Y is flexed out wider, so the tight end he could take an inside release. Because the 344 bench is run from the Base set so much, the choice route is diagrammed from the tight-end position in this chapter. Future chapters include explanations of Y and even Z and X running the Y route.

On 344 bench, the quarterback makes the 344 fake, pulls up quickly and hits Z or X if his pre-snap read of the flat player lets him know that he could hit that timing pattern. If he pre-reads Z, and the strong safety jumps it hard at the snap, the quarterback should know that Y is going to settle one yard inside of that particular strong safety for an easy completion. The tailback running the spot route should make it difficult for the Sam linebacker to have any influence on the play. COACHING POINT: You should not allow the quarterback to hitch on this throw. If he hitches, the timing will be off, making an interception possible.

Why should you run the bench route? One reason is that the force player is cheating on the run too much. If the force player is getting involved in a lot of tackles around the LOS, run the 344 bench at him. The force player will step up on the run, and find out he is much too late to get back out in front of the bench route. As a result, eventually you will slow run support! (Refer to Figure 12.12).

344 Caddy

Another 344 action pass is 344 Caddy. In 344 Caddy, the fullback and tailback have the same responsibilities as they do on 344 Bench. The pass protection, as on all 344's, is also the same. The receivers' routes, however, change. X runs a square in, or a dip route (i.e., the receiver goes straight downfield about ten yards—eight steps, plants his outside foot, runs a square in, and stops in the first open space), after climbing up field 10 yards. Because we go on steps for routes 10 yards and less, X takes seven steps. Many college teams, such as FSU, will run the dip route to 16 yards, but we simply don't have that kind of speed. Z runs a skinny post route, cutting on his seventh step, after attacking the corner's outside shoulder. Y drags across the field at a depth of six yards, coming underneath X on the route.

The quarterback makes the 344 fake, detailed in Chapter 8, and then sets up and progresses through his reads. Against a 3-deep zone, the quarterback should simply read the free safety. If the free safety backpedals, then he will be in good position to help out on the post with Z. Accordingly, Z is eliminated from the read. As a result, the quarterback goes to his second read, which is X on the dip route. However, if the free safety squats to help with X or to key the tight end crossing the field, (it should be noted that some defensive coordinators have that free safety key the second inside receiver), there is an opportunity to hit Z over the top for a big play.

If the read forces the quarterback to progress to X, the weakside linebacker should become part of the read at that point. As the quarterback looks to X, he should see the Will linebacker out of the bottom of his eyes. If the Will linebacker is dropping into the window that X is entering, the quarterback should throw the ball to Y on the drag, right underneath the Will linebacker. However, if the Will linebacker is walling off the crossing route by Y, the quarterback should be patient, hitch up in the pocket, and hit X with the ball as he enters the window between the linebackers (Refer to Figure 12-13).

344 Dip

While FSU has an arsenal of 344 action passes, we are limited in the number of plays we can put in at the high school level. Therefore, only a few are covered in this chapter, including 344 Bench, 344 Caddy, and 344 Dip. After the dip route, the "Q" route and a fullback delay are introduced. Later in the book, a screen off of the 344 action is also presented, but it is blocked much differently than a typical play in the 344 package. The 344 Dip employs the same exact blocking scheme for the offensive line and the fullback. The blocking assignment for the tailback involves one small change. After the tailback makes his fake, he should progress three yards up the field, and then break directly toward the strongside flats, similar to a quick-out route.

The X receiver can run one of two routes. He can be sent on a takeoff down the field, as FSU does, or you can make the adaptation I prefer at the high school level and have him run a shallow cross underneath the linebackers to draw their attention. Y then runs an 8-yard dip route. While the route can be sent deeper, I am most comfortable with the eight-yard depth because that is the level of speed that most average high school receivers possess. Z, who is usually a little quicker, runs a 10-yard dip route (square in) so that he is slightly deeper than Y.

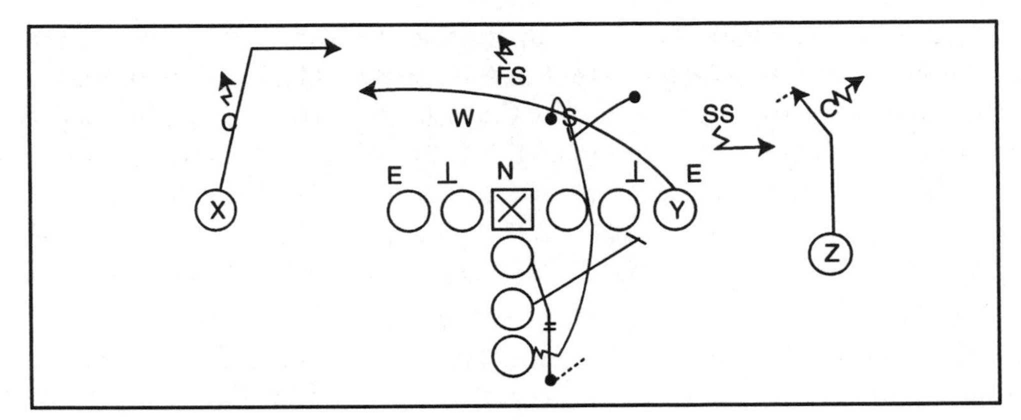

Figure 12.13—344 Caddy versus a 3-deep zone.

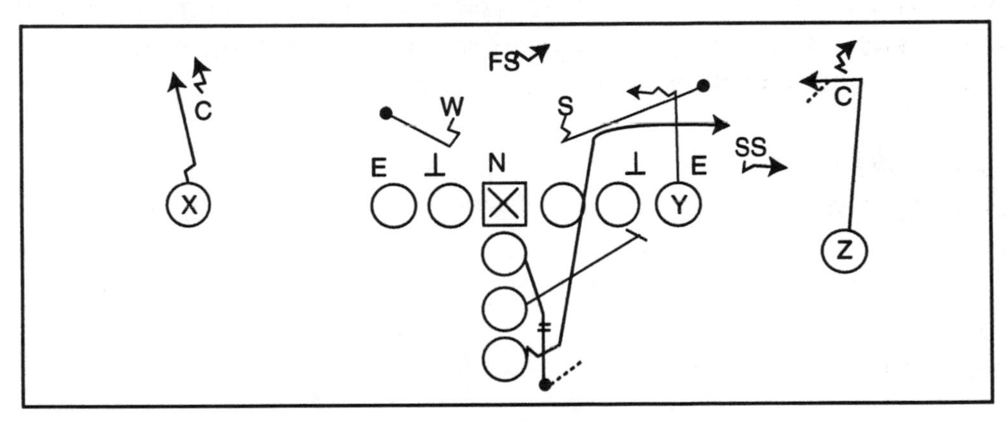

Figure 12.14—344 Dip versus a 3-deep zone.

The quarterback makes the 344 fake and sets up to progress through his reads. His first read is Y. If the linebacker has dropped with him, the quarterback should then progress to Z. The Z receiver will be open if the flat player jumps the tailback on the flat route. However, if the flat player drops in front of Z's route, the tailback will be open for an easy pitch and catch and should have a good deal of running room along the sideline (Refer to Figure 12.14).

344 Q

344 Q is a play-action fake used to stretch the field vertically. Again, the offensive line uses base 344 protection, while the fullback attacks the strongside end. With the same responsibility as on the 344 dip, the tailback progresses three yards up the field after the 44 fake, and then breaks toward the sideline on the strongside. When installing the 344 package, I recommend installing 344 Bench and Caddy together, and then 344 Dip and Q together to help the tailback learn his responsibilities.

On 344Q, the two wide receivers both run a post-corner route. Against a three-deep zone, X and Z both take a release at the corner, and then break to the inside on their seventh step. They continue to the inside until their tenth step, and then they break hard back to the corner of the end zone. Y runs a 6-yard drag route across the field. Because Y is in the flats to the weak sideline with X behind him on a corner route, and the tailback is in the flats to the strongside with Z behind him on a corner route, the field is stretched vertically for the quarterback.

The quarterback should make the normal 344 fake and set up. He has a choice of which side to attack, since the routes basically mirror each other. Your own preference may influence his decision. However, he has a high/low read on the play. He reads to hit the corner route over the top first, and then checks down to the flat route. Because the corner route takes longer to develop, the quarterback should be encouraged to hitch up into the pocket on this play. In order to keep the secondary honest against the I formation, this play should be thrown at least 7-8 times over the course of the season (Refer to Figure 12.15).

344 Fullback Delay

The final 344 play-action pass covered is the 344 fullback delay. This play is designed to catch the Sam linebacker jumping the tailback as the tailback goes to the flats, while the middle linebacker tries to wall off the drag route by Y. To make the play work, X should be sent on a takeoff to clear out, Z should be sent on a dip route, and Y should drag. The tailback should fake 44 and go to the flats like 344 Dip and 344 Q. The offensive line continues normal 344 blocking. The fullback, however, should block the defensive end for two counts, and then sneak vertically up the rail (i.e., outside the row of hashmarks). The quarterback makes the 344 fake, sets up, and looks off the linebackers. He then sticks the fullback with the ball in stride, while moving up the field. This play usually is effective a few times a season, especially if you hit the tailback or Y a couple of times to set it up.

Play Action Rollout 43 Dash

The last play-action pass included in this chapter from the FSU offense is the dash play. This play is set up with consistent fakes by the quarterback on the 43 play. He must always give the empty hand on the run play, and then pause. That action sets up this pass. FSU runs this play as a naked. However, in adapting it to high school, I have found it works better as a bootleg. In fact, we have even used this boot from the shotgun for big play after big play.

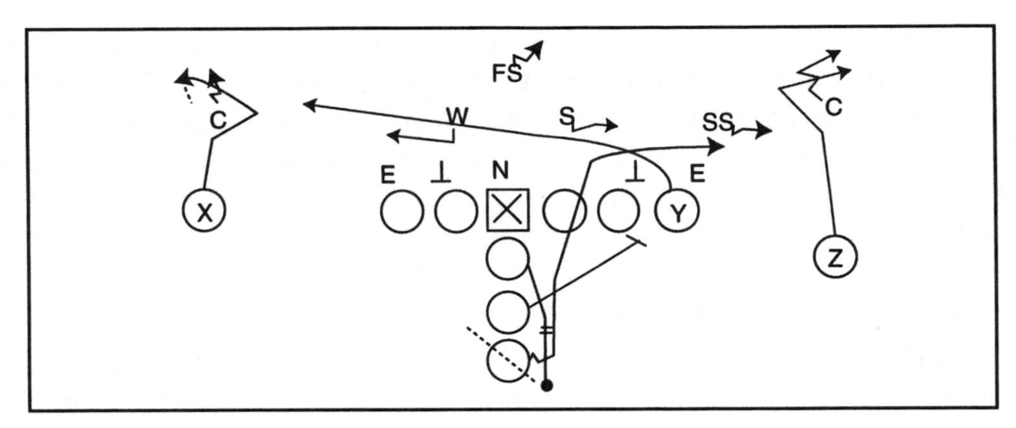

Figure 12.15—344 Q versus a 3-deep zone.

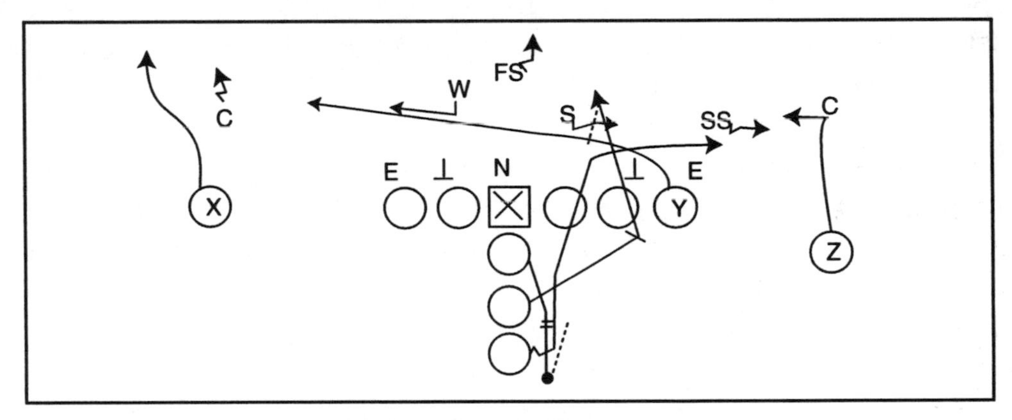

Figure 12-16. 344 Fullback delay versus a 3-deep zone.

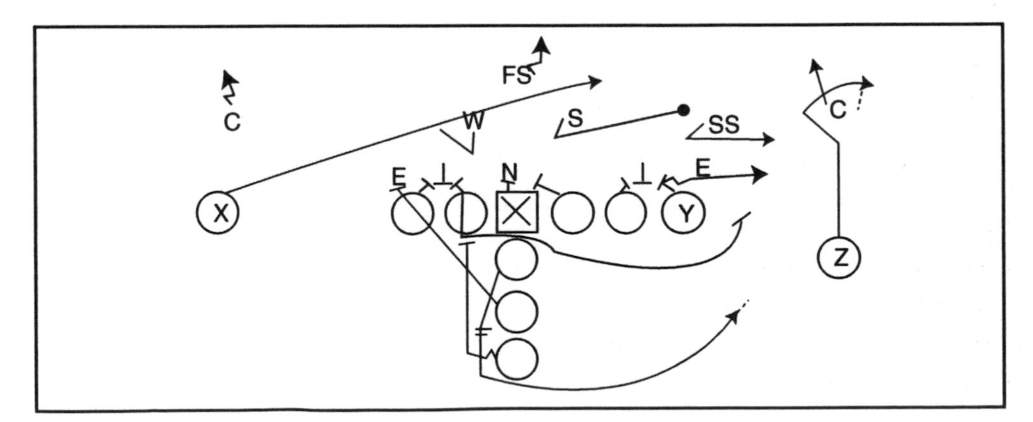

Figure 12-17. 43 Dash versus a 50 defense with a 3-deep zone coverage.

Again, to make this play work, the quarterback must freeze to sell that he has handed off the football. The quarterback's extended, empty palm is sometimes as effective as a bone-crushing block. However, the quarterback should be sure to safely tuck the ball away, just in case the defensive end doesn't buy the fake. The quarterback then reverses out and breaks contain looking to pass first and run second. Additional details on the quarterback's fake in this instance are presented in Chapter 8. On the fake, the tailback should also hunch over and attack the LOS just like he has the football.

The selling, however, isn't finished at that point. The tight end also has a selling job to do. The tight end should block down to enable the tackle be able to control him (the tight end) from getting up the field. He then releases directly toward the sideline at a depth of 3-5 yards and serves as the primary receiver. If you were in Panther (3-wide) on this play, Y would run a pigtail route (i.e., driving inside like a crossing route, planting his outside foot, and driving back to the sideline; also referred to as a bounce route or an arrow route) to sell a shallow cross, and then plant and drive back to the sideline at 3-5 yards deep.

X runs a diagonal route, aiming for a depth of about 12 yards and gaining separation as he accelerates across the field. Z runs a post-corner route exactly like he does on 344 Q. The tailback can either sneak across the field after his fake or run up into the line and pass-protect.

The pass protection on 43 Dash can be as a naked or a bootleg. We prefer to employ bootleg protection. Against a 50 with a strong 5-technique, it is important that the tight end give the 5-technique a good shot off the line, so that the strongside tackle can prevent him from moving up the field. The strongside guard blocks back on the nose, while the center blocks back on the 2- or 3-technique defensive tackle. The quickside guard pulls to the strongside for the boot, while the quickside tackle either helps on a 3-technique, or blocks solid on a 4i. The fullback attacks the defensive end at the snap (Refer to Figure 12-17).

With the exception of the quick-passing game, goal line, and trick plays, more than enough of the FSU I formation offense for a high school team to incorporate has been covered to this point. The next three chapters examine the quick passing game, the goalline package from the I formation, and the shotgun offense that has propelled FSU into the spotlight over the last few years. In fact, FSU's shotgun offense has become a solid portion of the Seminole's attack to go along with their I formation plays.

CHAPTER 13

FSU Passing Attack: The Quick Passing Game

The quick passing game can be a very useful tool to employ against blitzes and soft-zone coverages. As such, almost every offense has some version of the quick-passing game. Tulane, when Tommy Bowden was the Green Wave's coach, was very impressive using quick passes not only from under center, but also from the shotgun, putting to rest the myth that quick passes could not be used effectively from the shotgun. Florida State also uses hitches, slants, and fades from the shotgun.

I believe that the best way to run a quick passing game is to use steps, instead of yardage, to get the correct timing. With the exception of a goalline fade, all of our quick passes are thrown on a 3-step drop from under center and a pivot setup from the shotgun. The goalline fade from under center is thrown off of one giant gather step.

The quick passing game does not allow for a hitch step by the quarterback. For proper timing to be achieved, he must simply drop 1, 2, 3 steps, and throw. The first quick pass to be discussed is the hitch route. The receiver runs an 86 quick hitch route with his outside foot back, attacking the outside of the cornerback's shoulder, and then breaking back down the stem at five yards.

The route is a mirror for both X and Z on the play. The only way that situation changes is if the quarterback sees a different alignment by a corner on one side of the field and gives the receiver on that side a hand signal for an alternate route. The ball should be half way to the receiver when he turns around (Refer to Figure 13.1).

82 is the quick slant route. It is also run as a mirror route by X and Z. A three-yard stick route can be run by Y to clear out a throwing lane for the quarterback to hit Z with the ball. Again, the quarterback can change the receiver's route with a hand signal, if necessary.

The receiver should attack the outside shoulder of the corner, and then break on his third step to the inside at a 45-degree angle. The ball should be airborne before the receiver breaks (Refer to Figure 13.2).

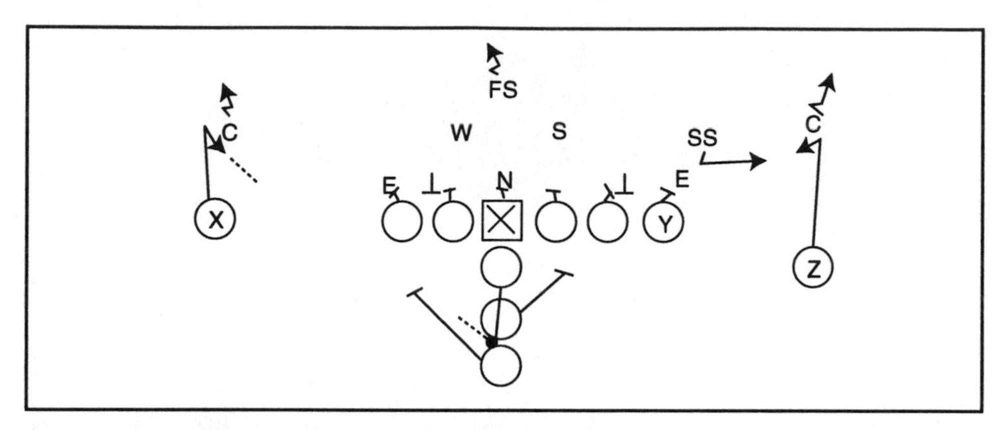

Figure 13.1—86, quick hitch versus cover 3.

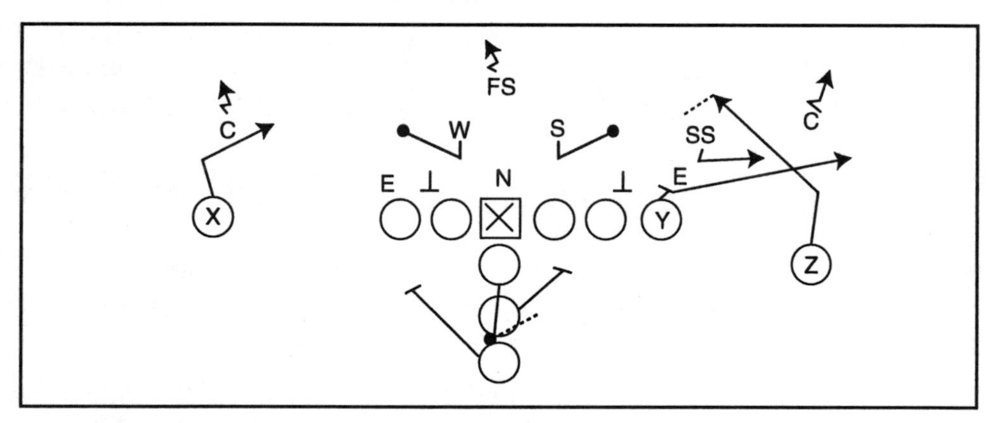

Figure 13.2—82 quick slant versus a 3-deep zone.

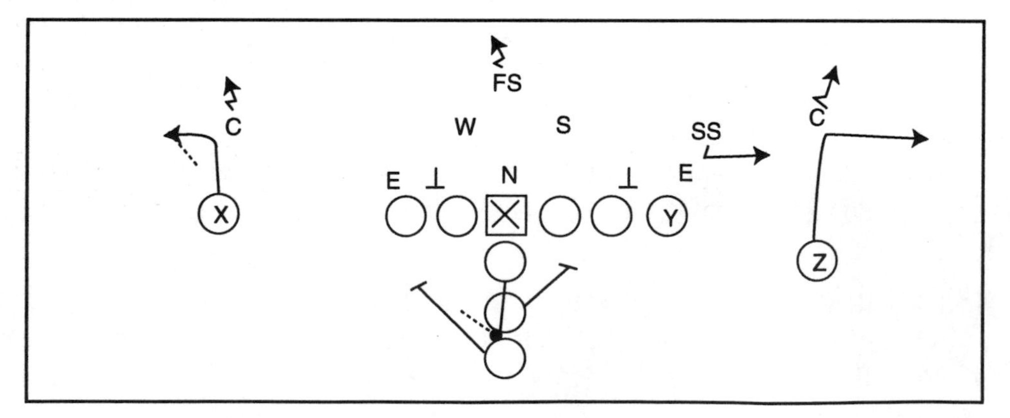

Figure 13.3—84 quick out versus a 3-deep zone.

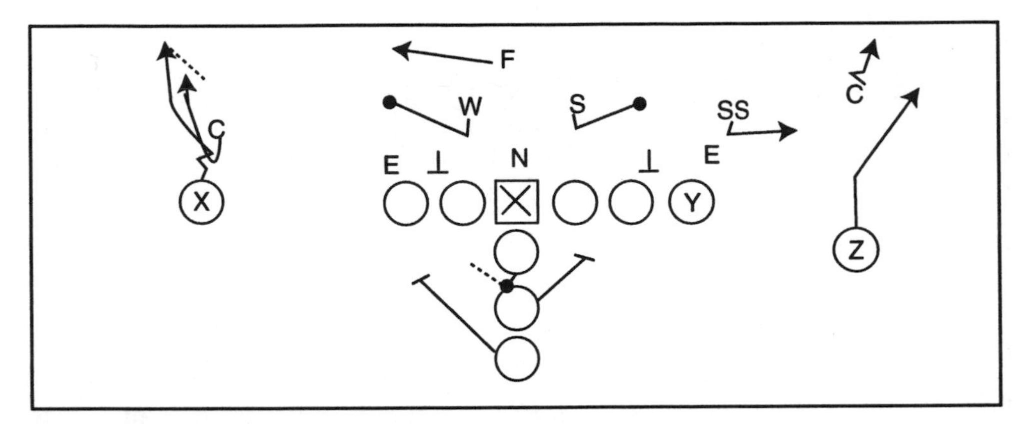

Figure 13.4—88 versus cover 92.

84 is a quick out. It's very difficult for a soft corner to ever get involved on the play. It should be thrown to the outside, at the receiver's shoulder level, and never behind him. X and Z both attack the outside shoulder of the corner for four steps, then throw their outside elbow back around to the quarterback, and snap their head around to find the ball that will already be in the air. The tight end stays solid on the route. This particular route is most effective when employed on the split-end side when the corner is soft (Refer to Figure 13.3).

The fade is one of the most difficult passes to defend when it is thrown correctly. On the fade, the receiver attacks the inside shoulder of the corner for the first two steps, and then explodes outside to a point 18-22 yards down the field, three yards from the sideline. This route actually lets us run away from the coverage of a 2-deep or 3-deep zone. While watching FSU over the years, I've learned that this pass is often intentionally under thrown, allowing the cornerback to run right past the receiver, who then leaps up for the ball at its highest point. To master this skill, it should be intentionally practiced during individual practice time with the quarterbacks and the receivers (Refer to Figure 13.4).

The pass protection we employ with the quick passing game involves aggressive cut blocking to keep the hands of the defensive line down. The fullback and the tailback protect off the offensive tackles on each side.

CHAPTER 14

THE GOAL LINE PACKAGE

The FSU offense is also very effective within the 10-yard line. The 3-step slant and fade routes are popular from the base "I" set in this area. However, there is also a goal line corner route that is very difficult for a cornerback to cover. In this instance, this play is referred to as "60 Goal Line."

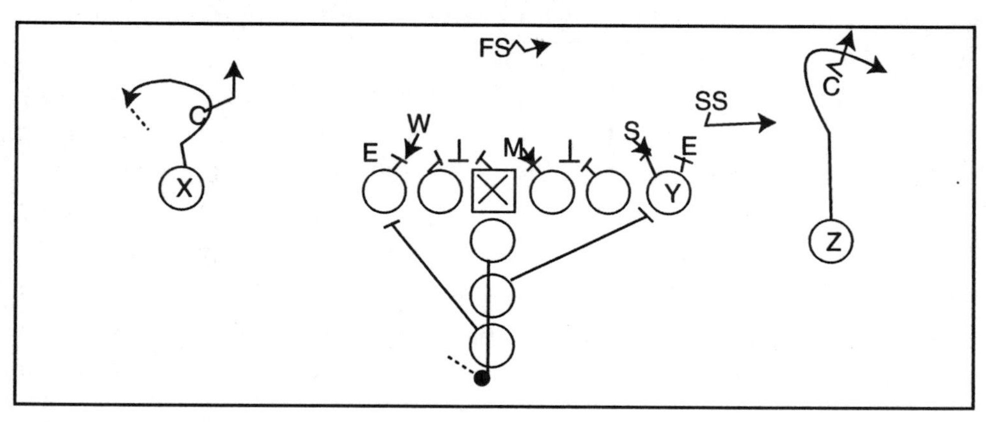

Figure 14.1—60 Goal Line.

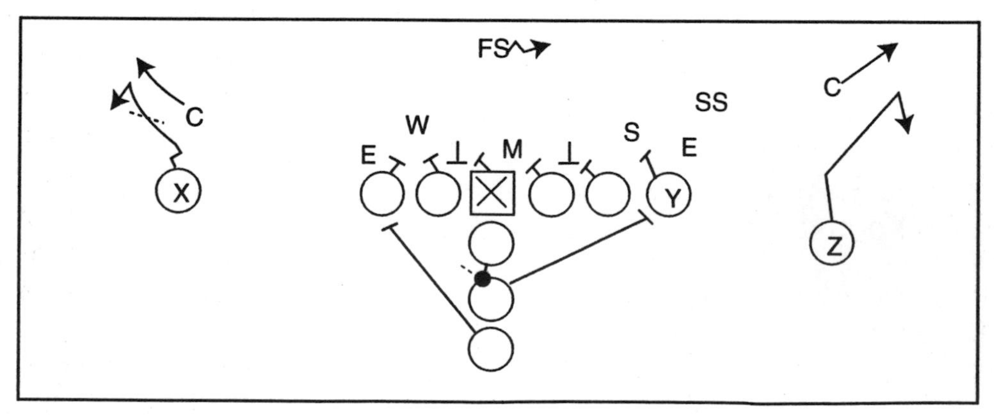

Figure 14.2—88 Stop.

60 Goal Line

On 60 goal line, the X and Z receivers both run the corner route, while the tight end stays solid to help maximize protection. The route is run to look as much like the slant as possible on the release, with the receiver taking three steps up the field, and then breaking on the slant toward the near upright of the goal post. When the receiver hits step number six, he throws his outside shoulder around and rolls out of the cut, breaking back toward the corner of the end zone. Frequently, the quarterback actually leads the receiver back toward the pylon in the front corner of the end zone to keep the ball away from the defensive back. As such, the receiver should be ready to react to the pass right out of his cut to the corner.

On 60 goal line, the quarterback takes a 5-step drop. He has a choice of which receiver to work with, depending on both the cushion and the wideside of the field. Both backs stay solid to help with protection. The offensive line follows the 560 protection rules. This play is one of three pass plays that are excellent to use from the 10-yard to the 4-yard line (Refer to Figure 14.1).

Another effective goal line pass play is the stop fade, (88 stop), in which both receivers accelerate toward the back pylon of the end zone, and then break the pattern off as the defensive back gets into their pocket to run with them with his back to the quarterback. The protection is the same as the 80 protection used on the three-step passes covered previously, with the tight end staying solid to help protect. The quarterback again makes a pre-snap decision concerning which cornerback to attack. He takes three big steps and then throws the ball to a spot to the outside hip of the receiver. The backs both attack the outside hip of the last protector on the line of scrimmage. At belly level, they should attack any defender coming free to keep the defender from getting his hands up and possibly deflecting the pass, since it is thrown more on a line than is the fade route (Refer to Figure 14.2).

A third pass that is effective at the goal line is the boot off the counter action. Running this play from the over set enables us to get two wide receivers involved in the route. The counter action is run just like 48, with the run action going back to the tight-end side. The quarterback follows the same actions as he does on both 48 and 48 boot (plays that were covered previously). Z, however, runs a choice route just across the goal line to get him into the end zone. X runs a corner route over the top of Z, going to the back pylon. The fullback works out into the flats at a shallow depth, getting his head around quickly for a pass. If the pass is thrown to him, it will be quick so he can turn up and score due to his leverage. The tight end climbs across the back of the end zone as a safety valve (Refer to Figure 14.3).

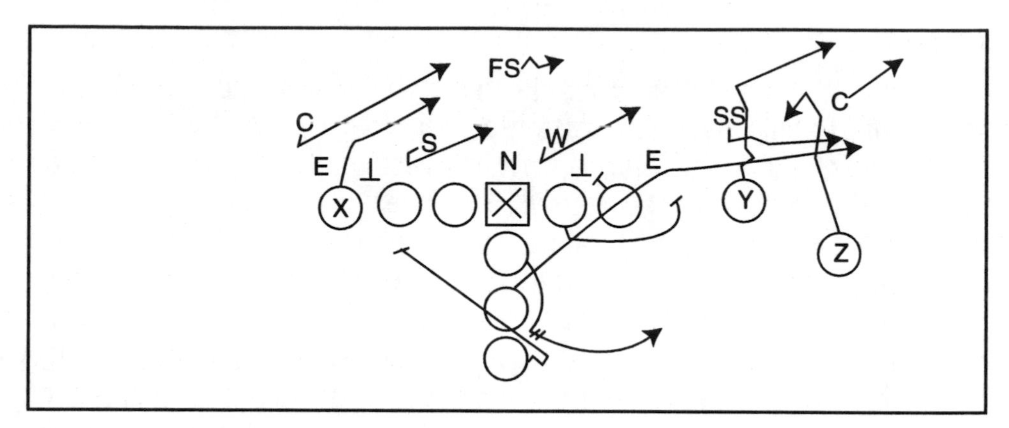

Figure 14.3—48 Boot Z choice.

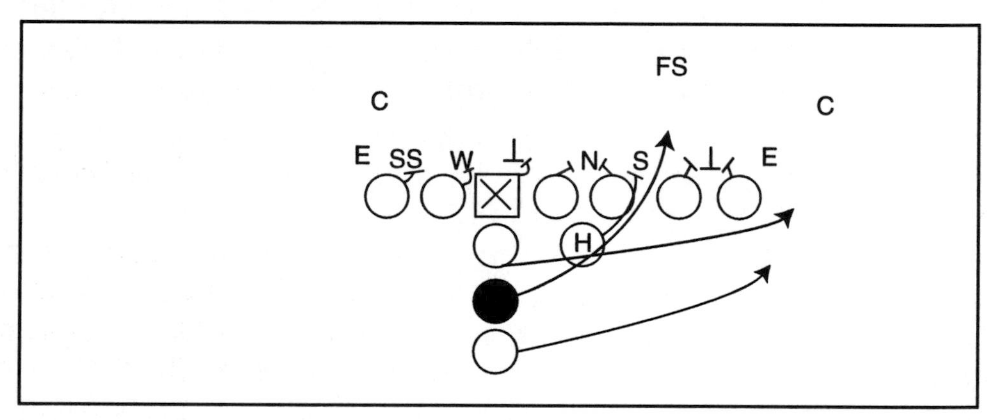

Figure 14-4. Heavy 34.

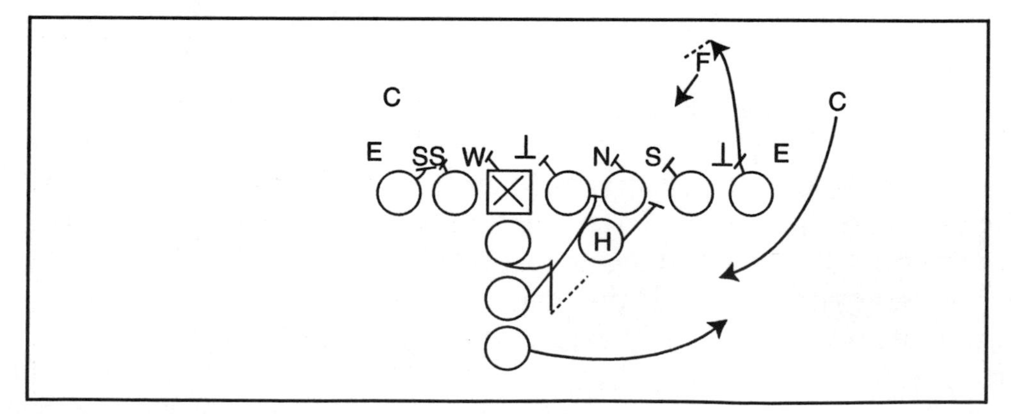

Figure 14-5. Heavy 34 Y dump.

The most used formation in the FSU offense once the ball gets inside the four-yard line is the heavy set, or trunks as we call it. This formation is a two-tight end, unbalanced set with an inverted "power" or "H" back that is usually set to the unbalanced side. The "H" back, however, can go in motion to get the end sealed for a weakside toss sweep. Two of the most often-used plays from this formation that work great at the high school level are 34 and 27.

On 34, the "H" back lines up at three yards deep, directly in the B gap. Because we are looking to get a push up front with man blocking, the "H" back should explode off the line and plow into the LOS to get some movement toward the goal line for the fullback. The tailback and the quarterback run the play exactly like 34 from the base set, while the fullback follows the "H" back into the line and looks for daylight while pumping his legs (Refer to Figure 14.4).

While the toss sweep can also be run from this formation, the next most effective play from this set is the tight end dump off of the 34 run action. Because the safety normally becomes so run-conscious if 34 is successful a couple of times, the tight end can usually find a big seam to work into in the end zone. The quarterback just sticks the ball in the fullback's belly, and then pulls up to hit the tight end on the dump off (Refer to Figure 14.5).

The final goal line play covered depends simply on the type of athlete you have at quarterback. If he is a good runner, a quarterback naked is an exceptionally effective play going back to the weakside of the formation. Someone in the box should be assigned to watch the backside end and corner to check to see if they are flying to the strongside on the belly (34). If they are, a 34 naked should be run. If your quarterback doesn't fit that mold, then a weakside sweep should be employed to slow down the backside pursuit (Refer to Figures 14.6 and 14.7).

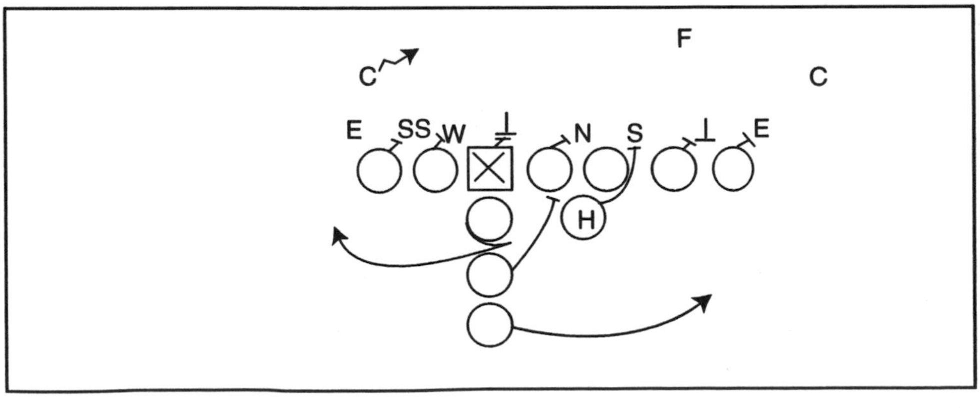

Figure 14.6—Heavy 34 naked.

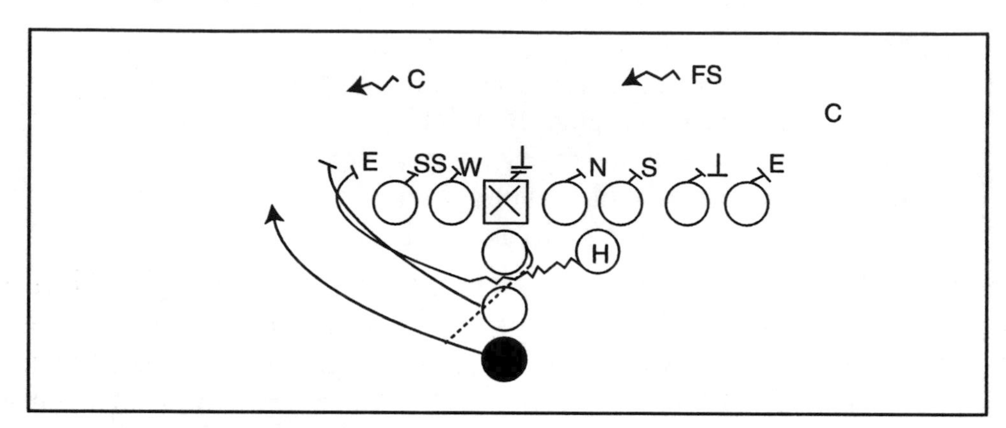

Figure 14.7—Heavy move 27.

The aforementioned are just a few of the plays in the FSU offense that can be effective in goal line and short yardage situations. Each of them is relatively easy to employ at the high school level and can fit in with most any type of offense.

CHAPTER 15

SHOTGUN FORMATION RUNS

Running from the shotgun formation can make a tremendous difference in the success that you have in this offense. Florida State found that out in 1992. Against Nebraska in the Orange Bowl that season, Nebraska placed its defensive ends so wide that the FSU offensive tackles couldn't block them. In inclement weather (rain), the 'Noles won the game anyway with a strong I formation running game. As a result, a decision was made to add shotgun runs for the 1993 season. Needless to say, that adjustment helped contribute to their national title that year.

During that same season, I learned the same lesson that the Seminoles had. Coaching at a small private school, I faced an opponent that placed its defensive ends so wide that we couldn't block them. We added a draw trap from the shotgun the next week and scored on an 80-yard touchdown the first play from scrimmage. The lesson to keep in mind is to run from the shotgun if you truly want to adapt your team to the FSU offense.

Many coaches think that adding shotgun runs to the playbook can cause the players to have too many plays to memorize. That simply is not true. In fact, many of the I formation run plays that you use can be employed just as easily from the shotgun formation. One example of an effective run play from the shotgun is the 44 with Panther personnel in the game (Refer to Figure 15.1).

44

The blocking on 44 from the shotgun is the same as it would be if you flexed the tight end from the I or went to the Panther set from the I formation. The only real adjustment that needs to be made is to have the quarterback give a naked fake around the opposite end following the handoff to the back. This action controls the backside defensive end. If the defensive end doesn't honor the quarterback, you should run a naked or bootleg to his side and that problem will be solved. Also, after the quickside tackle sets pass on the defensive end, he should give him a shot, and then climb to the backside linebacker. The quickside guard combo blocks the 1-technique tackle with the center, who chips off the 1-technique to the middle linebacker. The strongside guard turns out the 3-technique tackle. Because there is no tight end, the strongside tackle turns out the defensive end.

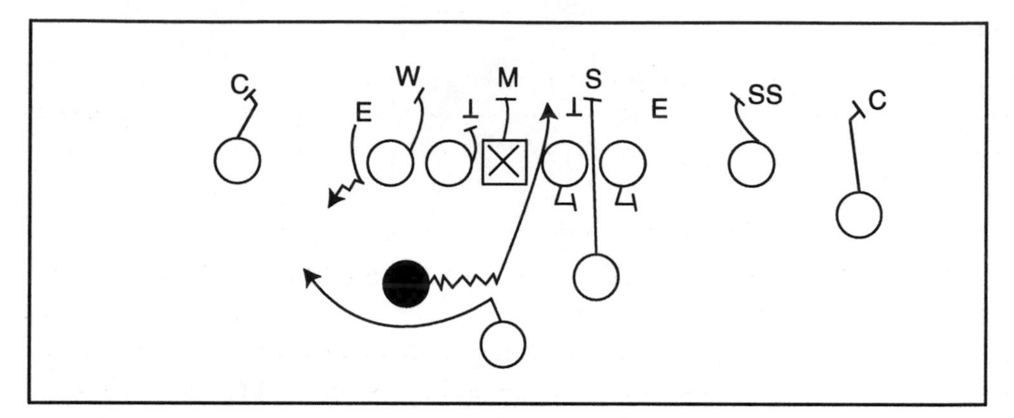

Figure 15.1—44 from Panther right shotgun versus a 4-3 defense.

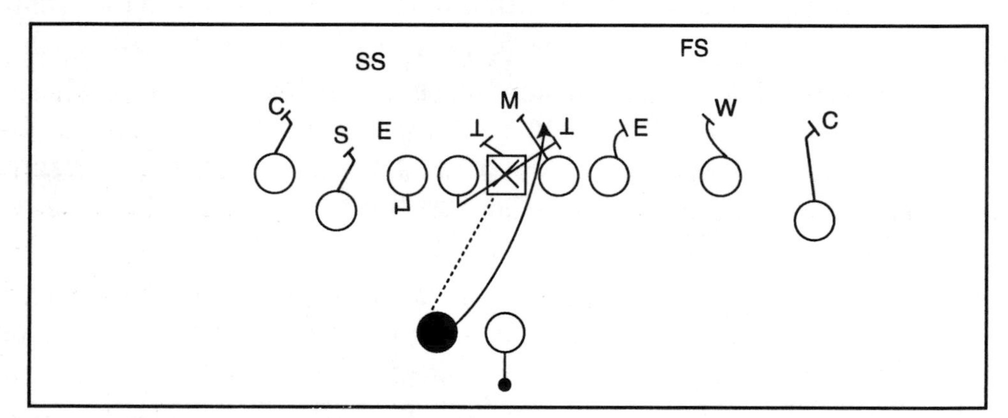

Figure 15.2—Shotgun inside-trap scheme.

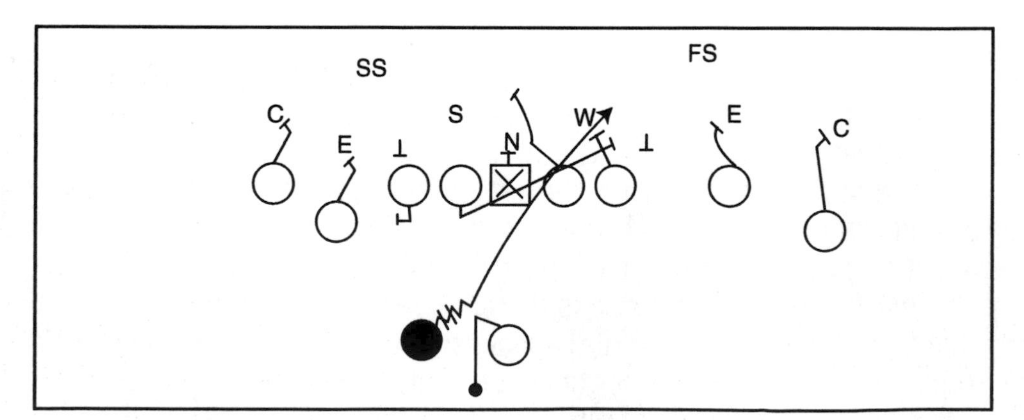

Figure 15.3—Shotgun trap versus a 3-4 defense.

Inside Trap

Another run you can use from the shotgun is the inside trap. We employ this run from the Rifle formation. This play can be blocked the same as any inside trap scheme you use within your the offense. Florida State adapted this into its offense as a direct snap to the back. At the high school level, it can be used either as a direct snap or a handoff. Because some high school coaches are more conservative than others, the handoff on the trap may be a better fit within their offense.

Against a four-wide offensive set, most defensive coordinators have gone to a 4-3 cover 2 or cover 4 alignment. That alignment usually presents a 3-technique and 1-technique defensive tackle along the front. Often, the Sam and Will linebackers walk out with the Y and T receivers in this formation. Therefore, Y and T must aggressively block to maximize the effectiveness of the trap. FSU was able to use this play against an excellent Miami team in 1993 on two separate third-and-long situations for big plays.

Against a 4-3 look, the center and strongside guard block down. The center is back on the 1-technique, while the strongside guard is covering the middle linebacker. The quickside tackle sets pass on the defensive end, and then proceeds to level two as the play develops. The strongside defensive end is turned out by the strongside tackle, who sets pass and does not let him cross his face to the inside. The quickside guard, who has the key block on the play, pulls to kick out the 3-technique defensive tackle.

If the play is being run as a direct snap, the running back catches the snap, and then follows the block of the quickside guard, cutting off his inside hip. The quarterback fakes a three-step drop, while looking back to the T and X receivers to influence the defense away from the run.

If the play is being run as a hand off, the tailback takes a lateral shuffle step, receives the ball from the quarterback, and follows the quickside guard. The quarterback then fakes a naked back to the quickside of the field. Figure 15.2 illustrates a shotgun inside trap versus a 4-3 front.

Shotgun Trap

Another common defensive front versus a four-wide receiver set, such as Rifle, is the 3-4. The tackles are widened out to either a 4i-, 4-, or 5-technique. On most occasions, the nose will align head up. That alignment leaves two linebackers in the middle of the defense. In reality, it doesn't matter because the trap is very effective against this defensive alignment as well.

When running a shotgun trap against a 3-4 defense, the strongside tackle blocks down on the Sam linebacker. The strongside guard chips off the nose to the backside linebacker, while the center blocks the nose. The quickside tackle sets pass on the defensive tackle, and then progresses to level two as the play develops. The quickside guard pulls out to the strongside defensive tackle and kicks him out. If the defensive tackle has been well coached to squeeze, it could turn into a wrap or log block.

The tailback should know that the hole against a 3-4 front will be slightly wider than against a 4-3 front. Furthermore the Y and T receivers should widen their splits to pull the outside linebacker/defensive end to slide out with them. As against the 4-3, both of these receivers must block the defenders very aggressively. The quarterback's basic responsibility does not change (Refer to Figure 15.3).

48 Counter

The counter, 48, can also be run from the shotgun just as easily as the I formation. We prefer to run the counter from the Pistol formation, thereby giving the field a spread look, but keeping the advantage of the tight end. The tailback can be placed to either side of the formation.

Many defensive teams will shade the nose weak and drop the defensive end off to the weakside in order to employ a 50 defense against this alignment. Most of the time, this defensive scheme is supported with a 2-deep coverage. All of the blocking rules for 48 from the shotgun are the same as for 48 from the I, with the exception of the fullback who is out of the game. The nose and the center will not have the "fill" support that the fullback normally offers. If the defensive tackle is making the play on the running back because of the lack of "fill" support, the back should be moved to the opposite side of the formation. FSU has really benefited from adding this formation. A team with an excellent tight end can also benefit from this particular formation (Refer to Figures 15.4 and 15.5).

Quarterback Keep

Another way to run the counter is to let the quarterback keep the ball himself. In order to achieve maximum success on this alternative for the counter, the quarterback should be the only back left in the backfield. You can either empty the back out with motion or line up in an open (5-wide) formation.

I prefer emptying out the back, placing him on the opposite side of the run. Because this action often gets the defense to moving around at the snap, it usually causes defensive confusion. The quarterback simply catches the snap, drops a step, and then follows the quickside guard's block. In 1995, we scored three times on 80+ yard runs using this particular counter play. It has also been effective on third- and long-plays. The blocking scheme stays the same (Refer to Figure 15.6).

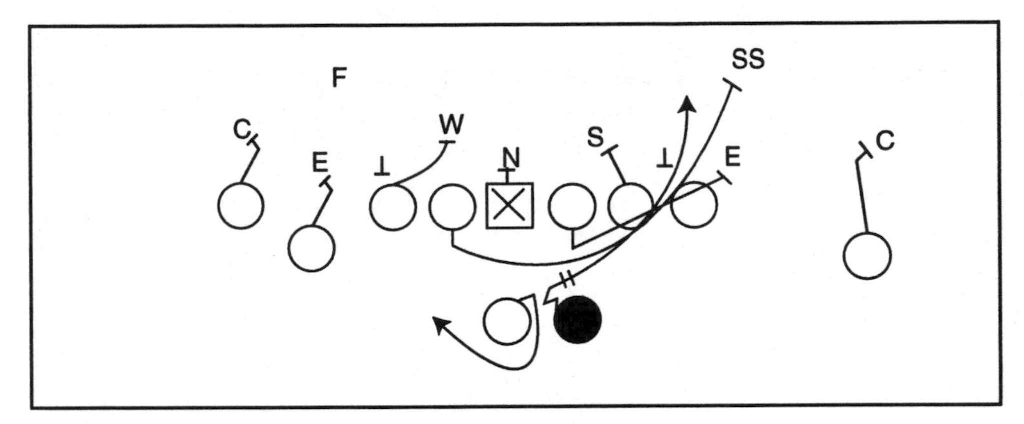

Figure 15.4—48 from shotgun versus a 50 defense.

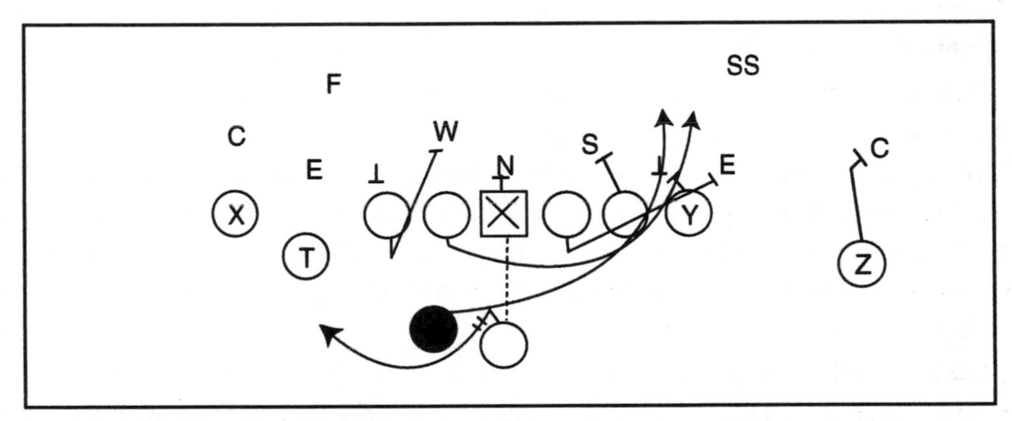

Figure 15.5—48 from the shotgun versus a 50 defense. (Note: The running back has been moved to the opposite side.)

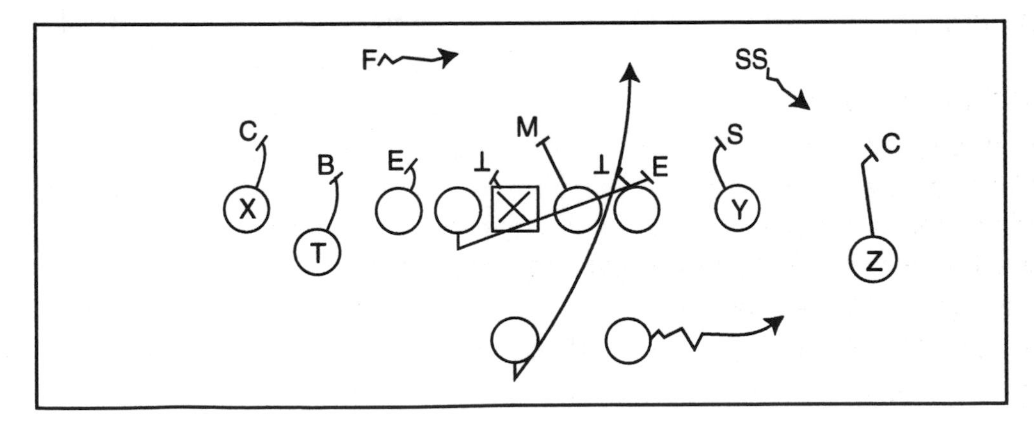

Figure 15-6. Counter play from an empty set with motion.

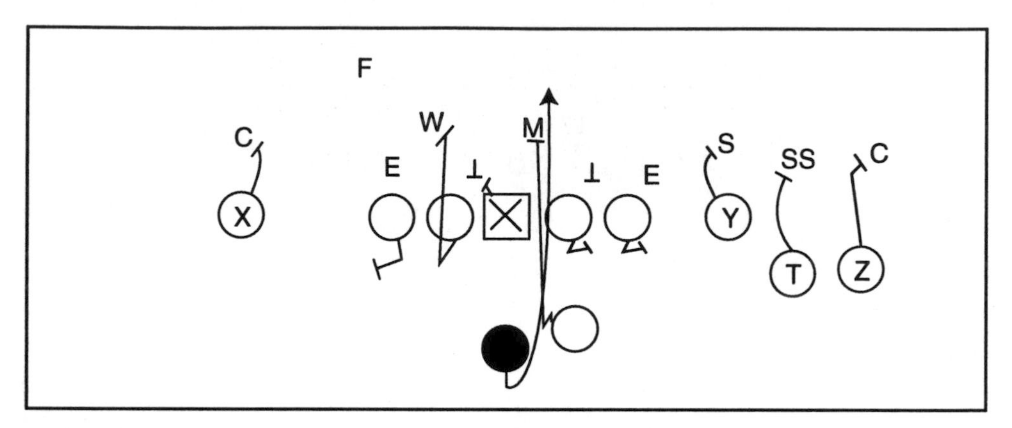

Figure 15.7—Quarterback lead draw from a Far formation.

Quarterback Lead Draw

Another shotgun run that is effective is the quarterback lead draw. We prefer to use the Far set on this play to spread the field more. On the quarterback lead draw, the strongside tackle turns out the defensive end. The strongside guard sets pass and turns out the 3-technique tackle, while not allowing him to cross his face. The center blocks back on the 1-technique, and the quickside tackle skips the 1-technique and climbs to the backside linebacker. The quickside tackle sets pass on the man on or outside him.

The key to the play is the block of the running back. He must attack the playside linebacker with low pads. The quarterback catches the snap, steps back, and then follows the running back's block. You should note how much the blocking on this play looks like 44 from the shotgun. You should keep in mind that you're not really adding anything to what your players have to learn. In recent years, both Florida State and Tulane have made a number of huge runs off the quarterback draw from the shotgun. The play can also be easily set up from this formation by running the shallow cross series a few times (Refer to Figure 15.7).

FSU also employs a variety of other draws within its offensive scheme. However, because the ones covered in this chapter easily relate to plays that are run from the I formation, they are easier to adapt to the high school football level. The point to remember is that if you want to enhance the shotgun-passing package of your offense, you must start by running from the shotgun effectively.

CHAPTER 16

Shotgun Passing Attack: Vertical Stretch Routes—the Smash

Due to FSU's their success with their "Fast Break" style of offense since 1992, many coaches relate Florida State and the shotgun together as a collective package, somewhat like people perceive biscuits and gravy as an inseparable tandem. Admittedly, it was the shotgun attack that first prompted me to investigate just how much of FSU's offense could be used at the high school level. That is one reason that I think the next few chapters of the book are so beneficial. I truly believe that if a high school coach dedicates the time and patience necessary to implement the shotgun attack the benefits will be well worth it. Keep in mind, though, that the I formation runs and passes, as well as the shotgun runs, that have been covered in this book to this point are also vital to the success of the shotgun.

The first shotgun route that will be examined is the smash route. This route has been a big part of FSUs offense for many years. For a high school quarterback, I cannot imagine an easier play to run. However, the play is complicated enough to be in virtually every college playbook in the country.

The smash route involves a simple read of the cornerback on either side of the field. The two outside receivers, X and Z, are running 5-step hitch routes. The receiver's technique is to attack the outside shoulder of the defensive back and then settle at five steps. Some coaches have the receiver drift inside at that point. I feel that is a mistake. If the cornerback reads and recognizes the inside route following the hitch, he could sink back and double cover the inside receiver.

The only way the receiver should be allowed to move inside is if the flat player responsible for getting under the hitch releases to the lower flats immediately. Then, the X or Z receiver could move inside only to the first available window for the quarterback to deliver him the ball. The receiver should settle down in that window and show the quarterback his numbers.

One way to prevent the flat player from moving out to the flats quickly is to have the Y and T receivers who are in Rifle (the preferred formation for this route) stem to the inside of the flat player on their release. If Y and T release to the outside, they escort the flat player to the smash route. This action not only increases the difficulty of completing the pass, it also increases the likelihood of an interception. It should also be noted that by stemming inside, the safety,(in a two-deep look) is forced to hold on the hash longer, thereby creating the opportunity for more separation when the receiver breaks his route to the corner. The threat of a broken arrow, a choice, and a corner route should prevent the safety from guessing. The Y and T receivers should break at 10 yards (eight steps if they're not jammed) back out to the corner the field. Each receiver should be prepared to adjust the angle of his route to the football, since the quarterback will undoubtedly attempt to lead him away from coverage.

The final route on the play is the check-down crossing route by the running back. On this route, the running back steps up at the snap and checks the Sam linebacker. If the linebacker comes, he meets him in the hole. If the linebacker drops into coverage, he should release three yards directly up the field and then break toward the weak sideline like a shallow-crossing route (Refer to Figure 16.1).

While the route can be run from the Rifle formation, the route can also be effective employed from the Open, or 5-wide receiver formation. That offensive alignment actually invites a blitz up the middle if the defense shifts to a 3-4 look. In that instance, the running back usually ends up wide open crossing the field. If the linebackers don't blitz, the quarterback progresses through his normal read, catching the snap five yards deep in the shotgun, checking for blitz, and then reading the corner. If the cornerback sinks, the quarterback should hit the smash. If the cornerback squats, the quarterback should hit the flag after hitching up in the pocket. If the linebacker comes, the quarterback should hit the running back crossing the middle after taking one gather step in the shotgun (Refer to Figure 16.2).

The pass protection on the smash route varies according to the protection call. The calls can be very simple. For example, 60's can involve maximum protection. In maximum protection, you must have two backs in the backfield. Therefore, most 60's are run from either the Base shotgun or Panther shotgun formation (Refer to Figure 16.3).

The strongside tackle sets pass on the man on or outside of him. The strongside guard sets pass on the defensive tackle, usually a 3-technique versus a 4-3. The center checks the middle linebacker and then helps with the 1-technique on the weakside. The quickside guard blocks on the 1-technique tackle, while the quickside tackle blocks solid on the defensive end. The fullback and tailback check the linebacker to their side, and then scratch where it itches.

Another common protection used with shotgun routes is the 460 protection. The 60 portion of the call lets the receivers know that the routes correspond with a 5-step drop or a shotgun 3-step. The 400 part of the call enables the offensive line to know that the running backs will check the linebackers, and then free re-

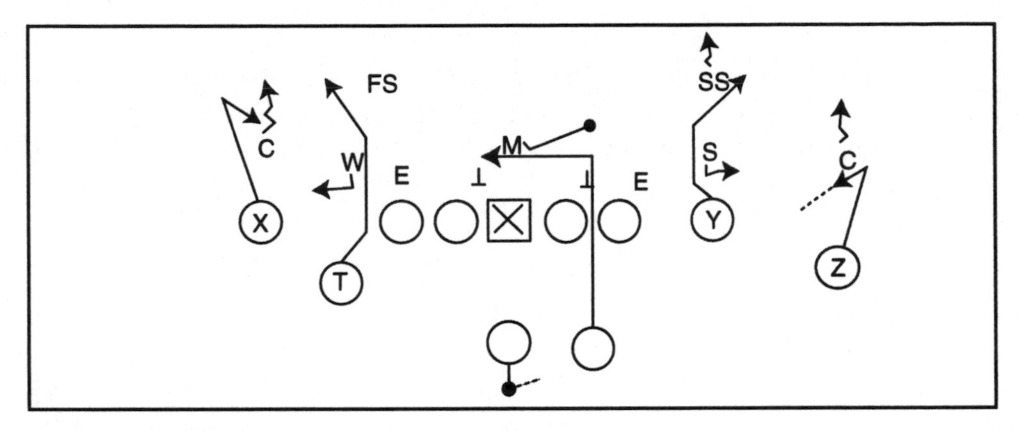

Figure 16-1. Smash route versus a 4-deep zone.

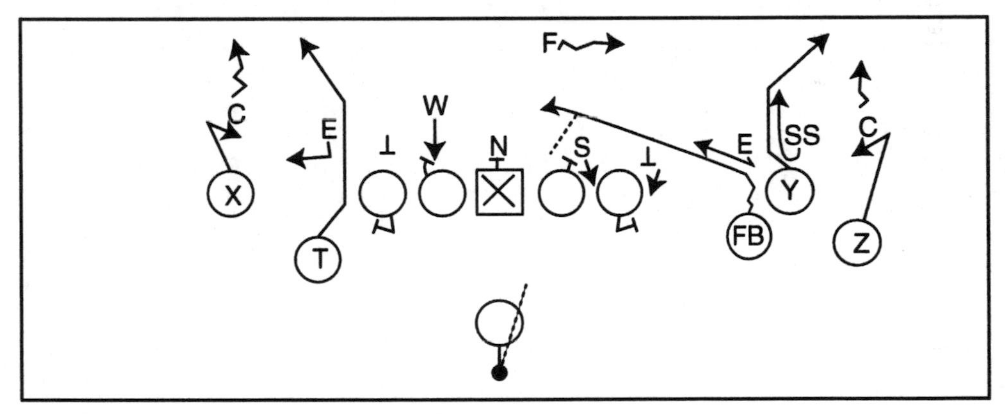

Figure 16-2. Smash route from an Open formation.

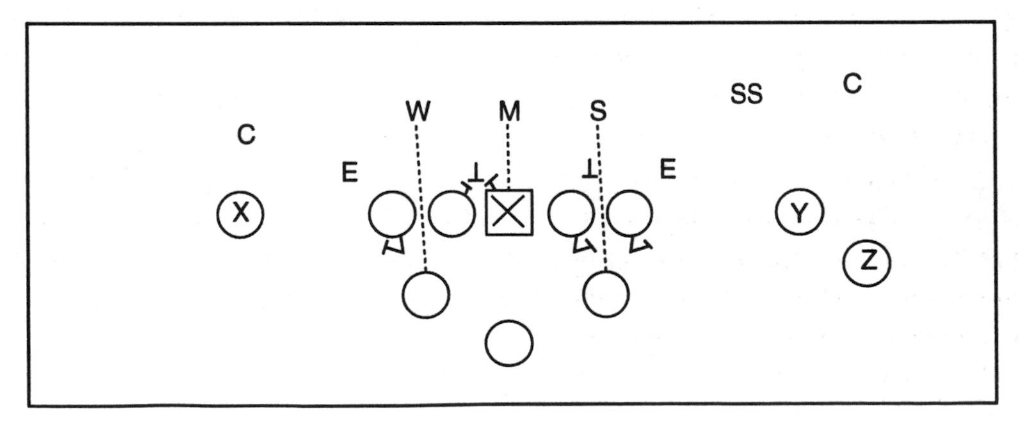

Figure 16-3. 60's protection versus a 4-3 defense.

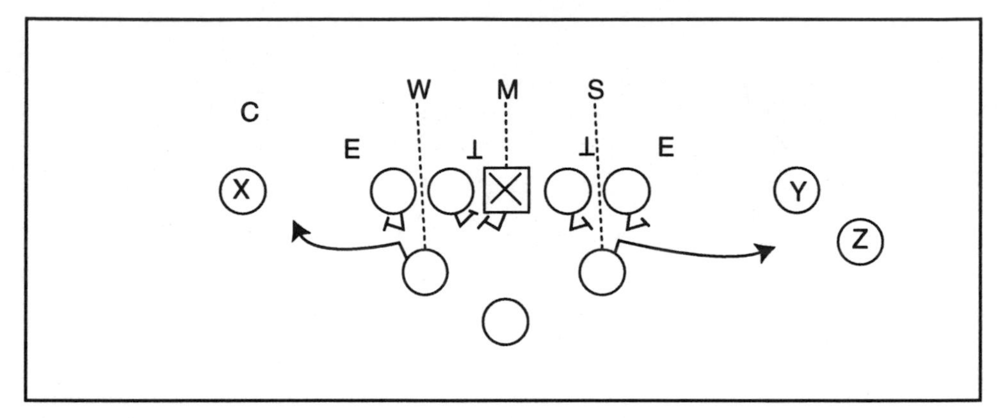

Figure 16-4. 460 protection from the Panther shotgun formation.

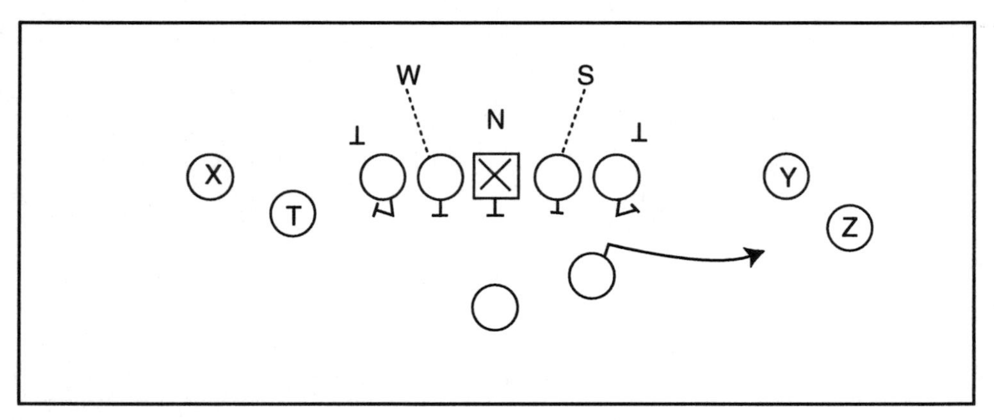

Figure 16-5. 500 protection versus a 3-4 front.

lease into their routes. The offensive line knows they have help versus the blitz, but no support from the running backs if a blitz is not executed. Otherwise, the offensive line responsibilities stay the same as 60 (Refer to Figure 16.4).

The only other pass protection for drop-back passes covered in this chapter is the 500 protection. The 500 protection lets the receivers know that the routes correspond with 5-step/shotgun 3-step patterns. However the offensive line now knows they are basically one-on-one. This protection is used with the 4- and 5-wide receiver formations. If a single back is in the backfield, he checks the Sam linebacker before releasing into his route. If the backer blitzes, he picks him up. If the formation has no backs, a hot route should be used to control a middle linebacker blitz (Refer to Figure 16.5).

When using the smash route, you will often face teams that like to bring the weakside outside linebacker in a 50 front. In response, you can do one of two things. First, you can have the inside receiver on the weakside (T) break his route

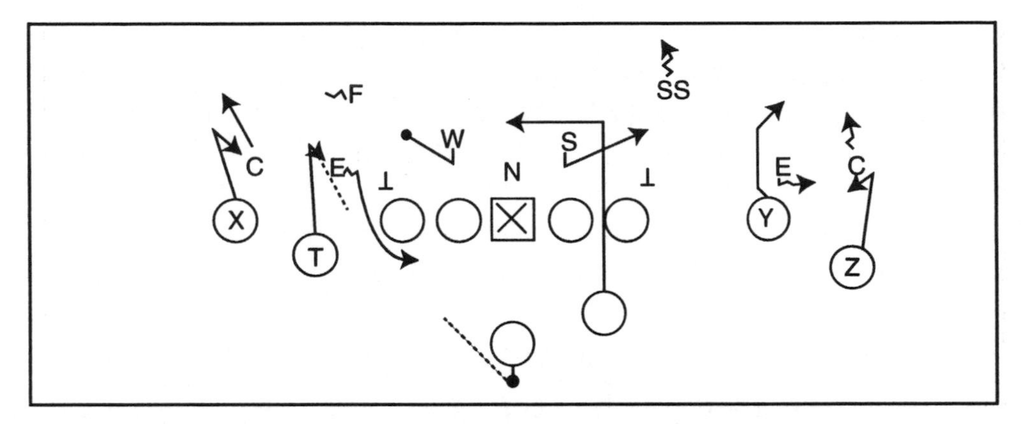

Figure 16-6. Rifle 560 smash with a weakside blitz adjustment.

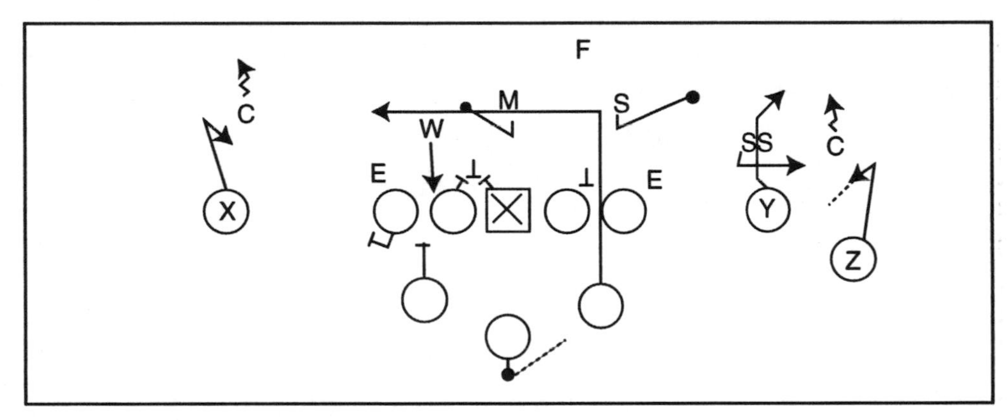

Figure 16-7. Panther 460 smash versus a weakside blitz.

of at five yards when and outside backer blitzes. It will be obvious when the blitz is coming from this source because the safety will cheat over T, and the linebacker will begin cheating in close to the snap. Figure 16-6 illustrates how to control the blitz with the hot on a 560 smash.

The second way to attack the weakside blitz is by using the Panther formation to get an extra blocker, and then call 460 smash. The running back can then pick up the blitzing linebacker, allowing the quarterback time to throw the easy completion to X on the smash route (Refer to Figure 16.7). Notice how the smash route is almost a natural hot route versus the blitz.

Even if the X and Z receivers encounter a hard corner, the play can still be very effective. The receivers should be coached to invite a collision on the defensive back's outside shoulder while driving up to five yards. When the receiver reaches that point, he should use a swim move with his outside shoulder to regain the inside position on the defensive back. The corner then has to go through the receiver's back to make a play on the ball, an action that should draw a flag.

The hard corner also offers the availability of more space for the inside receiver to use vertically. With the corner in the smash receiver's back pocket, he cannot sink back to help the safety. If the inside receiver is jammed, he should be coached to take an inside release, then straighten back up, and finally break to the corner at about 10 yards. A head-and-shoulders fake to the inside against the safety is fine if the receiver gets off the line quickly enough.

The Smash route stretches the field for the linebackers horizontally and the corners and safeties vertically. Correctly run pass patterns allow the quarterback to make a simple and quick read to deliver completions and move the chains.

COACHING POINT: The quarterback coach should work the quarterback on his "shortstop pivot" to maximize his quick release on the smash route to X or Z. In recent years, the Tulane quarterbacks have had probably one of the quickest releases I have ever seen using this pivot. On a daily basis, the quarterback should practice catching the snap, pivoting his feet, hips, and torso to the receiver in one quick movement, and then firing the ball to the receiver with high velocity. A quick release can help make the Smash route a dominant part of your offense.

CHAPTER 17

Shotgun Passing Attack: Vertical Stretch Routes—the Vertical

There was a time when the "GO" route was used only by wishbone teams on third-and-20 or in a Hail-Mary situation at the end of a game. Over the years, it gradually began to be used on second down to remind a secondary that was cheating up too much that they better back up or get burned.

It was only as recently as 1992 that the Florida State offense proved that the vertical could be an every-down pass play. Yes, even on first down and 10. Not only that, the vertical could become a relatively high-percentage pass play. Most high school coaches are looking for that type of play, because we do not always have the rocket-armed quarterbacks that so many colleges seem to have. One of the best factors about how FSU's offense has evolved to this point is the fact that a quarterback doesn't have to possess a rocket arm to be successful in the FSU offense.

While the vertical can be run from a variety of formations, it is most effective from a four-wide receiver set. That formation forces most defensive coordinators into a cover 2 or cover 4 look at the high school level. Rarely, is man under coverage seen at the high school level, although some high school teams possess the physical talent to use it. Even if we see man coverage, the vertical pattern is effective against it as well.

When coaching the 4 vertical route versus a zone look, the two outside receivers, X and Z, must hit a landmark approximately five yards from the sideline—25 yards down the field. It is important for the receivers to keep that landmark in mind, so that the field is spread as much as possible.

On the 4 vertical route, the T receiver should release down the field on the high school level hashmark. There is only one way he will ever see the football, and that is against a 3-deep secondary. If he stays on the hashmark, and the Y receiver releases on the hashmark as well, a free safety in a 3-deep zone look doesn't have much of a chance. The quarterback can give the free safety a look off or a pump fake to make him commit to one side, and then strike for a big play to the other (Refer to Figure 17.1).

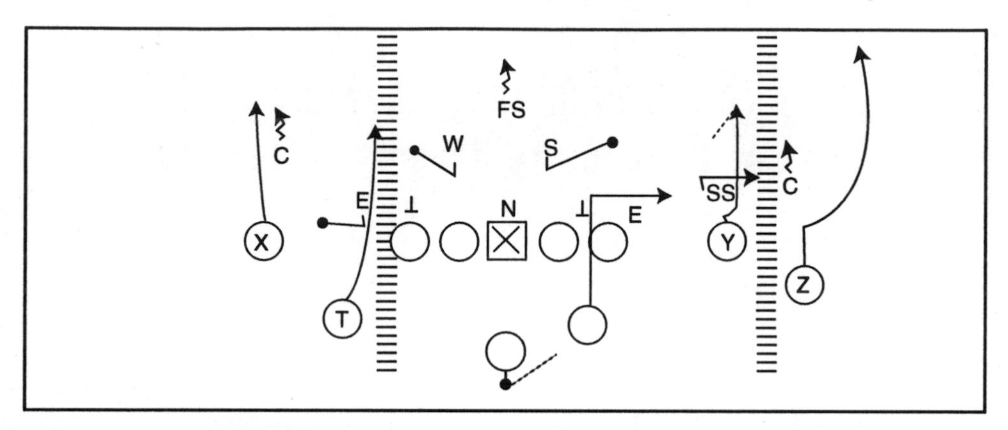

Figure 17-1. Vertical route versus a 3-deep zone.

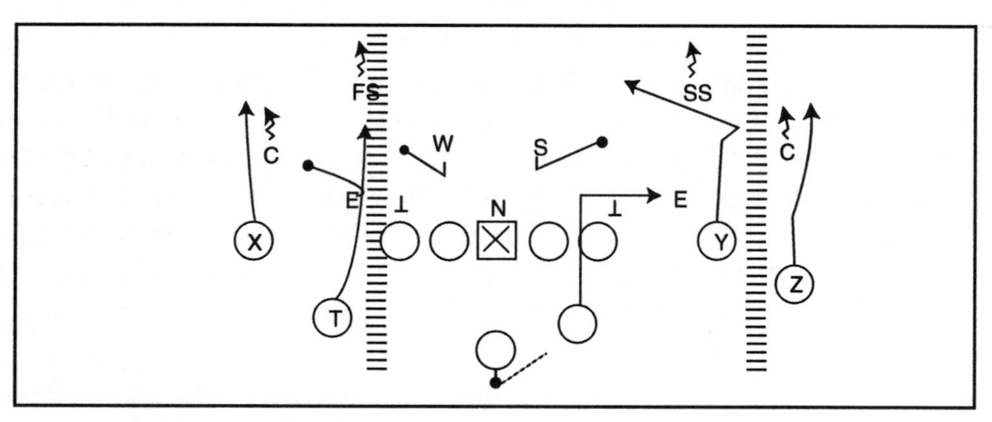

Figure 17-2. 560 vertical versus a cover 4.

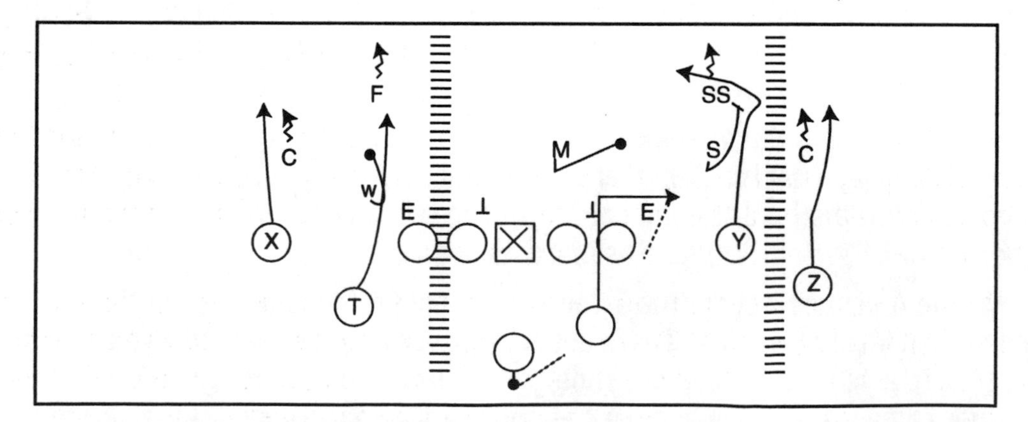

Figure 17-3. 560 vertical with a linebacker "wall" of Y. Note: because the Sam linebacker is walling off the broken-arrow, the flats are left open to the running back one-on-one.

Against a 4-deep look, the Y receiver has a vital adjustment to make. When he reaches a depth of 8-10 yards, and the safety over the top is at or near the hashmark, he should give an outside head-and-shoulders move, and then break inside the coverage of the safety. The safety has no backside help because T is running a vertical on the opposite hashmark. I've heard this route called anything from a tube route to an inside break.I prefer the term Broken Arrow. Coach Mark Richt of FSU uses that term for this route. This is the route that has made the 4 verticals such an effective and dangerous first-down play. The quarterback simply reads the safety over the receiver and then hits the receiver out of his break, leading him into an open window of the coverage. The ball is thrown on a line, just out of reach of the linebackers (Refer to Figure 17.2).

Eventually, a frustrated defensive coordinator may begin having the flat defender attempt to "wall off" the broken-arrow route. That action leaves the playside linebacker to match up on the running back out of the backfield. As a result, the back will have leverage and a lot of open field to run in if the quarterback recognizes this situation. The running back should check the playside linebacker for a blitz, and then proceed three yards up the field, breaking hard directly at the sideline on the strongside. Because that action is the exact opposite of what the running back does on 560 smash, the linebackers are left guessing as to which way he will go.

If the linebacker tries to wall off the pass, and the corner sinks, the quarterback finishes up his 3-step drop from the shotgun, hitches up, and delivers the ball to the running back. Most of the time, this situation turns into a broken-arrow-to the-tailback read for the quarterback. Both of these passes are relatively easy, even for a high school quarterback to make (Refer to Figure 17.3).

Should you ever throw the vertical to an outside receiver? Yes, depending on a couple of factors. First of all, if your receiver is a better athlete than the corner he is working against, the quarterback can intentionally under-throw the ball so that the corner will run by the receiver, and the receiver can out jump him for the ball. FSU does just that on a regular basis. It is also a pretty easy throw for a high school quarterback—certainly easier than slinging it down field 50 yards to a receiver in stride.

The second factor to consider is to hit the outside receiver versus a hard corner. In this situation, both outside receivers are being pressed. They make an adjustment on the vertical landmark to that of a fade, a route that is very difficult to defend against when a four-receiver formation is employed. Because of the threat of an inside receiver on a vertical route, the safeties will likely not be flying

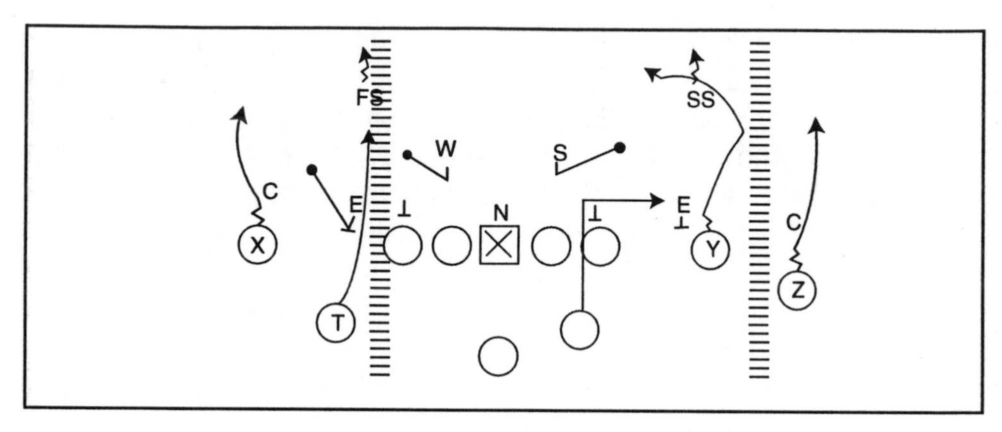

Figure 17.4—560 vertical versus cover 2. X and Z run fades.

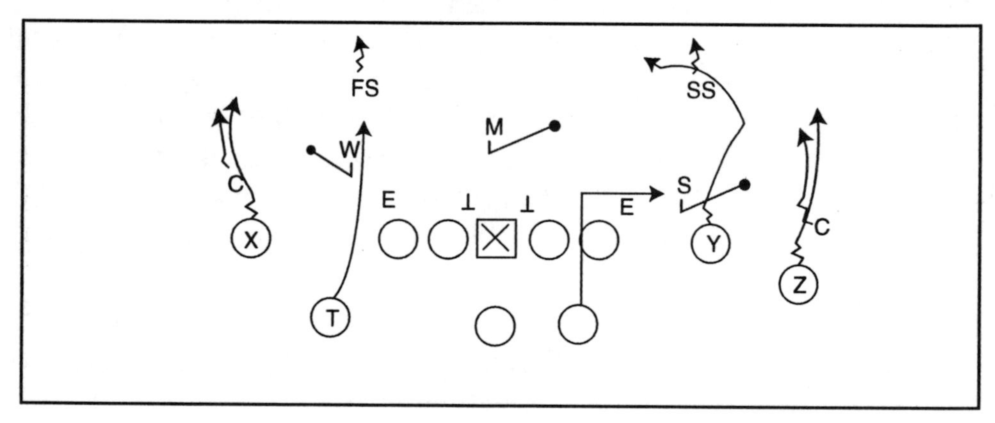

Figure 17.5—560 vertical versus a floating corner. (The corner sinks).

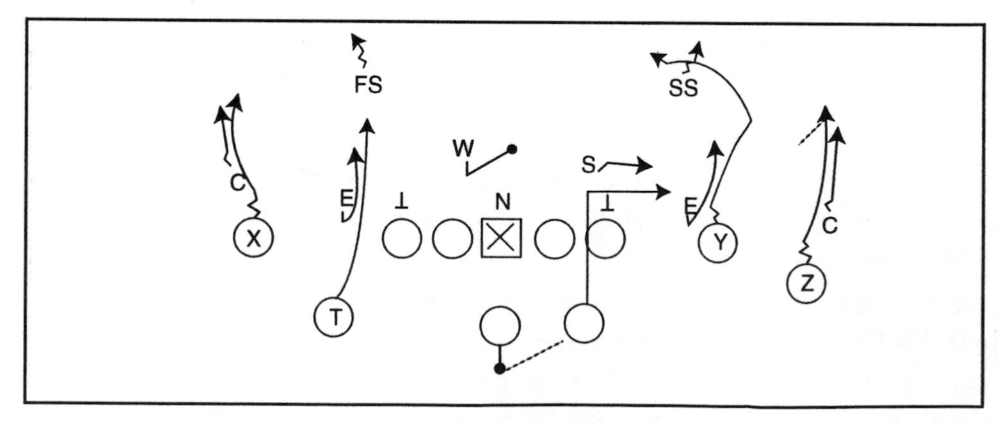

Figure 17.6—560 vertical from an Open right formation.

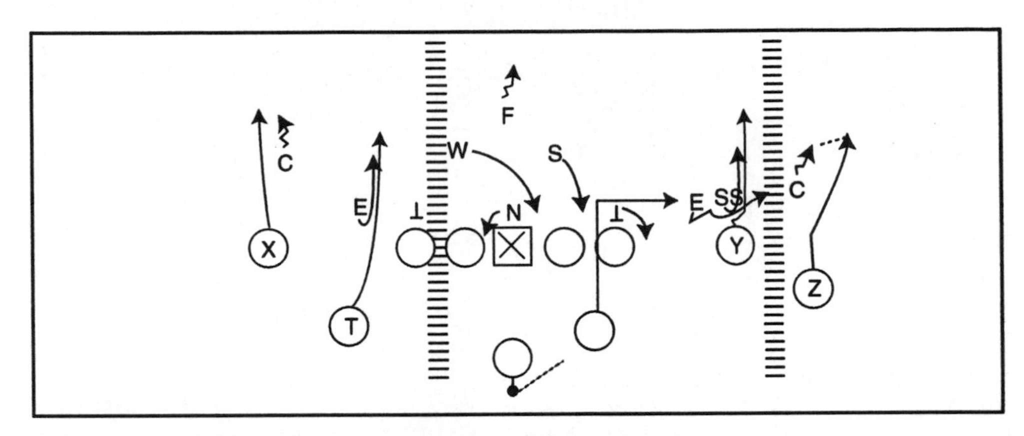

Figure 17.7—560 vertical from an Open right formation.

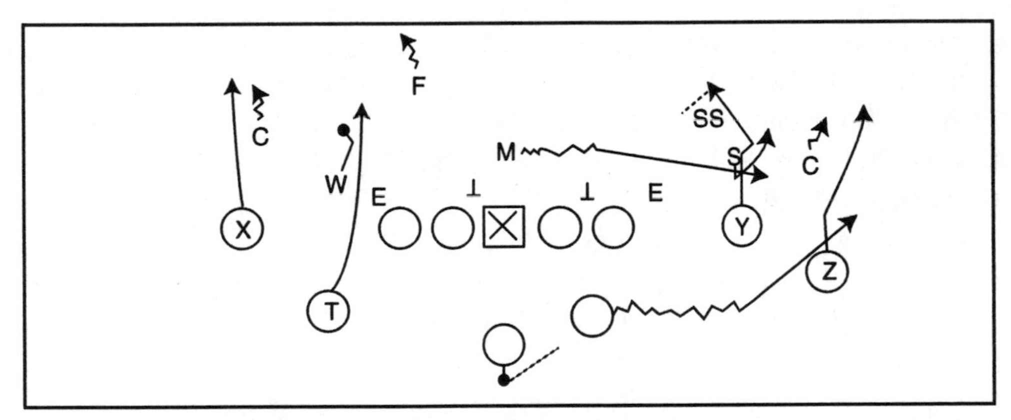

Figure 17.8—560 vertical from a Rifle right empty formation.

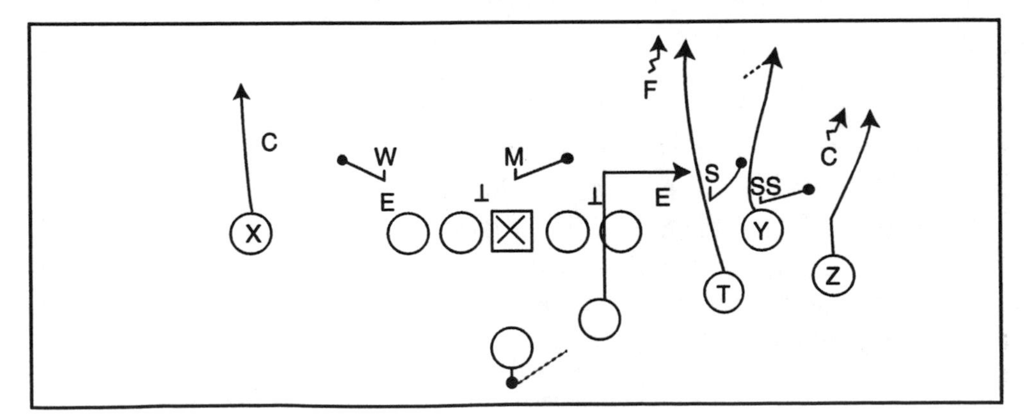

Figure 17.9—560 vertical from a right Near formation.

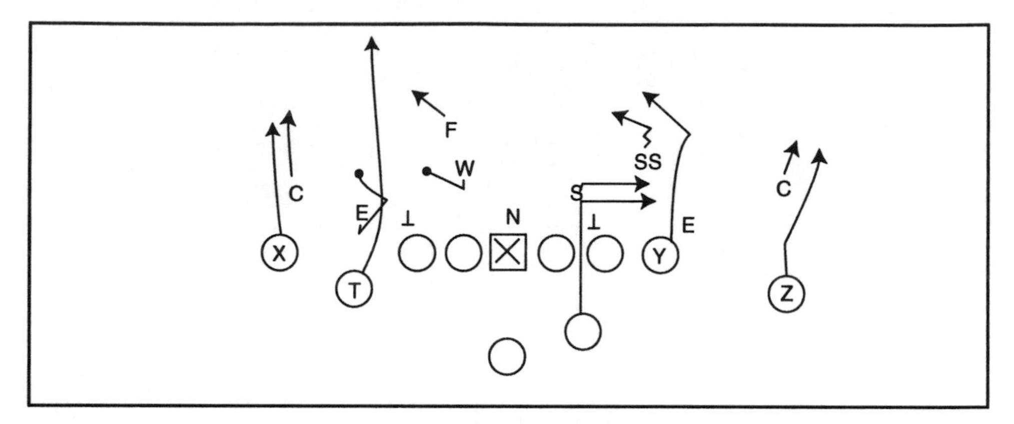

Figure 17.10—560 vertical from a right Pistol formation.

over the top of the corners to give help. That situation leaves a window open, 18-22 yards down the field, for the quarterback to catch the snap, pivot, and lay the ball out for the wide receiver. The receivers take an inside release at the corner, and then fight to the sideline aiming for a spot between 18-22 yards down the field, three yards from the sideline (Refer to Figure 17.4).

The cover 2 corner can also play a float technique. If the corner is "floating", he can either drop with the vertical by X or Z or he can jump the running back out of the backfield. While most college defensive backs can play this coverage very successfully,

Note: the safeties are faced with a difficult angle giving help.

many of the corners you face in high school cannot. On a 560 vertical, if the secondary has that cover 2/cover 4 look, the corner may be floating, especially if you have hit the running back a few times. The quarterback should then catch the snap and progress through his reads. If the Y receiver runs the broken arrow, and the linebacker doesn't have it walled off, the quarterback should throw the ball to Y. If Y is walled off by the linebacker, the quarterback should look to the running back. If the running back is open, the quarterback should deliver the ball quickly. However, if the corner has picked him up out in the flats, and the quarterback sees it, the quarterback should let the ball fly to Z. That is a play you may want to look for in the press box if the corners are jumping your receivers in the flats quicker than they should be (Refer to Figures 17.5 and 17.6).

The 4 vertical series can be run from other formations ranging from the Near and Pistol sets to the Empty and Open sets (Refer to Figures 17.7—17.10).

CHAPTER 18

Shotgun Passing Attack: The Choice Route

The choice-route combination appears to be a ten-yard curl and a stick route to the casual football fan. However, there is more to this route than simply telling X and Z to run ten yards up the field and turn around. Several keys exist to making sure a receiver is open on the play. This chapter reviews those keys.

One of the primary factors to be aware of concerning a choice route is that it can be run from a variety of formations. In other words, you can dictate what type of coverage you want to throw it against. Certain formations usually draw a certain coverage. The route is effective against a diverse array of formations—from Base formations (such as two wide receivers and a tight end), all the way to five-wide receiver formations. While most high school coaches are more likely to use the former than the latter, I encourage you to consider the choice route from a variety of formations.

After selecting the formations that best fit into your game plan, the next step is to be certain that the route combination is being run correctly. When it is, the quarterback should be able to make a simple read and toss an easy completion. The primary route to be taught is the choice route. While it is similar to a curl, it has to be modified (i.e., make an adjustment to ensure proper spacing between the two receivers involved).

The choice receiver should stem inside on his release from the line of scrimmage. This action gives him inside position against a defensive back who is covering him in zone coverage. The main goal of this receiver should be to finish his route one yard inside the curl/flat player of the defense. While he is gaining an inside position on his release and advancing ten yards up the field, the receiver should glance at the initial movement of the curl/flat defender. On most occasions, that defender will immediately jump the stick route being run by the inside receiver. This defensive tendency lets the choice receiver know there is only a limited distance he needs to travel inside on his break. That step also creates a quick-and-easy read for the quarterback, since the defender who could get in the throwing lane of the choice route has vacated that area to cover the stick (Refer to Figure 18.1).

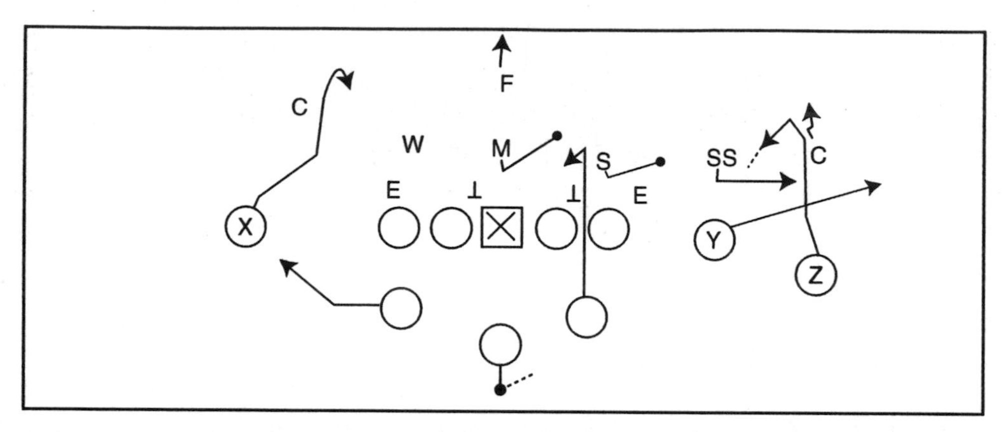

Figure 18.1—Note the movement of the flat players on both sides of the formation, thereby giving the choice receiver a shorter distance to travel to the inside.

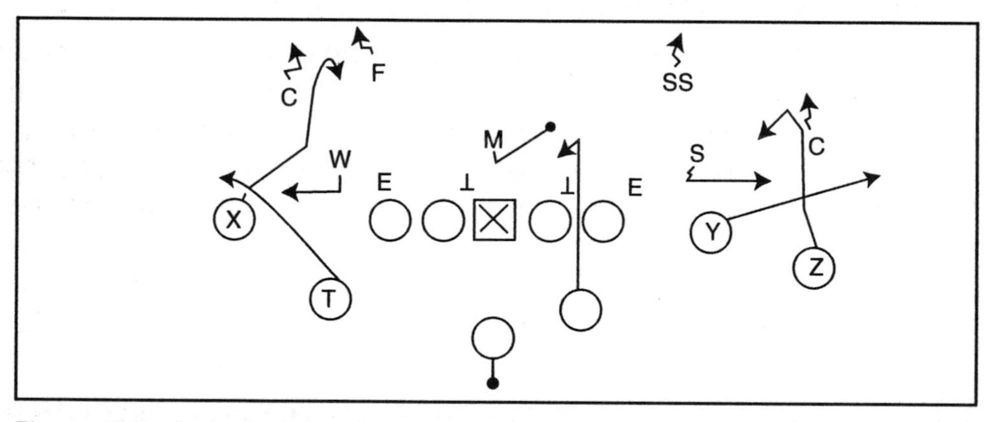

Figure 18.2—A choice route from a Rifle formation versus a 4-deep coverage in the secondary. Note: Z and X are working further to the inside due to the slow pursuit of flat defenders.

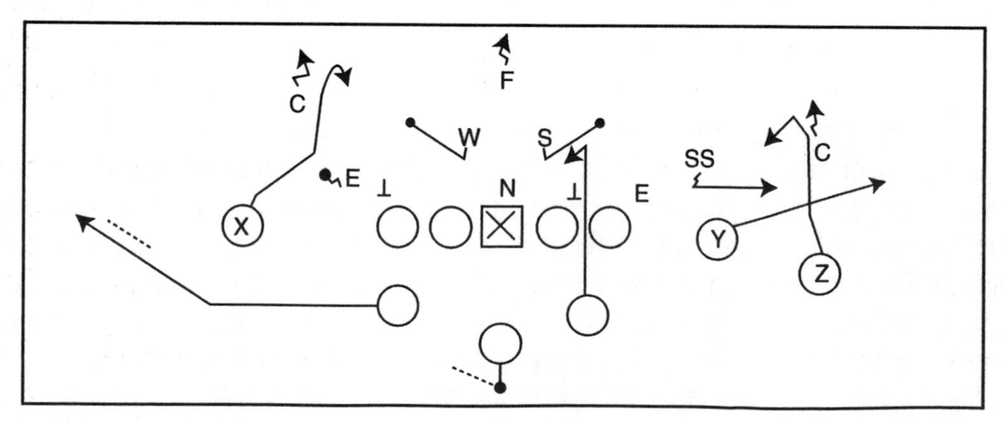

Figure 18-3. A choice route from the Panther formation. Note: the angle of the running back is parallel to the line of scrimmage on his release to a flare route.

On some occasions, the flat defender will react more slowly. Perhaps, the tight end is the stick receiver and gets hard nosed by the rush defensive end, or Y gets jammed at the line of scrimmage in either the Panther or Rifle formation. No matter what the cause, however, the X and Z receivers would then have to move further inside to finish the route at the landmark of one yard inside the curl/flat player. Once they break off their route at ten yards, they must work a little further inside and then back down the stem (Refer to Figure 18.2).

The inside receivers on the choice route, (Y in Base and Panther, and Y and T in Rifle and Pistol), also have landmarks to hit down the field. The route that they run is referred to as a "stick" route. It is a straight release route to a spot 5-7 yards deep at an angle all the way to the bottom of the numbers (Note: in Alabama, the yardage numbers are painted on the field). Once the receiver gets a clean release, he must get his head around to the quarterback as quickly as possible. If this pattern is thrown, the ball will be on the way to him rapidly. The quarterback will have read that the flat defender is hesitating rather than covering the pattern off the line. If the defender does not go with the stick route, the quarterback should set up quickly and deliver the ball before the flat defender can recover. The angle of the quarterback's release creates leverage for the receiver once he catches the football. If the ball is not delivered to the stick receiver, he should settle three yards from the sideline, showing the quarterback his numbers. However, if the quarterback scrambles toward him, he should turn up the field and run a go route. Charlie Ward hit Matt Frier during that situation for a long touchdown versus Miami in 1993.

If the formation happens to be Panther, the tailback takes on the responsibility of the T receiver's flat route. This objective is achieved with a flare pattern to the weakside of the field. It should be noted that the tailback explodes parallel to the line of scrimmage and does not bubble backwards. Once he approaches the halfway point to the sideline, he breaks at a 45-degree angle and prepares to receive the football. However, he never crosses the line of scrimmage unless the ball is delivered to him (Refer to Figure 18.3).

The fullback is also involved in the choice route. His involvement is not so much to actually catch a pass, but more to hold the Sam linebacker in his area in order to prevent him from being able to stretch and help out on the choice route if the route is forced inside. The fullback steps up and checks the linebacker at the snap. If the linebacker blitzes, the running back meets him in the hole. If the linebacker drops, the running back proceeds directly up the field and spots up at six yards.

The protection on the choice route is 460 from the Panther formation, and 560 with Rifle or Pistol personnel in the game. Detailed instructions regarding 460 and 560 protections were provided in Chapter 13.

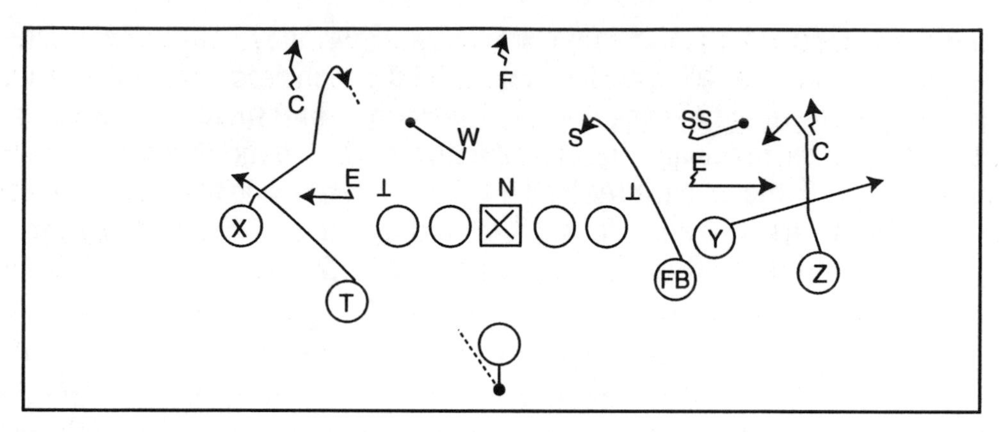

Figure 18-4. A 560 choice from an Open formation.

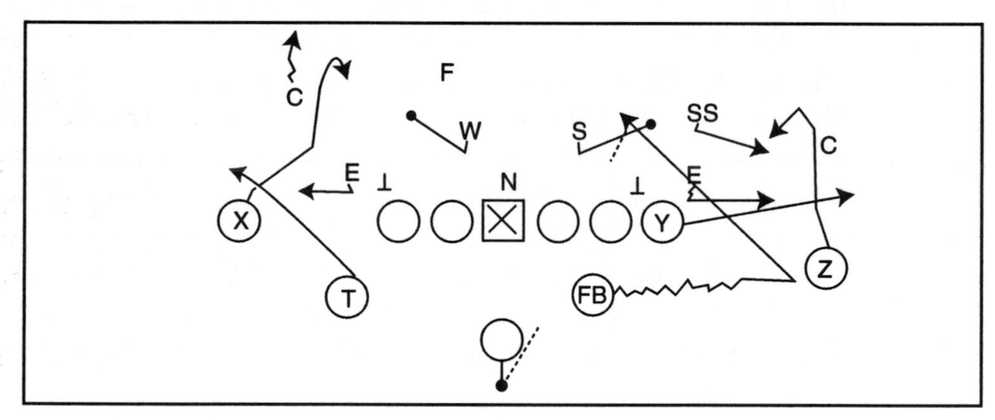

Figure 18-5. A 560 choice from a Pistol, empty formation.

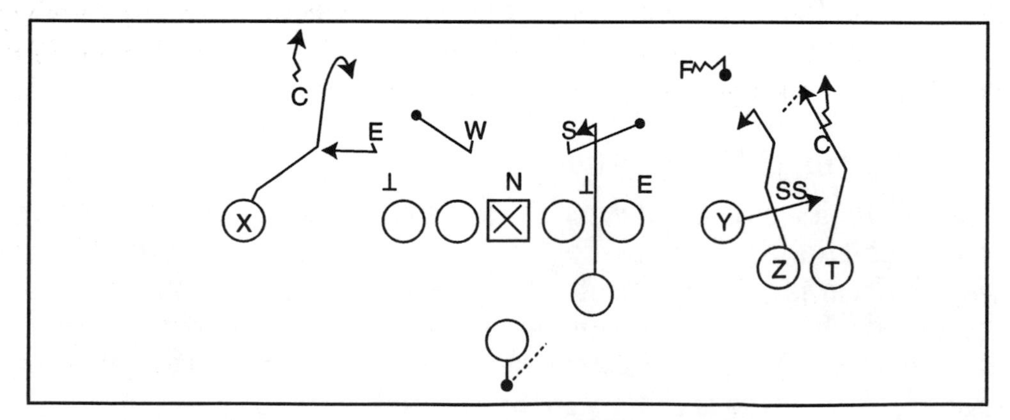

Figure 18-6. A 560 choice, T Skinny post from a Rifle Far formation.

The choice pattern is ideal to use with other formations. This section of the chapter presents three of the most effective formations in which a choice route can be employed. The first is the Open, or 5-wide receiver set. In this formation, the running back simply slides out into the slot on the strongside of the formation. His route is still a spot route, only in this instance he releases immediately into the pattern. Because there is no back to help protect, the quarterback must be ready to deliver the ball quickly if a blitz occurs. The running back should have a landmark of directly in front of the strongside guard when he spots up at six yards. This landmark puts him in a good spot for the quarterback to deliver him the ball against a middle blitz (Refer to Figure 18.4).

The next formation from which the choice route can be run is Pistol. This formation brings the tight end back into the alignment. If you choose, the running back can also be emptied out on this play. The ball, however, should be snapped within the first five yards of his motion so that he can break back to the inside on his spot route. The crossing and draw packages are so common from the empty motion that this action could confuse a defensive assignment (Refer to Figure 18.5).

The final formation to consider is the Far formation. When you run a choice route from a Far formation, T will have to be "tagged" with another route, because you cannot have two stick routes on the same side of the field. The responsibilities of everyone stay the same except for T. However, getting T spread out gets your Z receiver isolated on either a strong safety or a linebacker, thereby creating an opportunity for a big play over the top of the free safety if the free safety were to help on the choice route (Refer to Figure 18.6).

The choice route is an excellent addition to any offense. Over the years, FSU has made an incredible number of completions off this route. The choice route is also an excellent pass to adapt to the high school level. Because the route can really give a 3-deep zone fits, running it from a Panther formation might be an appropriate (and highly successful) addition to your offense.

CHAPTER 19

Shotgun Passing Attack: Horizontal Stretch Routes—The Bench

The bench route is an out route that is run with a speed cut. Used in both drop-back passing and on play action (344 Bench), it is one of FSU's top passing plays. It is set up with leverage by running the 560 vertical in order to make the corners weary of the deep ball.

On the bench route, the wide receivers, X and Z, each take an outside release, driving at the corners' outside shoulder, just like on a vertical route. However, when they reach their sixth step, they plant their outside foot hard to push toward the sideline and throw their elbow back around toward the quarterback as they snap their heads around. At that point, the ball should be halfway to the receiver out of his break, who should be in a perfect position to catch the football.

This action should all be done without the familiar patdown steps that so many teams use that can enable corners to react on the route and to make an interception (often for a touchdown). Because the bench route is a speed cut, 3- and 4-deep zone coverages can have a difficult time stopping the route. In fact, the best way to defend the bench route is to press the receiver so that he will run a fade instead of the bench. The fade creates an entirely different problem for a pressing corner.

As such, the bench route can be very effective with the outside receivers. However, there are effective inside routes that can compliment the bench route. Because the bench is a mirror route to both sides, the inside receivers are also on mirror routes to both sides. These inside routes, combined with the bench route, are the choice routes, that are run by the inside receivers. Because Y and T are lined up further inside than X and Z, they do not have as far to work inside to get one yard inside the curl/flat defender. The defender might even have to work a little to the outside to get that relationship.

Swing Route

The other route that can be combined with the bench route from the shotgun is the swing route by the running back. As was previously mentioned, the swing route should be run exploding toward the sideline to the half-way point, and then breaking at a 45-degree angle toward the line of scrimmage, but never crossing the LOS without the ball. Refer to Figure 19.1 for the 560 Bench route from a Rifle formation.

The bench route can also be run from the Panther formation. Because two backs are in the backfield, you should adjust to 460 protection in this instance. The fullback should check the Sam linebacker and then swing to the strongside. The tailback checks the weakside backer and then progresses up the field to eight yards. At that point, he should slide either inside or outside to get one yard inside the curl/flat player. All other assignments stay the same. The use of this formation will most likely draw a 3-deep zone look. Refer to Figure 19-2 for a 460 Bench route from a Panther formation.

On occasion, the Panther formation will draw a half-zone/half man coverage. At Texas Tech, we referred to that defensive alignment as cover 92. This particular coverage forces the X receiver to convert the Bench route to a fade. Because most of the time, a blitz is also evident from that coverage, the tailback might have to pick up a blitzing linebacker on his side. The routes to the strongside stay the same. Y is matched up one-on-one with a safety as he runs the choice route, and Z is getting single coverage on the bench. This sequence is almost a guaranteed 1, 2, 3 step and throw the bench for the quarterback because no one will get underneath the bench. However, you should make sure that the quarterback, as with all bench routes, doesn't hitch up. A hitch will ruin his timing and might lead to an interception (Refer to Figure 19.3).

The bench can also be run from the Pistol formation and the Base formation. I would not recommend it from either a Near or a Far formation because they both make it too congested to the strongside for an out route. Because this offense is based on simplicity, congestion can complicate the quarterback's reads.

COACHING POINT: The quarterback should be coached to pre-read the coverage to see if one of the wideouts is being pressed. If a wideout is pressed, he should convert to a fade or a takeoff route. If neither wideout is pressed, the quarterback can also choose a side to which to throw based on an unusually large cushion by the defensive back. Otherwise, the quarterback should read from Z to Y and to the running back on the swing, all the while reading the curl/flat defender to determine where to deliver the football.

When the quarterback catches the shotgun snap, he should always take a quick 3-step drop and deliver the ball immediately to the bench route if it is open. There should never be a hitch step on the bench route. It is a timing pattern. As such, the quarterback should not hitch up on timing patterns. He should be aware that if the bench isn't there, Y is settling one yard inside of the defender who is sprinting underneath of Z. The running back is an outlet. If the back also is covered, the quarterback should simply throw the ball over his head and out of bounds. This pass should be practiced in skeleton drills, since it can be exceptionally effective in a no-huddle situation.

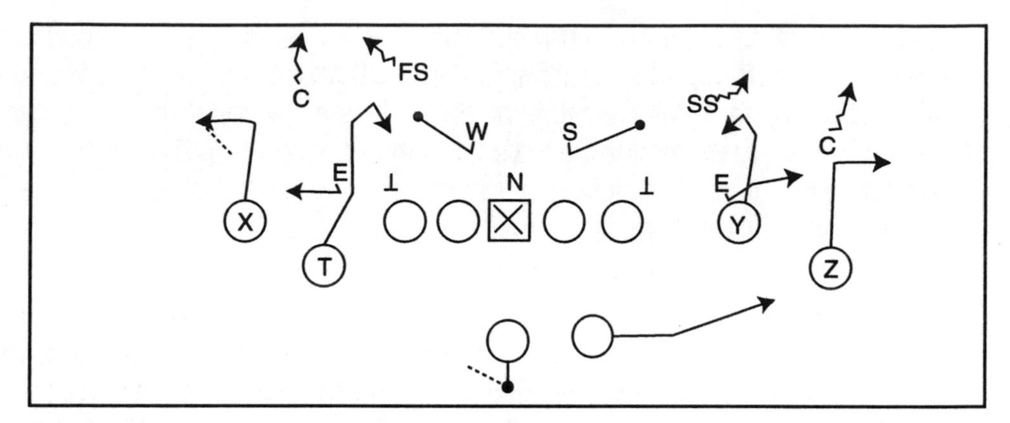

Figure 19.1—A 560 Bench from the Rifle formation.

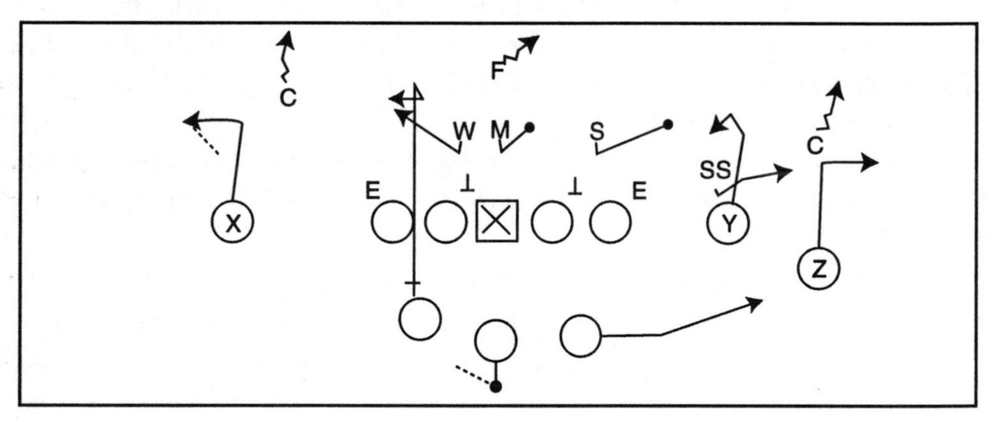

Figure 19.2—A 460 Bench route from a Panther formation.

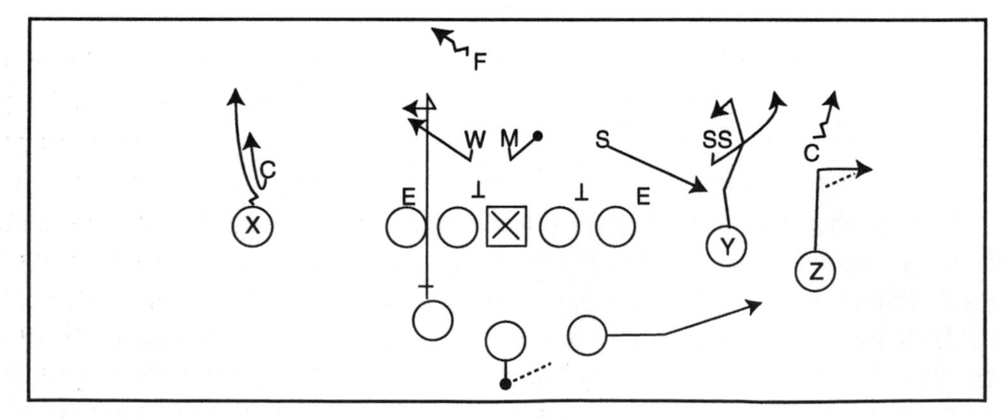

Figure 19.3—A 460 bench versus a cover 92.

CHAPTER 20

THE SHALLOW CROSS SERIES: Z CROSS

In the previous chapters on shotgun passes, the focus was on throwing medium and long-range passes. The chapter examines the shallow-cross series—a series that is used in conjunction with those plays. When an offense concentrates on throwing out routes, verticals, and flags, the area of concern with the defense begin to move back slightly. Linebackers begin dropping a step deeper and a little more quickly. Corners play a little softer (i.e., become more outside conscious).

The shallow cross series is a series of short-to-intermediate passes that are designed to frustrate defensive backs, stretch linebackers horizontally and vertically, and absolutely wear out a pass rush. The series has built-in sight or hot adjustments for blitz situations and features patterns that can be run from a variety of formations. It also allows for a shallow cross to come from each of the four receivers when in the Rifle or Pistol formation, or from Y and Z when in the Base and Panther formations. Refer to Figure 20.1 for a 560 Z cross as run by FSU.

On the Z shallow cross in the FSU offense, the playside, as on all crosses, involves a shallow crossing route, a choice route, and a swing by the running back. This situation makes the read easy for the quarterback on all shallow crosses, no matter which receiver is running the cross. The quarterback should always read the crossing route first, the choice route second, and then check down to the running back third.

The choice route should be run exactly the same as it is by the receivers on the 560 bench or 560 choice. The receiver's primary objective should still be to settle one yard inside the curl/flat player. The swing route is more vital on the shallow cross series than on any other combination of routes with which it is used. The swing receiver will always check the playside linebacker, then progress immediately into the route. The swing receiver should make sure not to bubble back, as some teams doing a cheap imitation of the crossing series tend to do. If the quarterback hits the running back on the run, the back should have lots of sideline left to work with to outrun the player assigned to cover him. Who can forget the fourth quarter comeback of FSU versus Florida in 1994 when the running backs received swing pass after swing pass and always seemed to find running room after the catch (Refer to Figure 20.2).

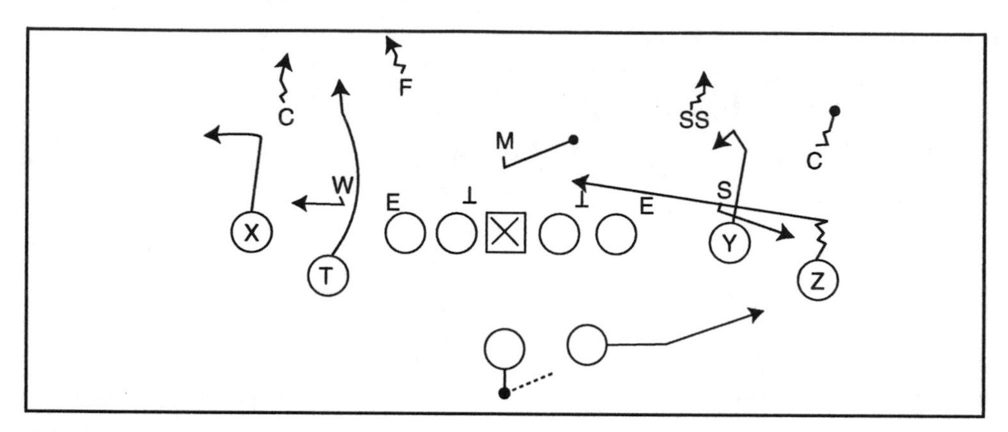

Figure 20-1. 560 Z cross from the Rifle formation.

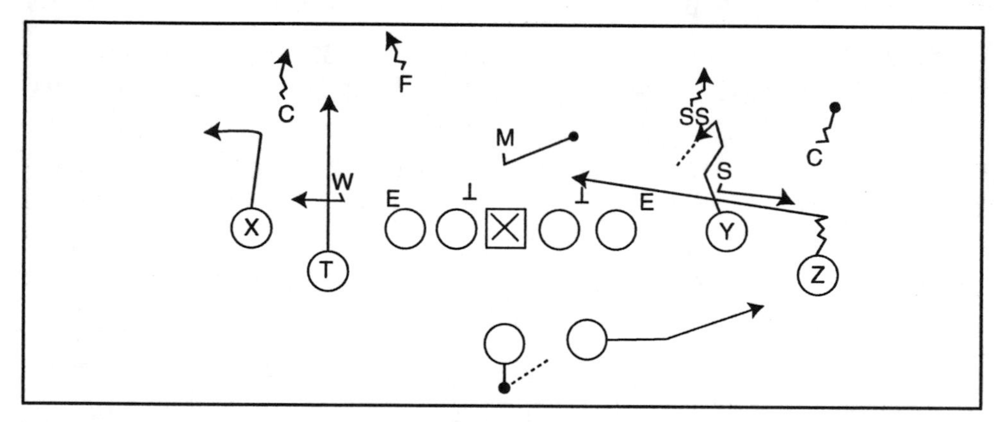

Figure 20.2—560 Z cross. Note the path of the back after catch.

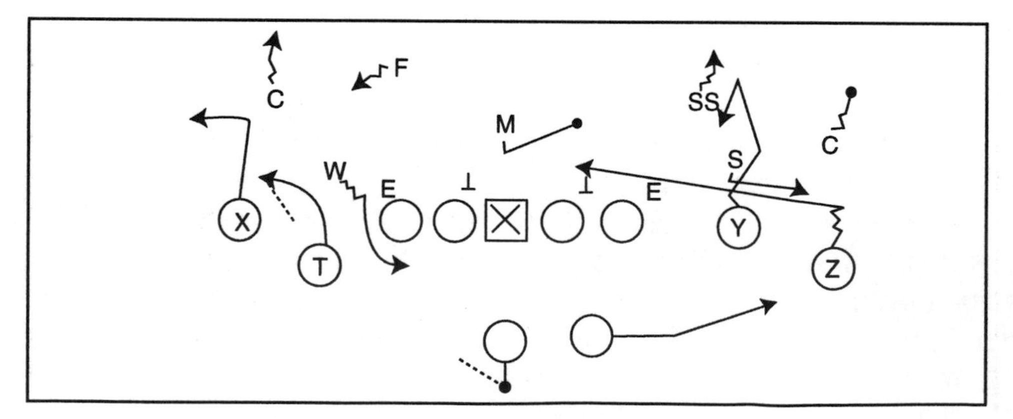

Figure 20.3—A 560 Z cross with FSU's blitz adjustment.

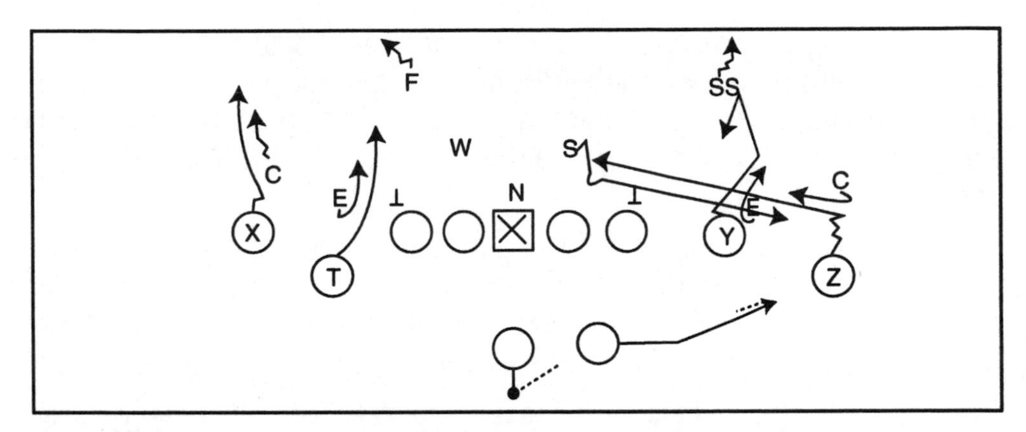

Figure 20.4—A 560 Z cross versus a hard corner.

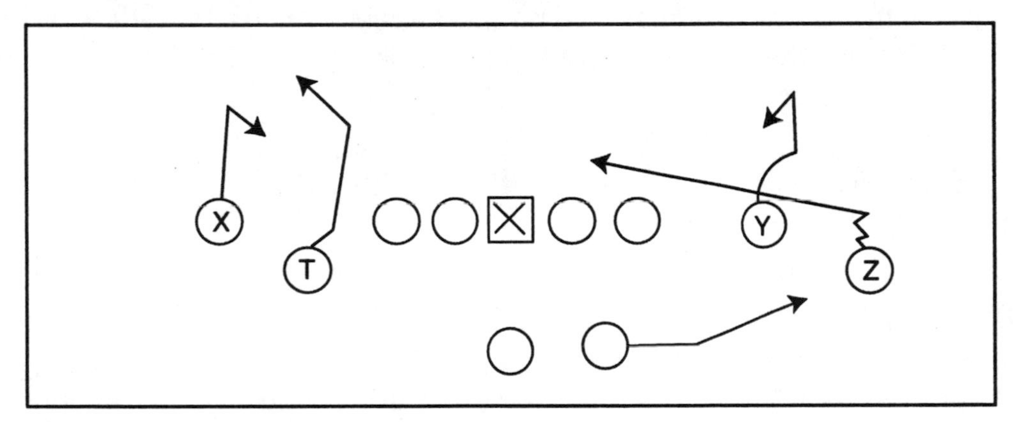

Figure 20.5—A 561 Z cross modification.

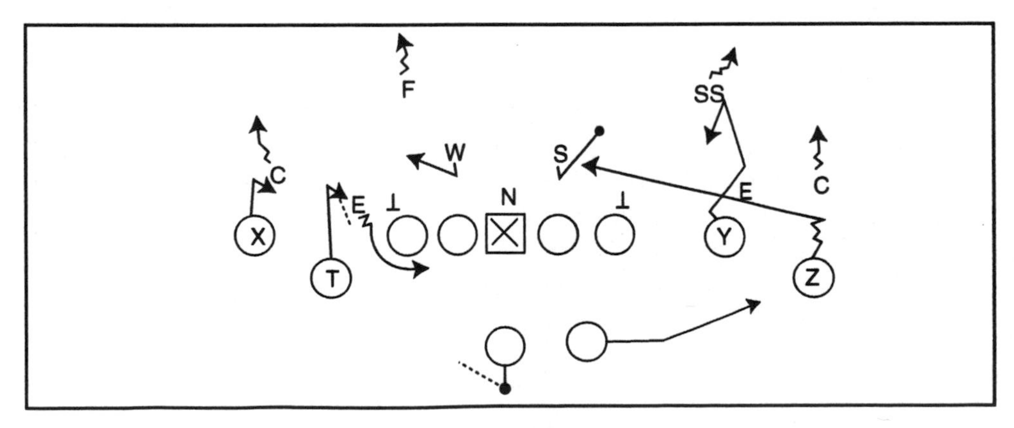

Figure 20.6—A 561 Z cross versus a weakside blitz.

When running the shallow cross, the Z receiver should release up the field under control versus a zone coverage. He can take one normal step or three short choppy steps and then cross the field at a depth of three yards underneath the linebackers. He should make eye contact with the quarterback when he is ready for the football.

If Z faces man coverage, his thinking should change. At this point, his goal should be to get off the line as soon as possible to the inside and gain separation from the defensive back as he continues to accelerate across the field and to make eye contact with the quarterback when he is ready for the football.

The quarterback should look to see if dropping linebackers have vacated an area for the crossing receiver. If they have, the quarterback should stick the ball on the receiver's numbers. He should not throw the ball too high, since such a throw could lead to a tipped interception. If no area has been vacated out, the quarterback should read the flat player to determine if the ball should be delivered to the choice or the swing. Y is on the choice on the 560 Z cross, and Z runs the cross.

The backside routes run by FSU on 560 Z cross are a bench by X and a vertical by T. If the Will linebacker blitzes, T breaks his route off to a quick out (Refer to Figure 20.3).

Another adjustment that could be forced with these backside routes occurs when the corner presses X, forcing X to convert to a takeoff (Refer to Figure 20.4).

To modify the 560 Z cross to the high school level, I gave considerable thought to how all these adjustments could cause confusion. Subsequently, I identified two possible backside-route combinations that would decrease the amount of possible adjustments by our receivers. The way we put them together was to employ either the smash concept, with which the receivers would already be familiar, or the choice concept, with which they were also already familiar.

The first adjustment could be designated in a number of ways. For example, you could have the first adjustment called 561 Z cross—the 1 in 561 referring to the first adjustment. Initially, for example, the first adjustment affects the smash. The playside of the cross stays the same, with Z on a cross, Y on a choice, and the running back on a swing. The backside runs the smash route. X runs five steps and hitches up, while T runs the inside-release flag route. Refer to Figure 20.5 for an example of this modification. You should keep in mind that there are simple ways to modify the offense without having to make too many adjustments.

On the other hand, one blitz adjustment still has to be made even on 561 Z cross. If the backside linebacker blitzes off of T, then T should simply stop his route at five yards and turn around (Refer to Figure 20.6).

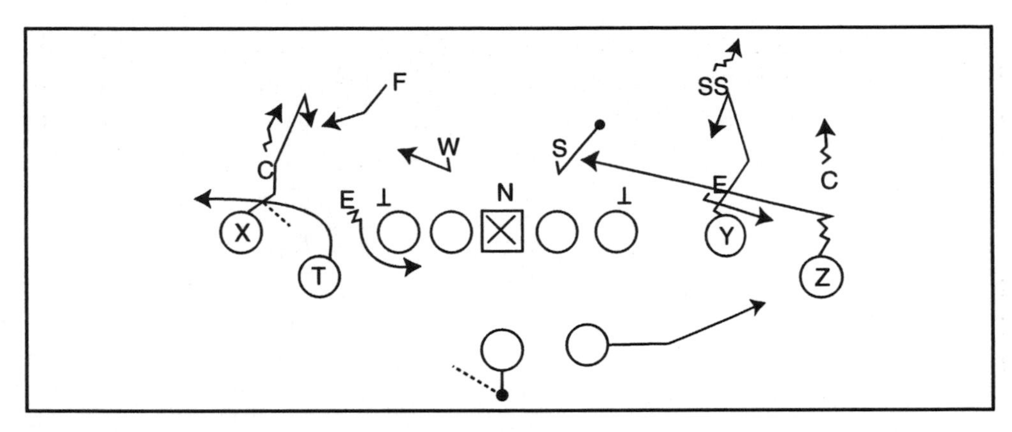

Figure 20.7—A 562 Z cross modification.

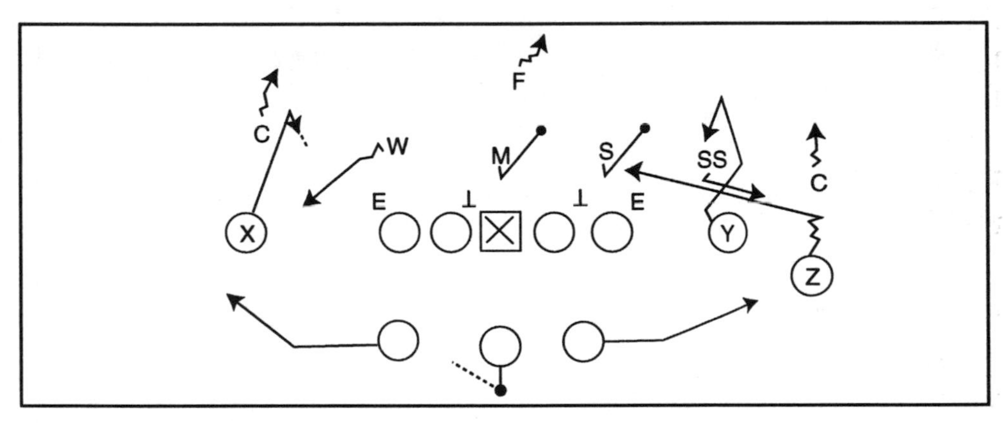

Figure 20.8—A 462 Z cross from the Panther formation.

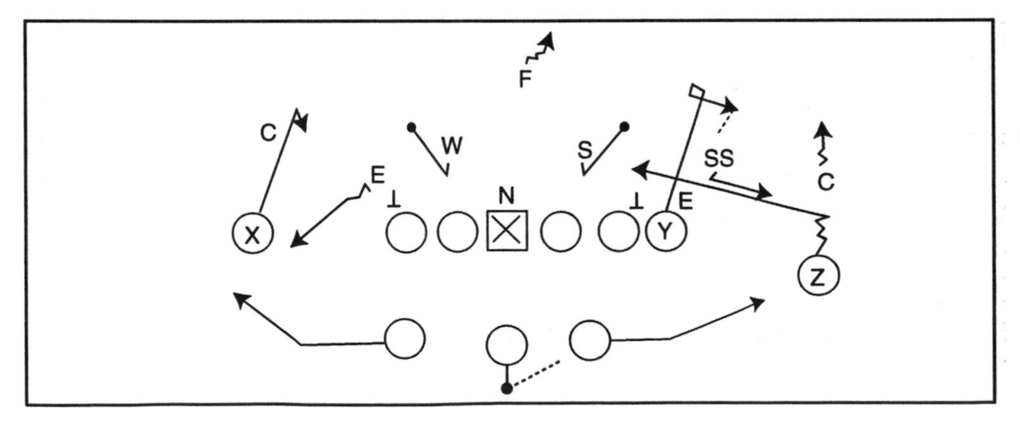

Figure 20.9—A 462 Z cross from the Base formation.

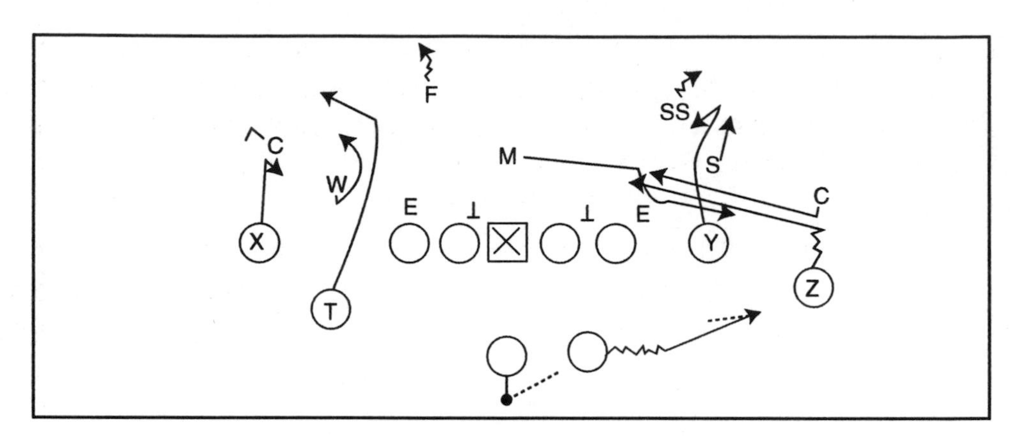

Figure 20.10—A 561 Z cross from the Rifle empty formation.

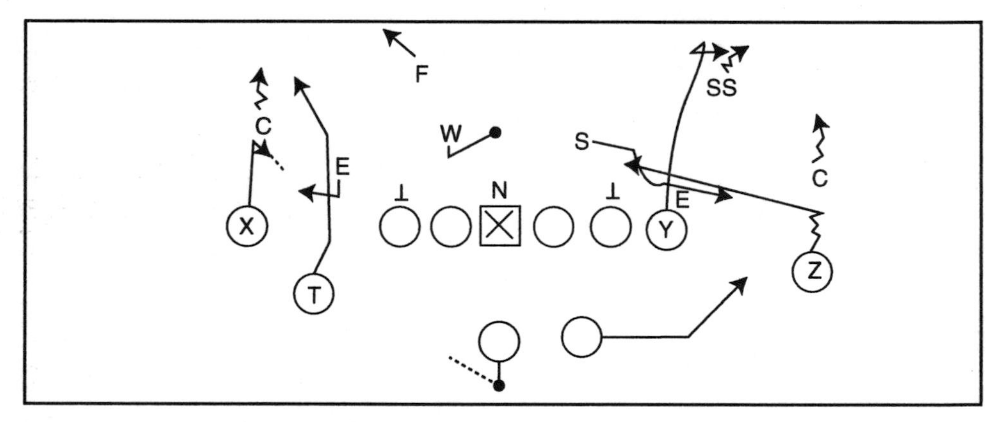

Figure 20.11—A 561 Z cross from the Pistol formation.

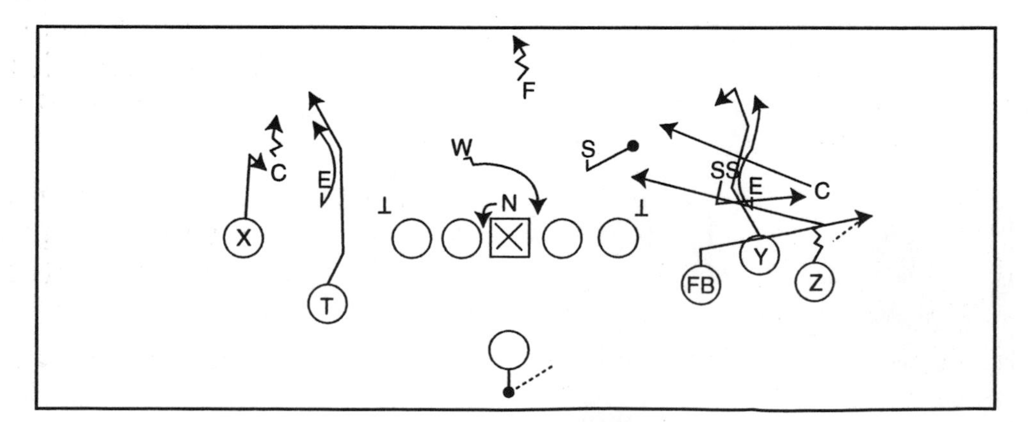

Figure 20.12—A 561 Z cross from an Open formation.

The second adjustment employs the choice as the backside route combination. This play, the 562 Z cross, works especially well with the inside crosses that are discussed in future chapters. X runs the choice route, while T runs the stick. Because the stick is a natural hot route, no blitz adjustment has to be made on the backside with this play (Refer to Figure 20.7).

While FSU uses the bench/vertical combination on nearly all of its base crosses, I recommend using the backside adjustments of 561 and 562 for the remainder of the crossing package because they adapt much easier to high school football. The Z cross can also be run from the Panther, Near, and Far formations. The Panther formation is discussed first, again using the 561 and 562 modifications. With the Panther formation, the 562, (or choice modification), on the backside is preferred. While the bench pattern used by FSU is an option, a hard corner or cover 92 forces the receiver to convert the route. The choice route requires no conversion versus a hard corner. Because we are in the Panther formation, the 500 protection changes to 400. As a result we are looking at 462 Z cross (Refer to Figure 20.8).

462 Z cross can also be run from the Base formation. On this play, the tight end runs the choice route. He should work to the outside on his release in order to prevent the Sam linebacker from being able to cover him. He works up the field and slides back outside to the choice landmark (Refer to Figure 20.9).

The ability to run the pattern from a variety of personnel groups; such as Panther, Rifle, Base, and Pistol as well as from others, allows a tremendous amount of pressure to be put on a defense that has only a week to prepare for all those offensive looks. If the plays are installed carefully, you can see that they are really easy to learn. For the offense, it's the same play over and over. The same types of routes and reads repeated. But for a defensive coordinator, it can provide for a long few days of practice. In turn, it may lead to a blown assignment somewhere on game day. Figures 20.10 through 20.15 illustrate Z cross from a variety of other formations—with and without motion from the running back.

Frequently, the linebacker slides out with motion, creating a tremendously large vacated area for Z to simply make a catch and run in the open field. Figure 20.11 demonstrates the 561 Z cross from the Pistol formation. This alignment utilizes the tight end back in the formation.

The Open formation is very effective with the shallow cross series. It also sets up a quarterback draw.

The Pistol formation can be a very effective for crossing series. Furthermore, it can help set up a counter blocking scheme for a quarterback draw.

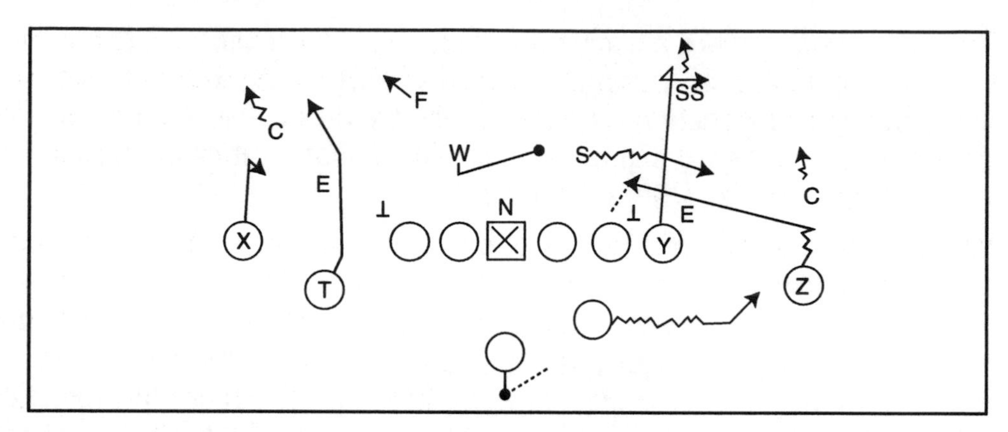

Figure 20.13—A 561 Z cross from a Pistol Empty formation.

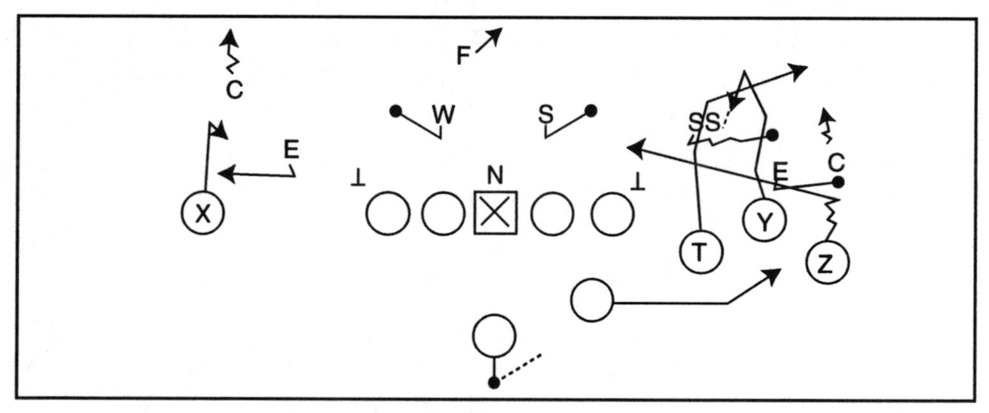

Figure 20.14—A 561 Z cross from a Rifle Near formation.

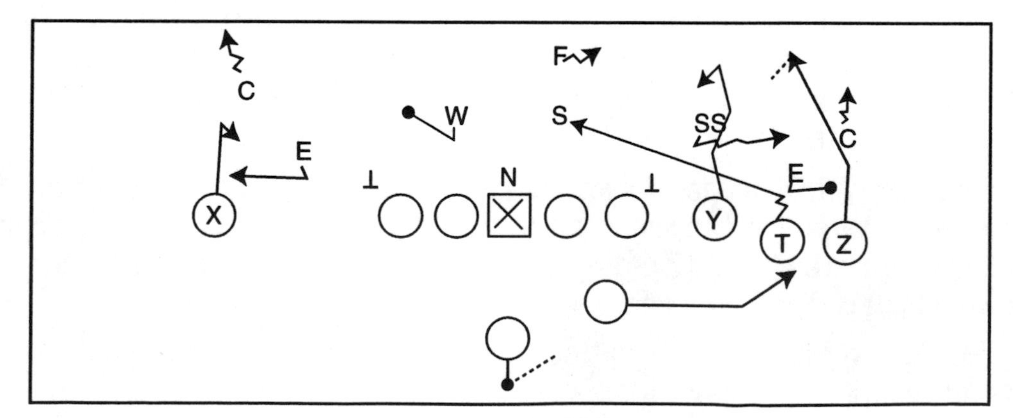

Figure 20.15—A 561 Z cross T post, from the Rifle Far formation.

The question arises concerning whether the shallow cross can be run from the trips formation. The straightforward answer is yes, you can. You should simply line up the T receiver in the slot and send him on the same route he would run on the other side of the field, a flag. He doesn't have to have a tagged call here; he just runs the same route from the other side of the field.

From the Far formation, T's route should be tagged. Because he is too wide to run a flag route, T should run a post. If the free safety jumps the choice route, the post should come open behind him. If not, T should go through his normal cross-package reads.

The 561 Z cross...one play, two backside-route options, and numerous formations to employ it. Every coach should be able to find a way to use Z cross in his offense. In reality, it can't be any simpler than this particular package from the FSU offense. Furthermore, it is very easy to modify this package to the high school level. Remember, the quarterback always has the same read, no matter what formation the offense lines up in. He reads cross first, choice second, and the swing third.

CHAPTER 21

THE SHALLOW CROSS SERIES: Y CROSS

On the Y cross, the inside receiver runs the crossing route. The Y cross is read the same as the Z cross, checking from cross, to choice, to the swing route. Because Z runs the choice route, the receivers are just swapping responsibilities. At the high school level, I recommend using the 562 modification that was discussed in the previous chapter. That modification gives the backside of the play a stick route by T, which pulls the linebacker out to the flats and away from the shallow cross and a choice route by X (Refer to Figure 21.1).

As can be seem in (Figure 21.1), the modification to 562 pulls the flat player out, vacating a pretty large area for the Y receiver on the cross. If the inside line-backers drop, this pass is a "gift". If the Sam linebacker were to jam Y to the inside, the choice route opens up for the Z receiver. In fact, during the 1998 season, the choice receiver opened up on this same play for our offense, enabling our receiver to make 11 easy catches for 150 yards on the same play. That doesn't begin to mention the success FSU has had with it over the years. The T receiver, running a stick route, also creates for an easy hot throw if the Will linebacker blitzes.

As can be seen, all of the different packages begin to mesh together to create an explosive type of offense. Y cross can also be run from the Panther and Base formations if you want to get two backs into the formation. I recommend using the 462 modification on the backside of the play. A hot is not really needed, because the back in the backfield checks for blitz before releasing into the pattern. Keep in mind that the "400" part of the call means there are two backs in the backfield to check for the blitz before releasing. Refer to Figure 21.2 for a 462 Y cross from the Panther formation, and Figure 21.3 for a 462 Y cross from the Base formation.

The Panther and Base formations are more likely to draw coverages such as a 3-deep zone or a cover 92. You can also run the Y cross from other formations, including, Open, Rifle empty, Pistol, Pistol empty, and Near formation. These formations spread the field considerably more than either the Rifle or the Panther formations, thereby allowing the crossing receiver to have a larger area of open field following the reception. Refer to Figures 21.4 through 21.8 for a 562 Y cross from the various formations.

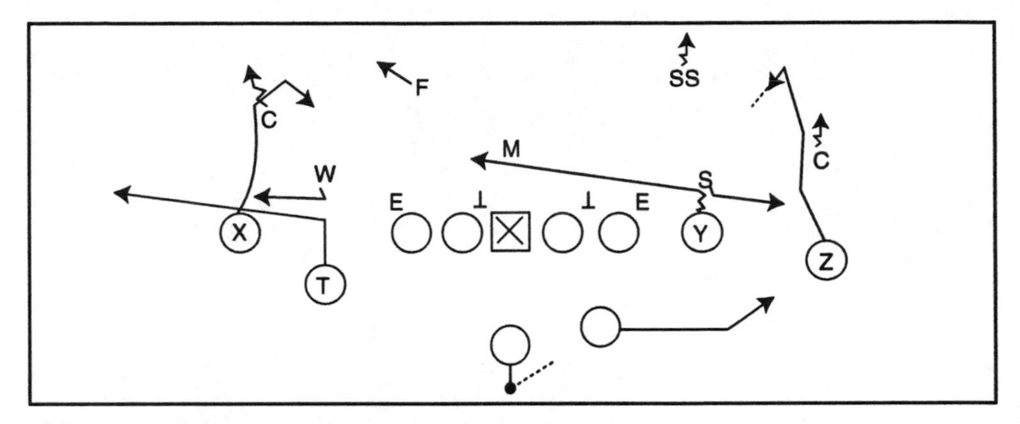

Figure 21.1—A 562 Y cross from a Rifle formation.

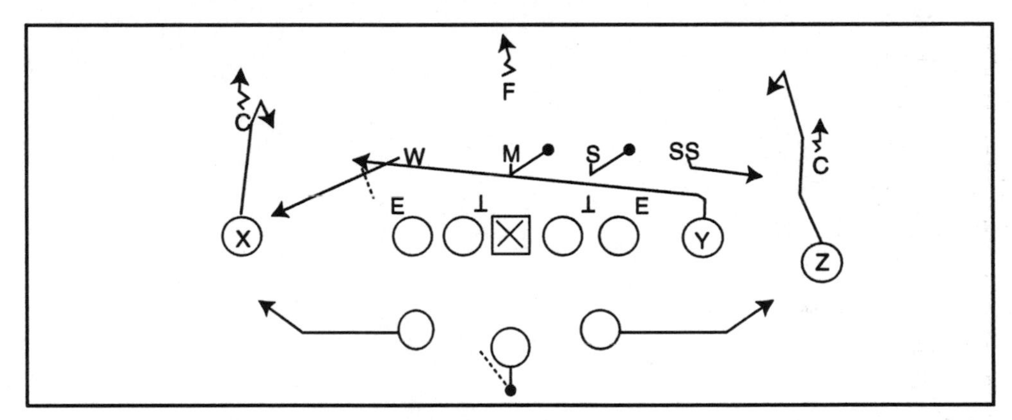

Figure 21.2—A 462 Y cross from the Panther formation.

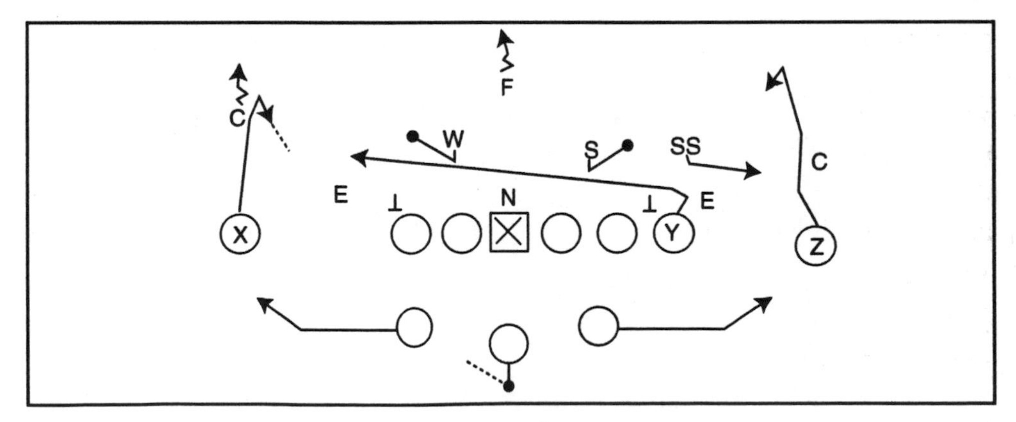

Figure 21.3—A 462 Y cross from the Base formation.

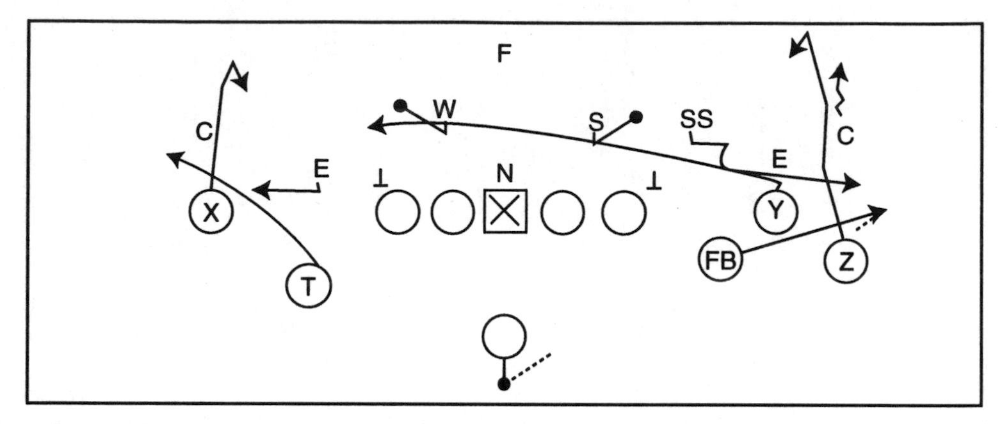

Figure 21.4—A 562 Y cross from an Open formation.

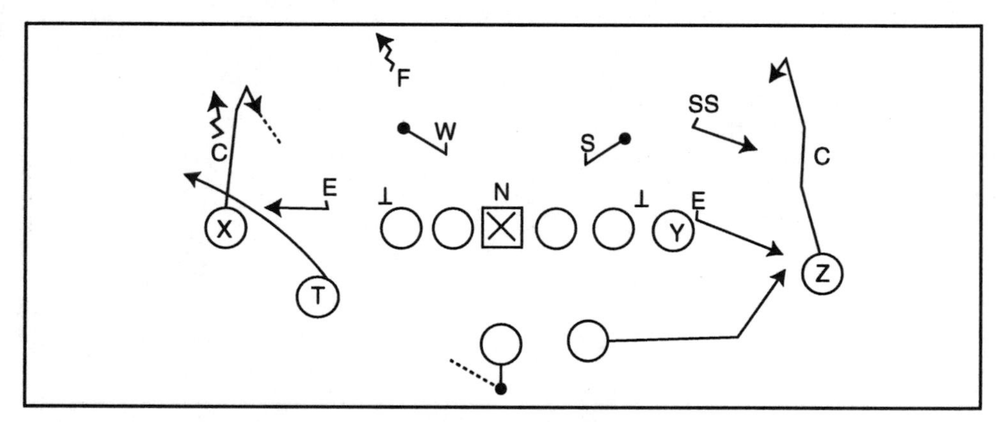

Figure 21.5—A 562 Y cross from a Pistol formation.

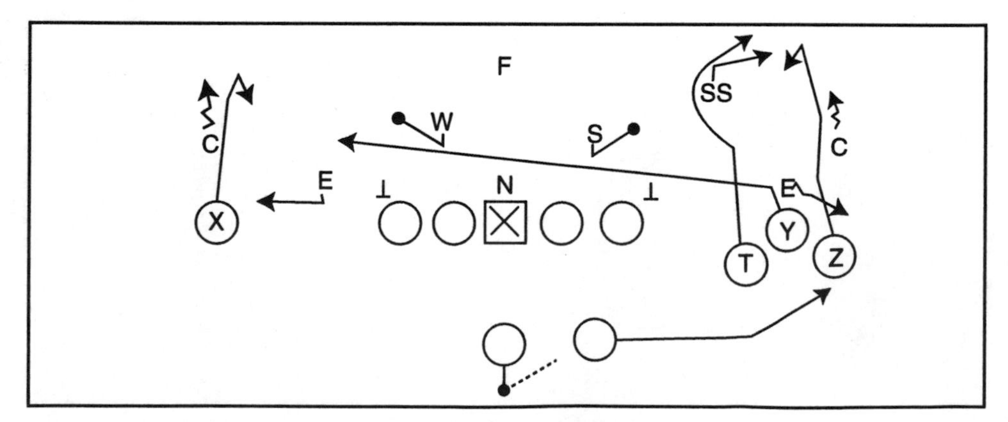

Figure 21.6—A 562 Y cross from the Near formation.

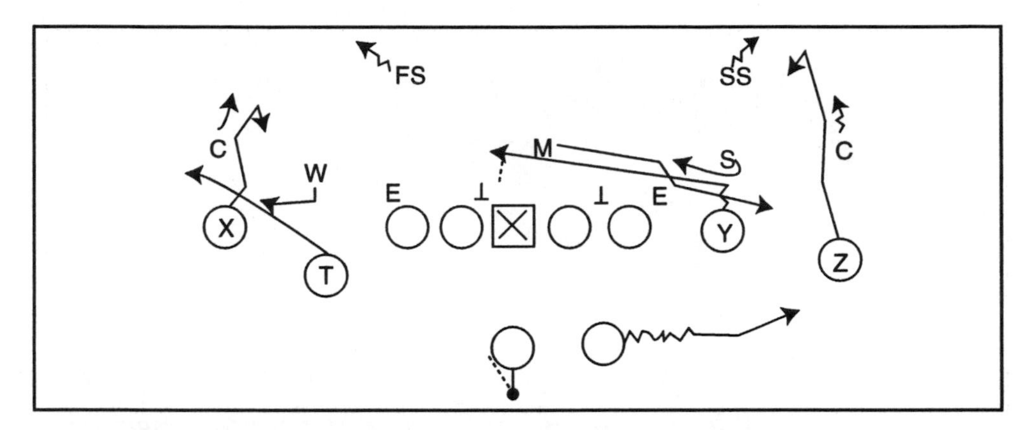

Figure 21.7—A 562 Y cross from a Rifle empty formation.

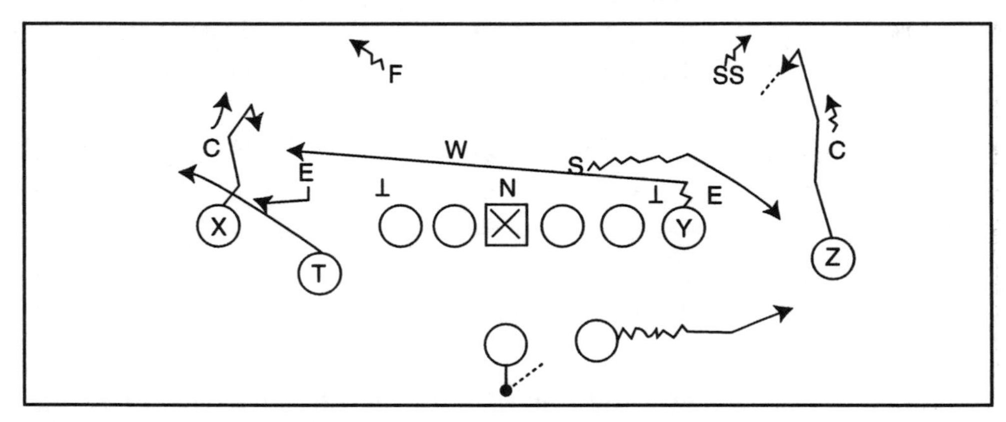

Figure 21.8—A 562 Y cross from a Pistol empty formation.

COACHING POINT: Y like Z comes across the field under control on the crossing route at a depth of three yards against a zone coverage. If he faces man coverage, he should accelerate off the line of scrimmage with an inside release to gain as much separation from the defender as possible.

CHAPTER 22

The Shallow Cross Series: X Cross

The X crossing route is the outside cross from the short side of the field. It is run just like the Z cross, except that it runs from the boundary out to the wide side of the field. X takes the same type of release as Z against both zone and man coverages. As a result, X and Z can take reps together during individual practice time—a step that can enable you to make better use of the existing time available for practice.

The only limitation on the X cross is that it is only run from the Rifle or Pistol formations. Our four-receiver sets are not lined up into the boundary because the sideline becomes a friend to the defense. Because X is on the boundary side of the field 90 percent of the time, we do not use formations that present trips to his side. Among the formations with which X cross will never be used are Near, Far, Panther, and Base.

On 561 or 562 X cross, the T receiver runs the choice route. The running back aligns to the boundary side for the swing route. The backside can be the 561 combination, which is the smash, or the 562 combination, which is the choice. Both routes are very effective backside options on the X cross. Figure 22.1 illustrates the 561 X cross from the Rifle formation. It should be noted that the FSU offense refers to weakside crosses as a 200 package. This package aligns the running back to the boundary side. To keep from complicating things, we recommend employing the base protection of 500 for the X cross. You might want to make an "opposite" call for the running back.

The running back can also be put in motion on an X cross. Figure 22.2 illustrates an Empty 561 X cross. Having discussed an X cross with a 561 modification from a Rifle formation, the next step is to review the 562 modification from Rifle and Rifle empty formations. Refer to Figures 22.3 and 22.4.

The final formation in which an X cross can be utilized is the Pistol formation. Either a Pistol or a Pistol empty formation can be employed to run the X cross. The 561 or 562 modifications are also possible alternatives, although I prefer the 562 with the tight end in the game. Figures 22.5—22.8 diagram each of the four possibilities.

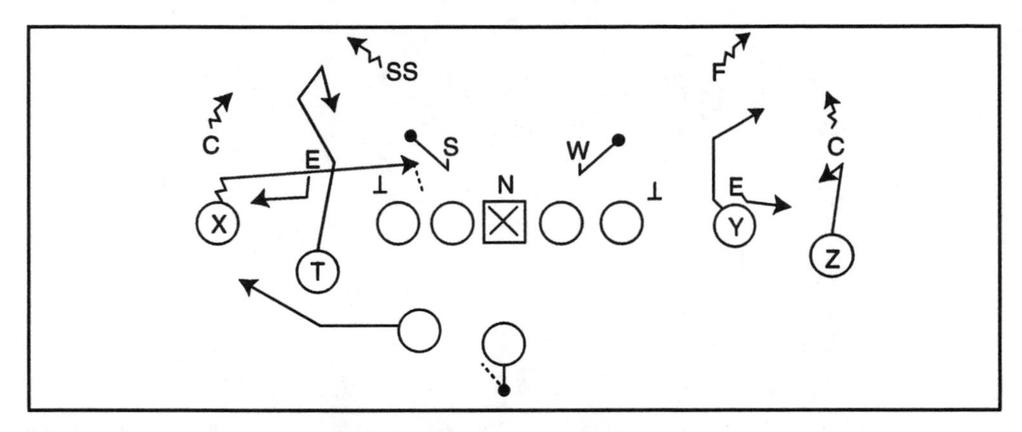

Figure 22.1—A 561 X cross from a Rifle formation.

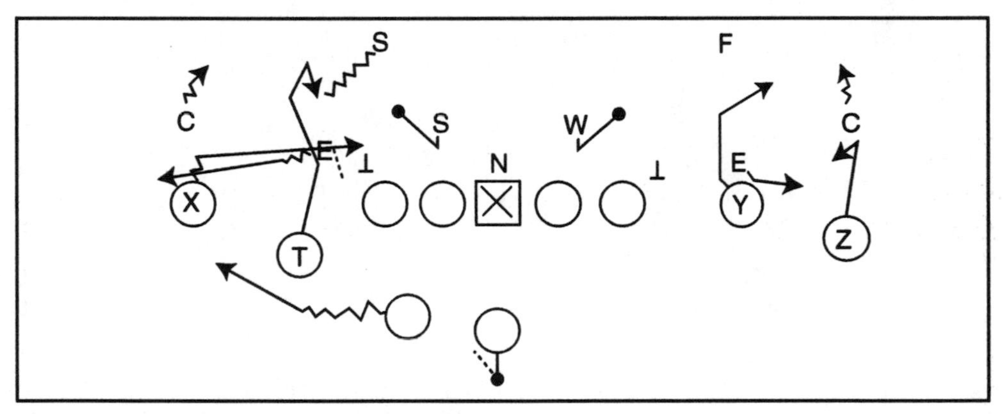

Figure 22.2—A Rifle empty 561 X cross.

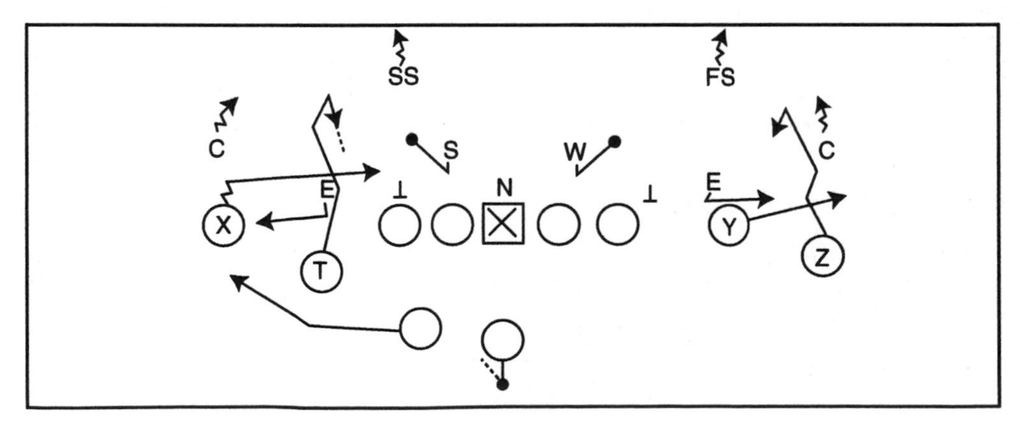

Figure 22.3—A 562 X cross from a Rifle formation.

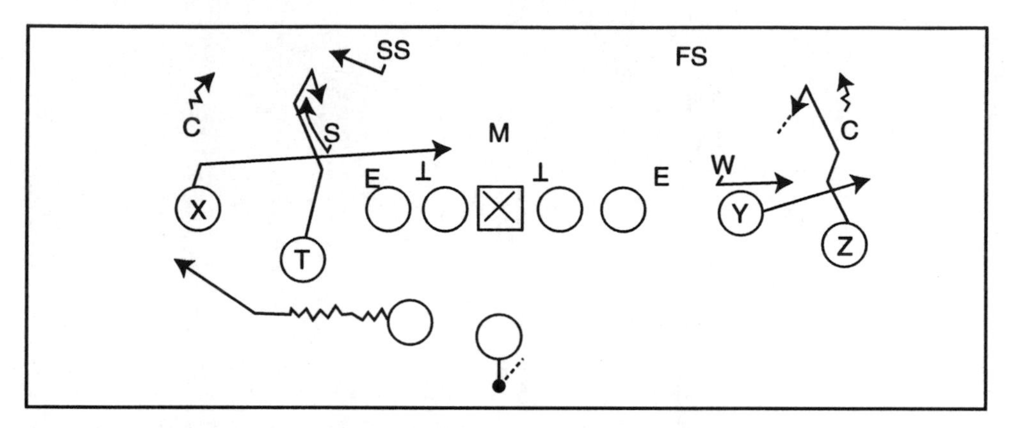

Figure 22.4—A 562 X cross from a Rifle empty formation.

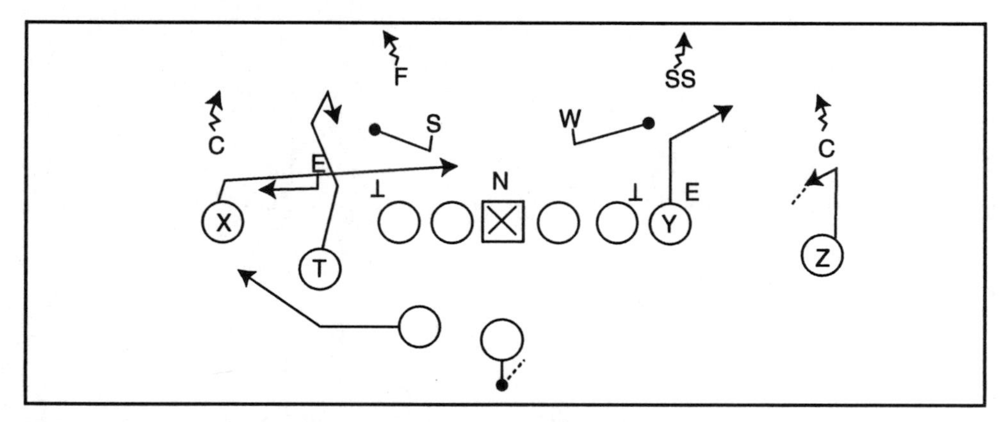

Figure 22.5—A 561 X cross from the Pistol formation.

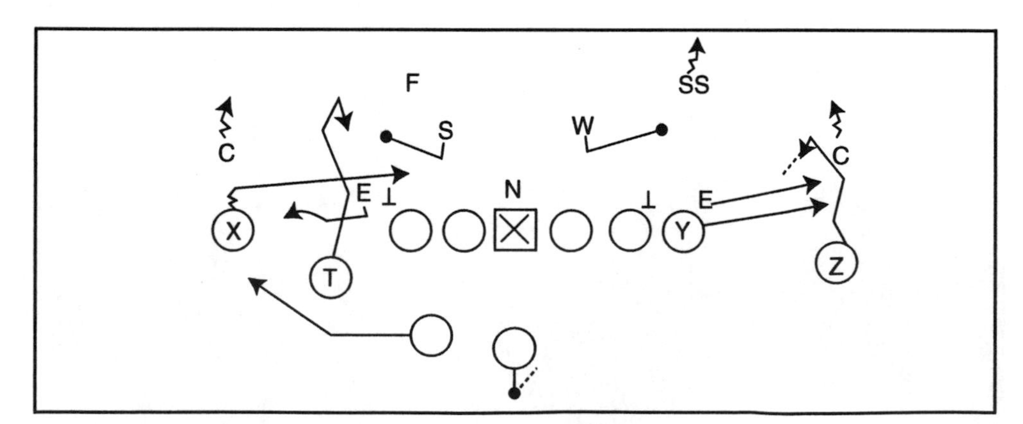

Figure 22.6—A 562 X cross from the Pistol formation.

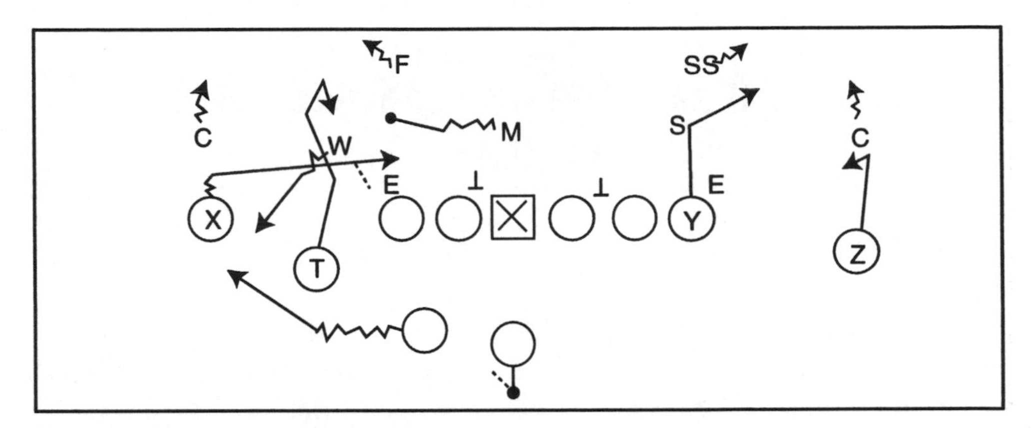

Figure 22.7—A 561 X cross from the Pistol empty formation.

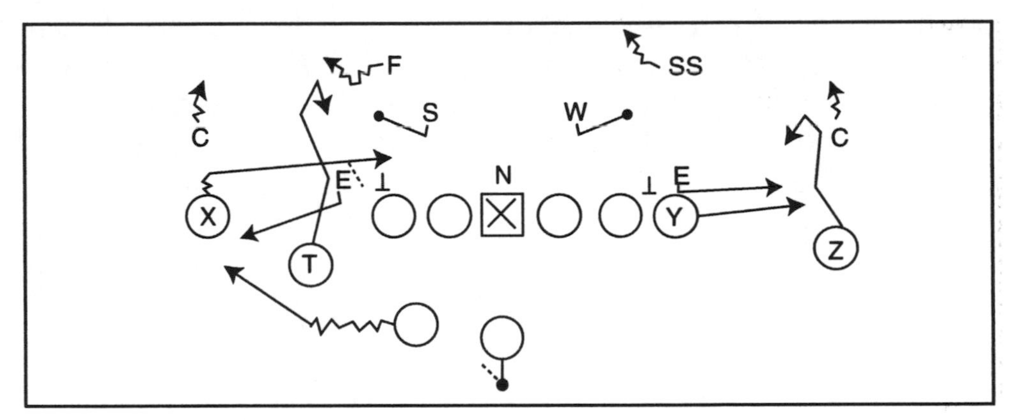

Figure 22.8—A 562 X cross from the Pistol empty formation.

CHAPTER 23

The Shallow Cross Series: T Cross

The T cross is run like the Y cross, with the inside receiver doing the crossing route, and the outside receiver doing the choice route. It is run from the same formations as X cross, since T is also on the boundary side of the formation.

The T cross can be run with the 561 or 562 modification on the backside of the route. I recommend using 562 because the Y receiver will pull the outside backer out with him on the stick route. With the cross being run toward the wide side of the field, a large opening is created for T. Figures 23.1—23.8 illustrate a T cross from the Rifle and Rifle empty formations with the 561 and 562 modifications and from the Pistol and Pistol empty formations with the same modifications.

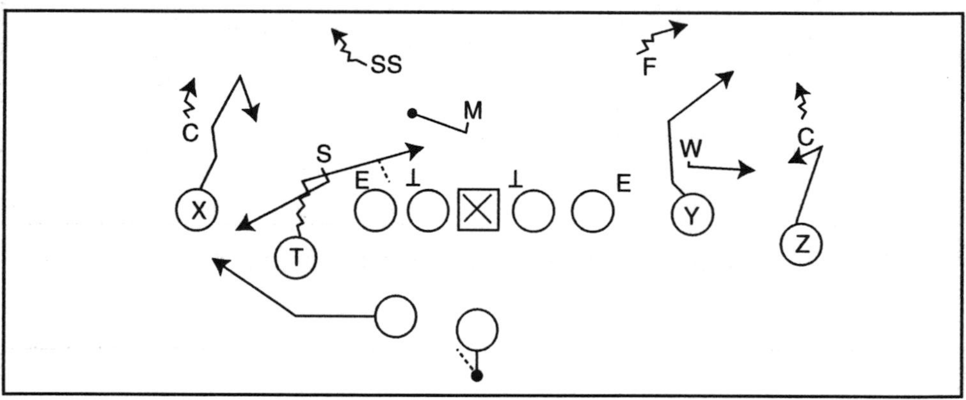

Figure 23.1—A 561 T cross from a Rifle formation.

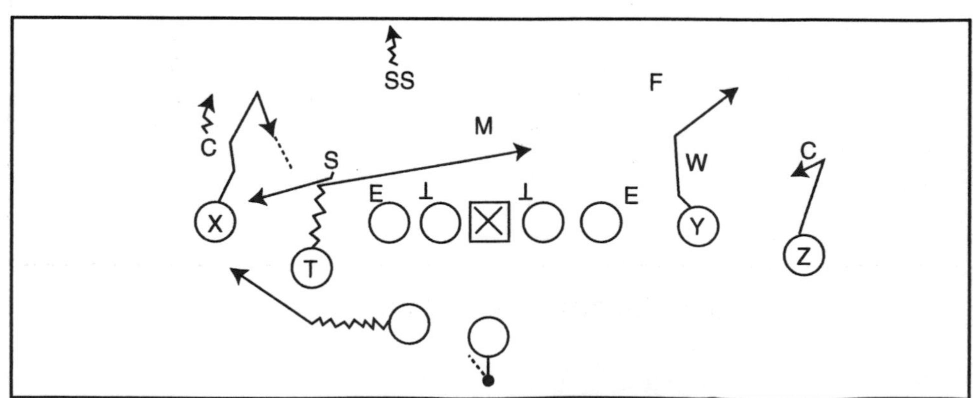

Figure 23.2—A 561 T cross from the Rifle empty formation.

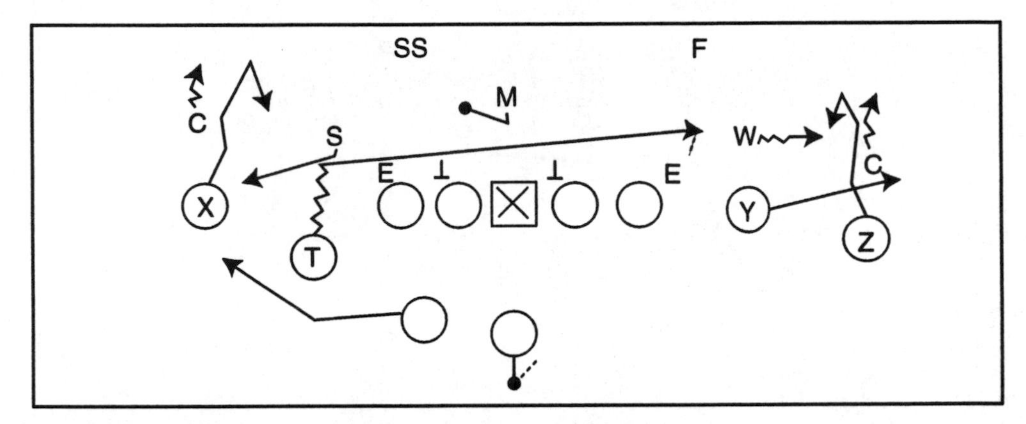

Figure 23.3—A 562 T cross from the Rifle formation.

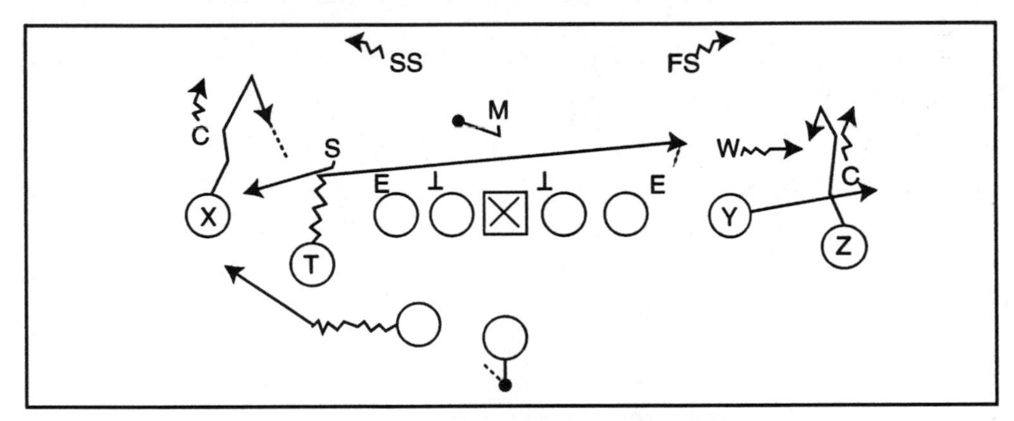

Figure 23.4—A 562 T cross from the Rifle empty formation.

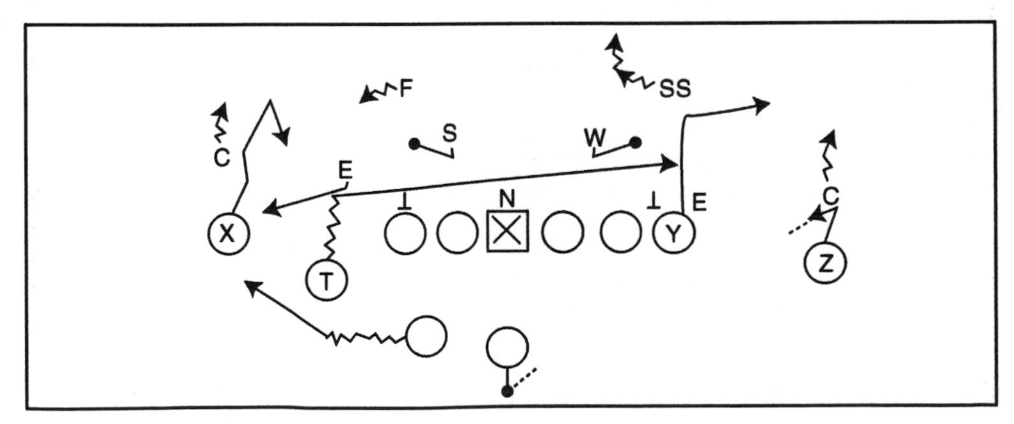

Figure 23.5—A 561 T cross from a Pistol formation.

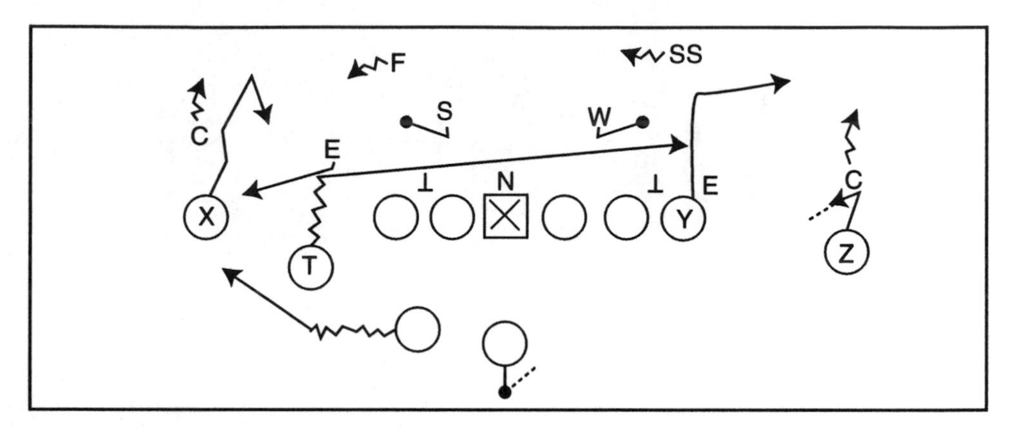

Figure 23.6—A 561 T cross from the Pistol empty formation.

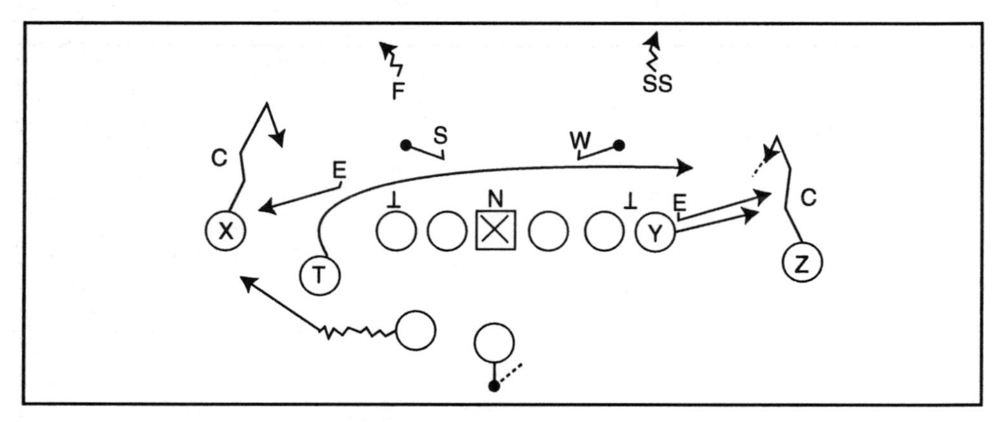

Figure 23.7—A 562 T cross from the Pistol formation.

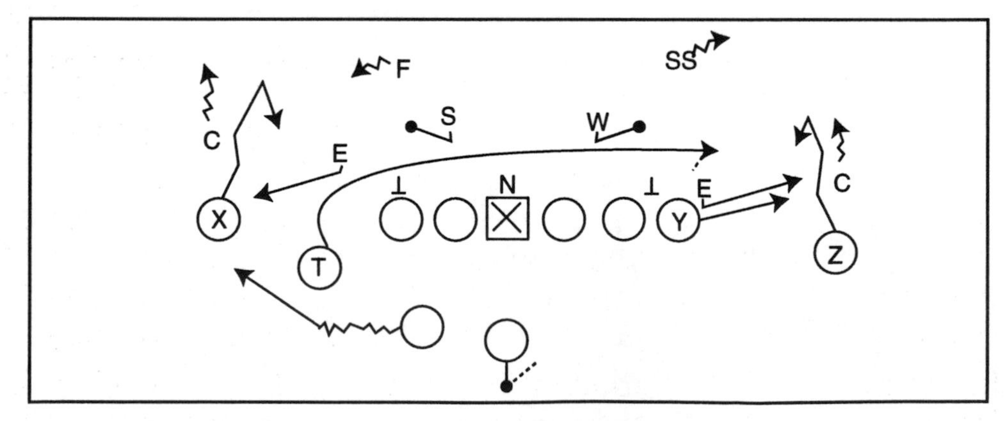

Figure 23.8—A 562 T cross from the Pistol empty formation.

COACHING POINT: On 562 T cross, you should spread Y and Z out an extra couple of yards in order to help clear out for T on the crossing route.

CHAPTER 24

The Shallow Cross Series: Red Zone Adjustments

A few adjustments can be made in the shallow cross series to make it even more effective within the red zone. The first two adjustments deal with the X and Z cross. FSU has been using these adjustments for quite a while. Personally, I'll never forget seeing an adjustment made at an Auburn practice under then coach Terry Bowden. The Auburn offense, nearly identical to the FSU offense, was going against the first team defense. The offense had used several crossing routes during the scrimmage. I heard the defensive coordinator begin yelling to the safety to "sit on that curl", referring to the choice route by Y.

As a result, the safety sat on the curl, but Y wasn't running a curl. Instead, Y gave an inside head-and-shoulder fake and then broke to the corner. Of course, he was wide open for a big play. FSU uses a 563 Z cross to take advantage of just such a play by the defensive secondary. It can also be run with X, on a 563 X cross. These two plays can be run from a Rifle or a Rifle empty formation, while the X cross can also be run from a Pistol (Refer to Figures 24.1—24.5).

Although the quarterback still reads the cross first on both the 563 Z cross and the X cross, the second read now becomes the flag route being run by the inside receiver. This play can also be very effective if the playside cornerback is jumping the swing route when he sees the outside receiver running a crossing route. This play really can be a back breaker for a defense.

Additional adjustments can be made by crossing the two inside receivers. While most people have credited teams like Kentucky and BYU for this route, FSU began using 560 Expo in the 1993 season. While, Kentucky currently runs the play far more often than the Seminoles do, FSU continues to employ it effectively.

The "Expo" route can be run from the Rifle, Pistol, Panther, and even Base formations. With Base and Panther, the running back should run a crossing route from the backfield. The Expo route is effective from all of these formations.

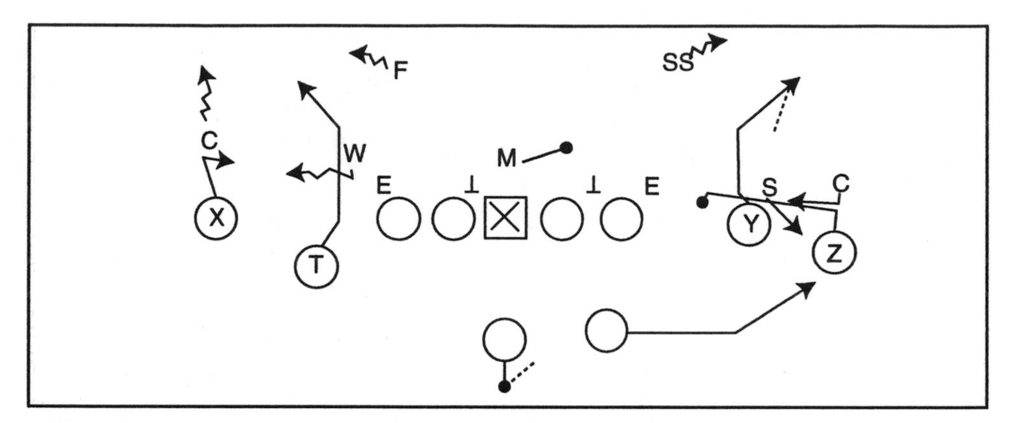

Figure 24.1—A 563 Z cross from the Rifle formation.

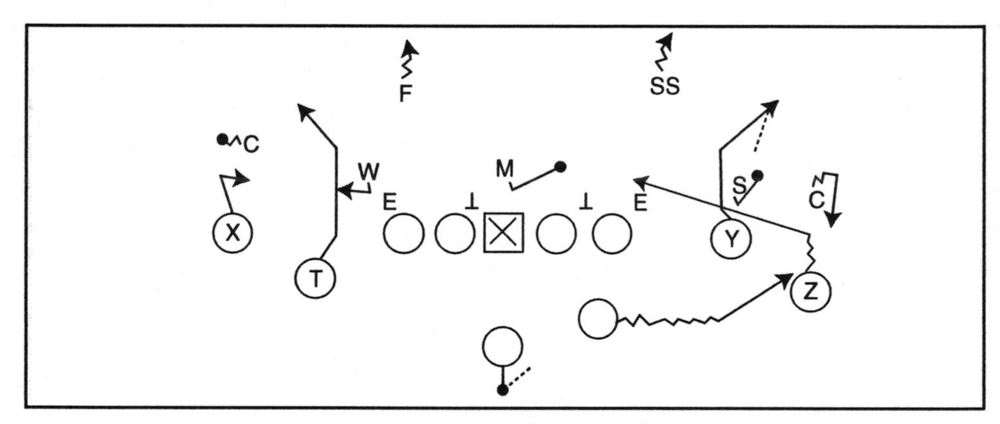

Figure 24.2—A 563 Z cross from the Rifle empty formation.

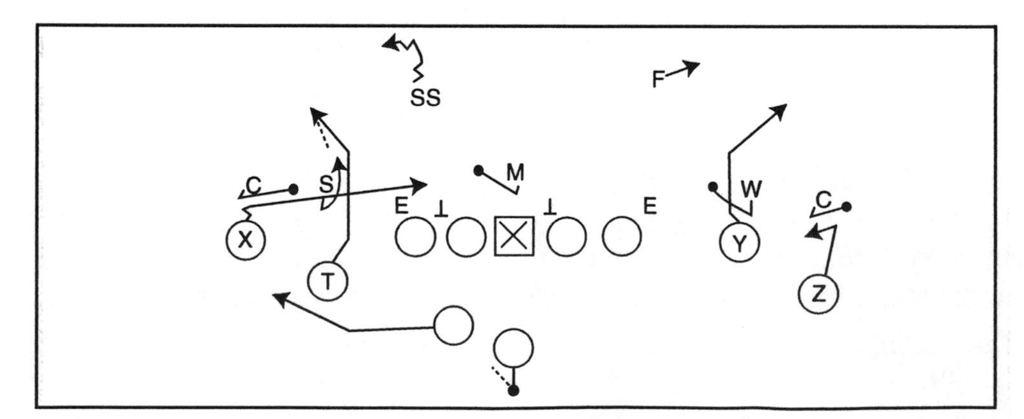

Figure 24.3—A 563 X cross from the Rifle formation.

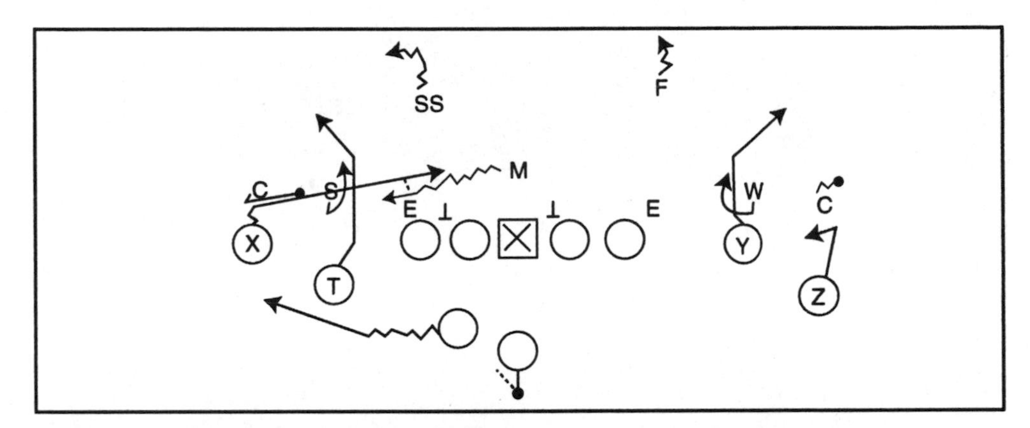

Figure 24.4—A 563 X cross from the Rifle empty formation.

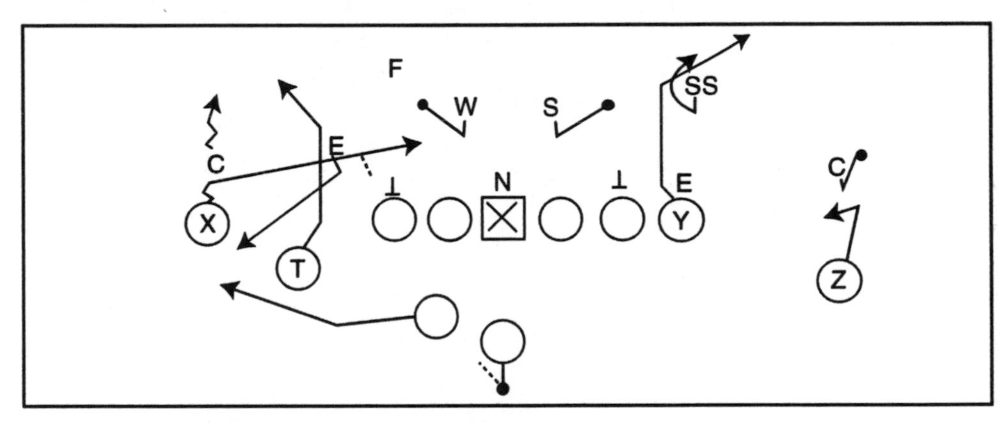

Figure 24.5—A 563 X cross from the Pistol formation.

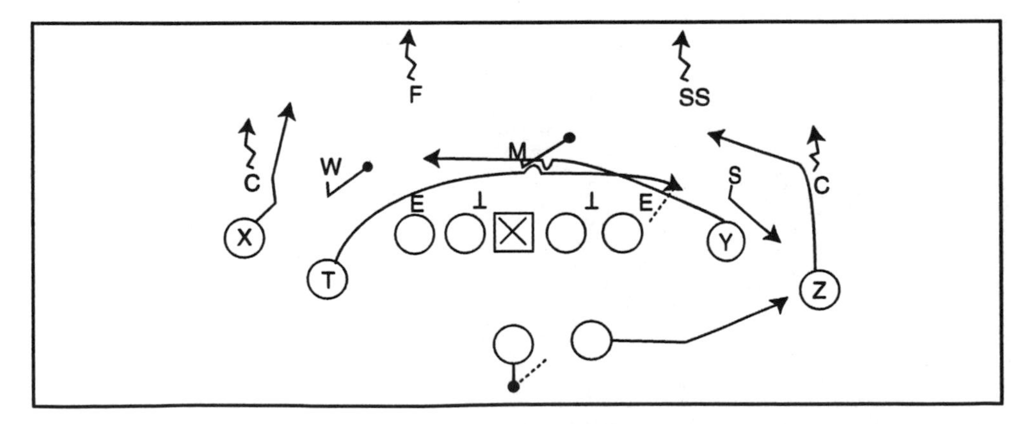

Figure 24.6—A 560 Expo from the Rifle formation. Note: T and Y intentionally rub shoulder pads as they cross in order to screen off any defender who might be chasing them.

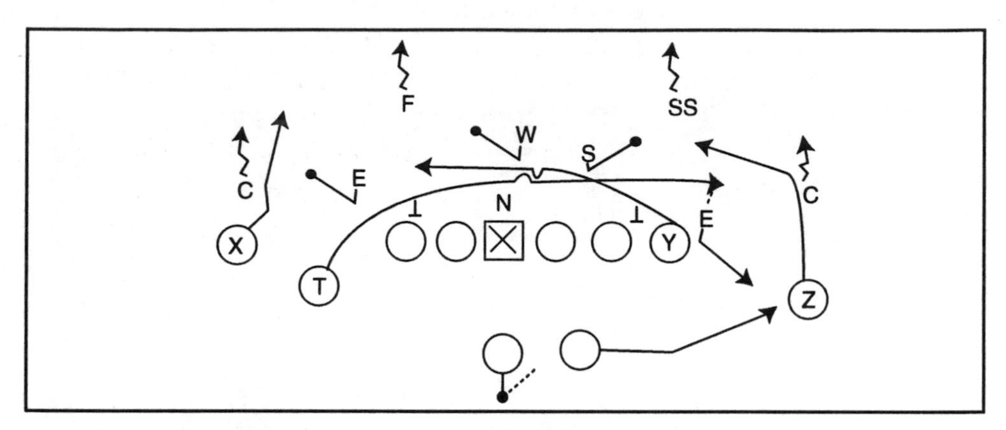

Figure 24.7—A 560 Expo from the Pistol formation.

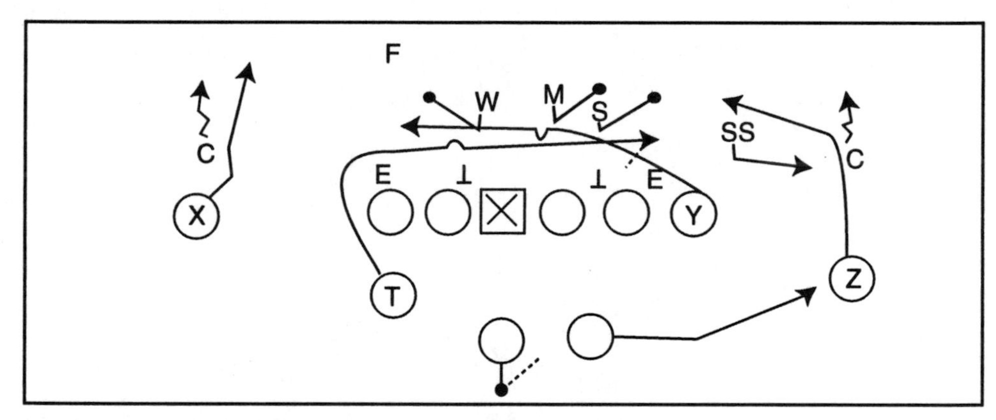

Figure 24.8—A 460 Expo from the Panther formation.

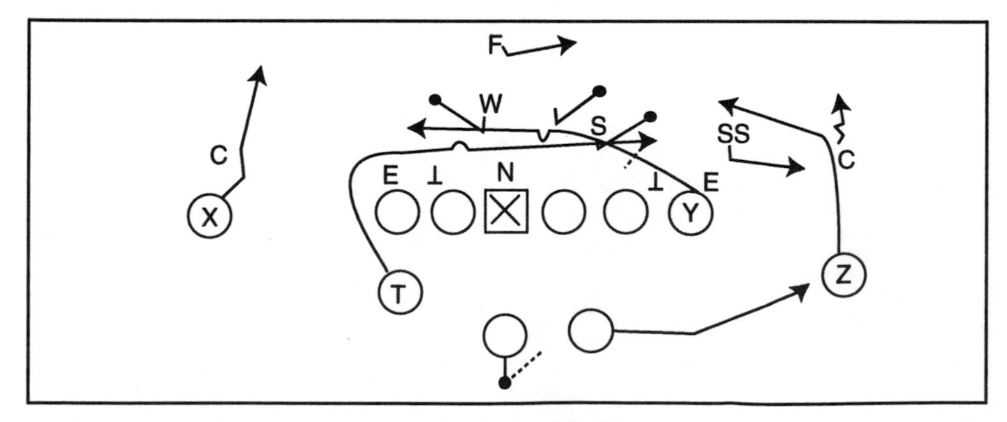

Figure 24.9—A 460 Expo from the Base formation.

On the Expo route, X runs a 7-step post route. Z runs a 15-yard dip route, and Y runs a shallow cross. If the formation is Rifle or Pistol, the T receiver runs a shallow cross, coming under the crossing Y receiver and rubbing shoulder pads as they cross each other's path. The T receiver then continues to work across the field, working into an opening against a zone and making eye contact with the quarterback when he is ready for the football. If the play is run from the Panther or the Base formation, the tailback circles out of the backfield, and then runs a crossing route under Y, using the same procedure as T. Figures 24.6—24.9 illustrate the 560/460 Expo route.

On the Expo route, the curl/flat defender will be pulled out by the swing route. The quarterback should look from the cross coming from the backside, to the dip, to the swing route. Kentucky has proven that this play can be one of the top routes in an offense. The Seminoles had good success with this route against Notre Dame in the 1993 game. This play is yet another indication of the flexibility of the FSU offense.

CHAPTER 25

Shotgun Passing Attack: Rollout Passes

Moving the pocket is important no matter what offense you are running. If the quarterback is always setting up in the same spot, the defense can pin their ears back and tee off on him. Florida State has always been one of, if not the best, rollout teams in the country. FSU's quarterbacks are sound at throwing on the move, and FSU's offensive scheme is solid. Even before the "Fast Break" was developed, FSU was moving the pocket and rolling out their quarterbacks. However, the shotgun has attracted more attention to the 'Noles and to their rollout-passing game.

The most commonly used play within the FSU rollout package is "Smoke". Any coach who has ever attended an FSU or other Bobby Bowden coaching clinic is familiar with this play. Every year, it is one of the most featured plays of the clinic session—vivid testimony to the continued effectiveness of the play.

Smoke is a straight rollout used to the wide side of the field. It is most commonly employed from the shotgun formation. While Z is the primary receiver on the play, the quarterback always reads from high to low. In other words, he reads the corner to see if the corner sinks far enough to cover the deep flag run by Y. If he does, the quarterback checks back down to Z for an easy completion.

The route Z runs is called a slide route. On the slide route, Z takes an outside release path from the top of the numbers (aligned slightly wider than usual) and runs a 10-12 yard route. Z's landmark should be the bottom of the numbers. In other words, he runs the route very similar to the first part of a takeoff. When he reaches his landmark, he plants his outside foot and pivots back down the stem. This route is effective against both press and zone coverage.

As was previously discussed, Y is on a deep flag route behind Z. The spacing between Y and Z is greater because Z has cheated slightly wider in the formation. This spacing makes it very difficult for the flat defender to get underneath the slide route. As a result, the quarterback can read the corner on the run and can have plenty of room to get the ball to Z after reading the corner. The X receiver runs a square in from the backside. The only other route that would be used in Smoke is a drag route by T if the formation is either Rifle or Pistol.

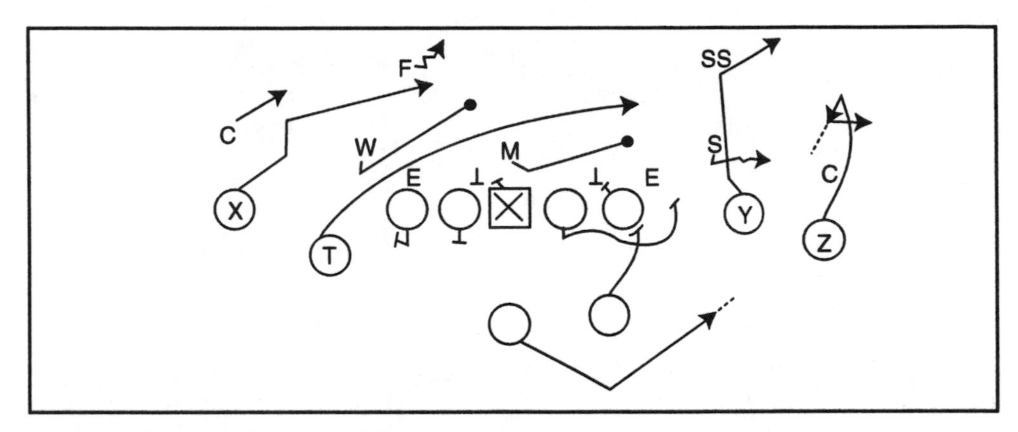

Figure 25.1—Smoke from a Rifle formation.

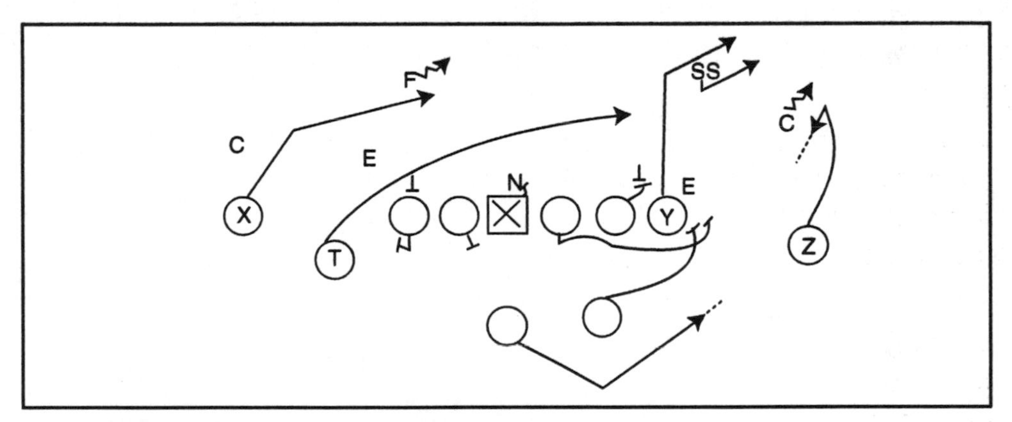

Figure 25.2—Smoke from a Pistol formation.

Smoke can be run from most types of formations. Before the ball can be thrown effectively, however, the offensive line must pass protect. The most important block of the entire play comes from the fullback who cuts the defensive end. However, in Alabama high school football that is not legal. As a result, we coach the fullback to attack a landmark of the outside front of the mid-section of the contain defender. As long as contact is made above the waist initially, the fullback can slide down on the contain player and, hopefully, get him to the ground. However, he cannot lose contact with him at anytime.

On Smoke, the strongside tackle blocks down, and the strongside guard pulls out and looks for a scraping linebacker. The remainder of the offensive line hip protects (i.e., protects off of their inside hip), while the tailback gates the backside pursuit.

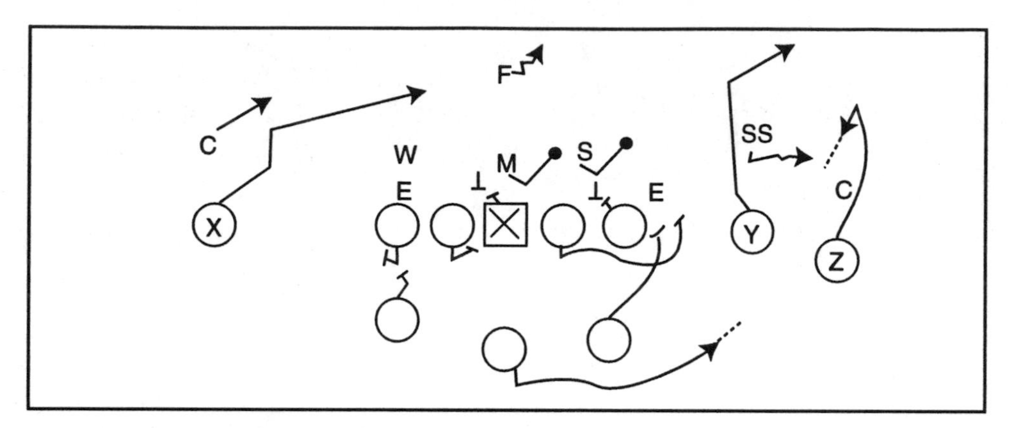

Figure 25.3—Smoke from a Panther formation.

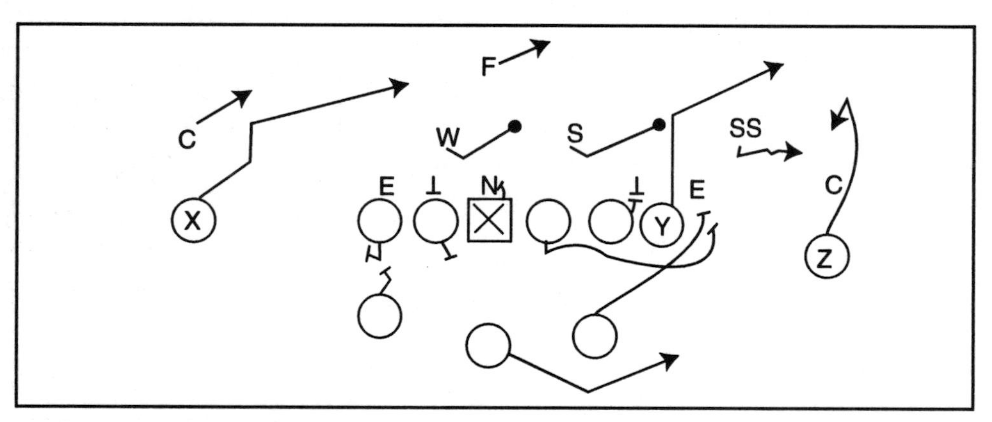

Figure 25.4—Smoke from a Base formation.

The quarterback catches the snap five yards deep and gains depth as he rolls out to seven yards. Once he reaches seven yards, he attacks downhill, directly at the number one receiver. His shoulders must be squared up with the receiver to deliver the football. Figures 25.1—25.4 illustrate Smoke from a variety of formations.

Smoke can also be run from the Near formation. On the Near formation, T must change his route to a seam in order to hold the safety in the middle of the field. That action eliminates the drag route T used from the backside (Refer to Figure 25.5).

Smoke is a great play in the no huddle offense when you want to speed up the tempo, or when you want to catch the defense before they get lined up. The no huddle is discussed in greater detail in Chapter 29.

Smoke can be run with a few tricks. One example is the play—Smoke A hide. This play is Smoke with a little twist to it. In Smoke A hide, the tailback (in a panther formation) makes a poorly executed block when he gates the backside contain player. If you run Smoke often enough, the contain player will usually be charging hard at the quarterback.

After his futile blocking efforts, the tailback simply sneaks outside and shows his numbers to the quarterback so that the quarterback can deliver the ball to him.

On the Smoke A hide play, the quarterback rolls outside the tackle, stops, and delivers the ball back across the field to the tailback. Either you can have the quickside tackle and quickside guard scoop down two gaps, and then pull outside to lead on the support players, or you can just leave the tailback out there and let him run after the catch. During our 1994 season, we didn't pull the quickside blockers out, but still had six touchdown passes off of the play. FSU used to run the play a lot, but I haven't seen them run it since the National Championship game against Nebraska in 1994. Auburn used it, under Terry Bowden, for a 30+ yard gain against Florida in the 1997 season. The play is illustrated in Figure 25.6.

Another trick play off of Smoke is also a hide—Smoke Y hide. Base is the formation employed with Y hide. Auburn scored a touchdown with Y hide against Florida in 1996, while FSU used it against LSU in a crucial victory during the 1991 season.

On Smoke Y hide everything is done the same as Smoke from the protection to the routes, with the exception of Y. Y collapses as he steps down to block on the play. He then crawls to an area on the opposite side of the field. Usually Y is all alone. In turn, the quarterback rolls out, sets up, and then throws back across the field to a wide-open Y (Refer to Figure 25.7).

Another trick play off of Smoke is the play (Smoke Twist) that burns those free safeties who go flying over the top of the flag route, when they key the second inside receiver. This play can just about make the free safety "twist" himself into the ground. The Smoke Twist can be run from either the Panther or the Rifle formation.

To set up Smoke Twist, Smoke should be run a couple of times. Eventually, the free safety will begin to cheat over the flag when he sees the quarterback begin to roll out. You should then come back and run the Smoke Twist, sending Y on a post corner-post route for a big play. FSU has used this play so many times over the last few years, especially in the three Sugar Bowls they have appeared in during the last five years.

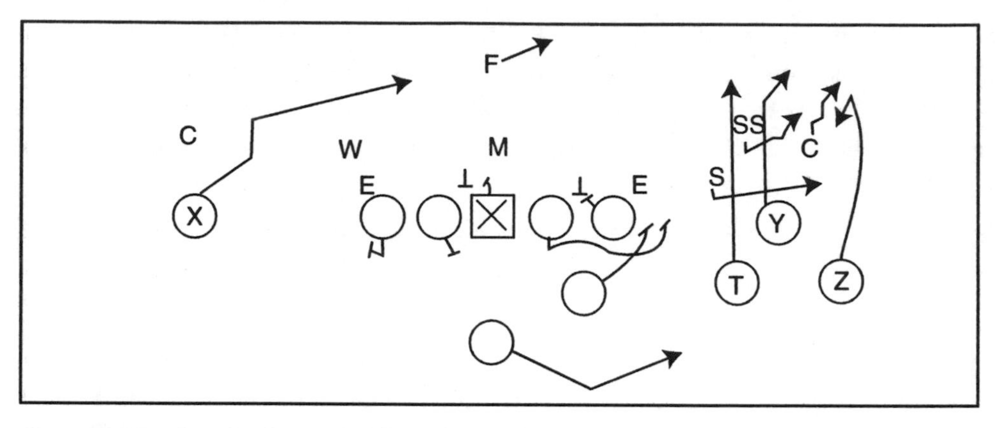

Figure 25.5—Smoke from the Near formation.

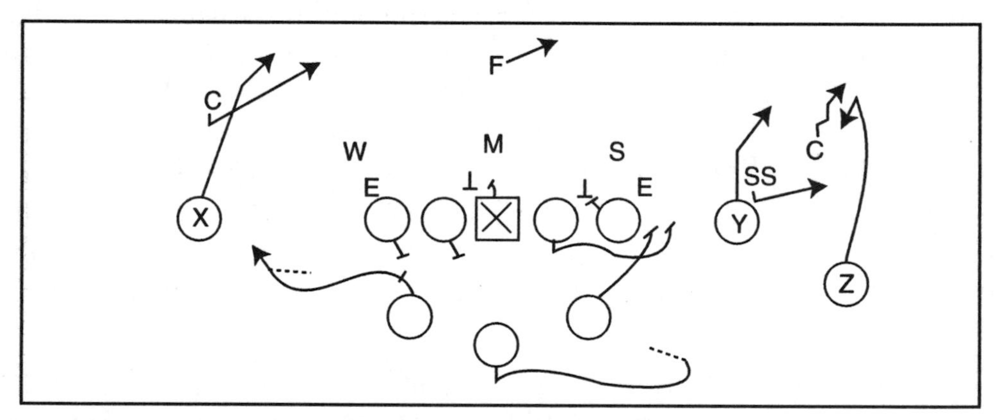

Figure 25.6—Smoke A hide from a Panther formation.

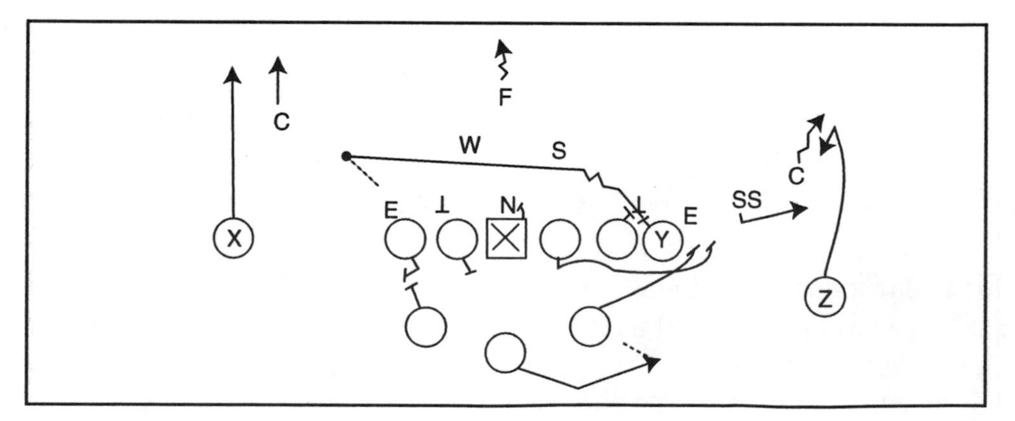

Figure 25.7—Smoke Y hide.

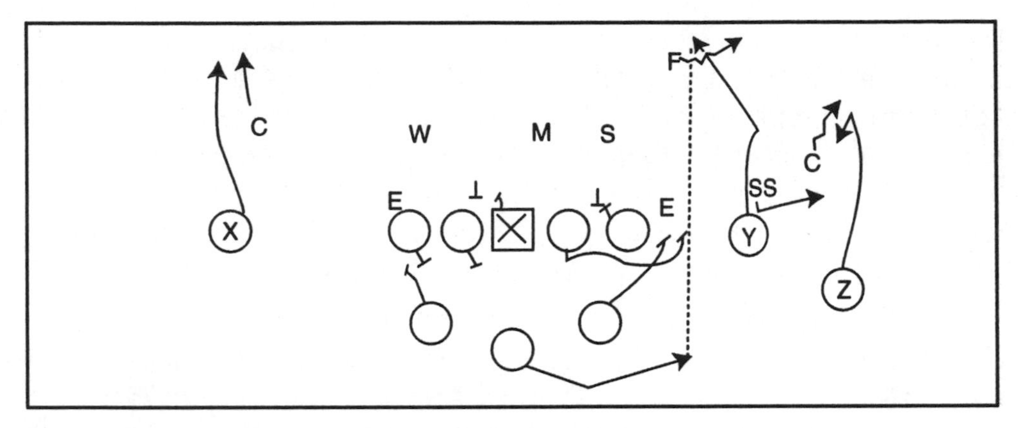

Figure 25.8—Smoke Twist from a Panther formation.

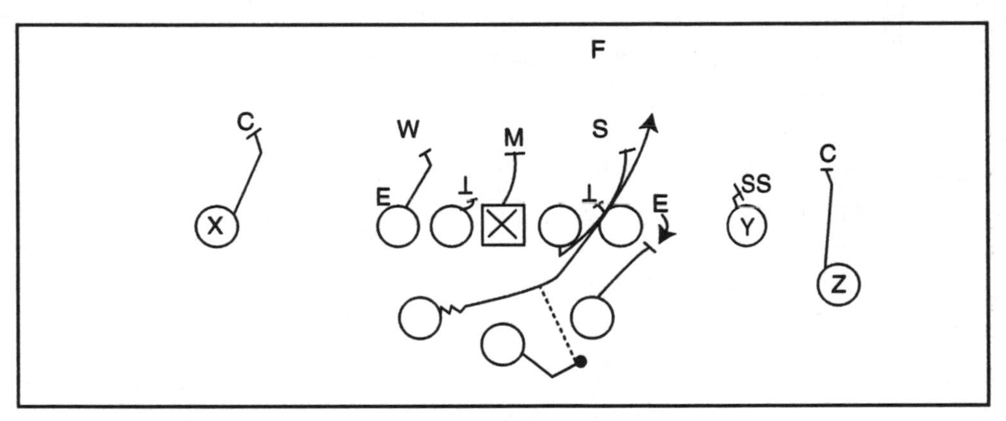

Figure 25.9—A Shuffle pass from the Panther formation.

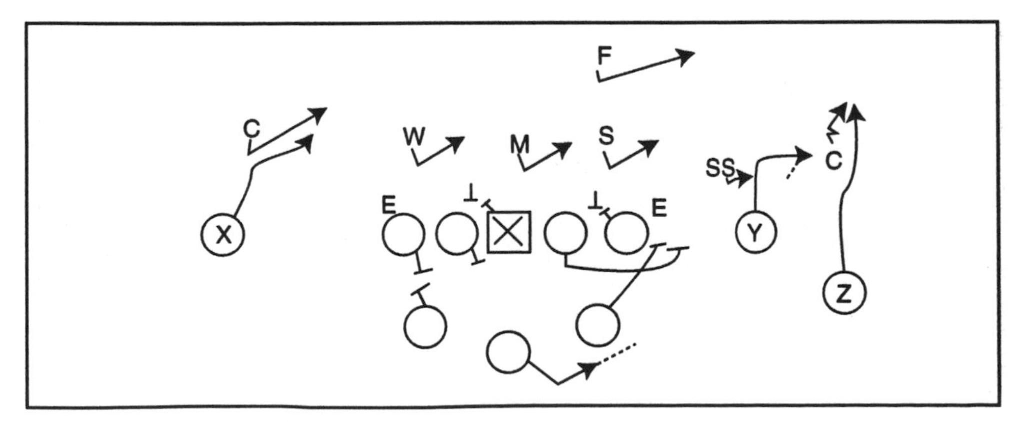

Figure 25.10—Lightening from a Panther gun formation.

Smoke Twist is relatively easy to adapt to the high school level. Perhaps the most important thing to do is to make sure that the quarterback plants his feet and steps into the throw so that there is not a wounded duck flying around for anyone to grab. I recommend sending X straight down the field to hold the backside corner away from the play. If you run the play from the Rifle formation, you should have T do the same as X, because you will probably be dealing with twin safeties. That opposite safety must be held on the hash.

On Smoke Twist, the quarterback should roll out, set his feet, and quickly look the safety off to sell that Y is running a corner route. The quarterback should then turn the ball loose, leading Y away from the safety (Refer to Figure 25.8).

Another trick play off of Smoke is the shuffle pass. The shuffle pass play tends to be open after the fullback has been sealing off the defensive end time after time. As a result, the end will begin to widen to make the fullback's block more difficult. On 96—the shotgun shuffle pass, the fullback then kicks that defensive end out. The strongside tackle blocks down, much the same as on Smoke. The strongside guard pulls. But instead of looking for a scraping backer, he wraps the playside linebacker. The backside of the offensive line will scoop. The quarterback catches the snap and takes the first three steps of the rollout, and then plants on his outside foot and steps directly toward the tailback who is coming underneath him for the shuffle pass. When the tailback receives the shuffle pass, he hits the hole at full speed for a possible big play (Refer to Figure 25.9).

One final rollout pass is the Lightening play. The Lightening play is blocked exactly like Smoke. Only two routes change on the play. In this instance, Z runs a vertical, giving a stutter step at about 10 yards to get the corner to squat. The Y receiver runs a bench route from the inside receiver spot. These changes provide a second option of routes from the basic rollout package (Refer to Figure 25.10).

CHAPTER 26

Shotgun Passing Attack: Gun Play-Action Passes

For the shotgun to operate at its most effective level, you must have a solid running game from it. I do not mean a token draw here or there. You need a sound running package such as the one discussed previously. Running from the shotgun can help you have a balanced attack and can enable you to take advantage of the various defensive alignments that are usually employed against the shotgun. Just look at the FSU and Tulane offenses over the last few years with their shotgun-run attack. The question arises concerning what running has to do with play-action passing from the shotgun? The answer is straightforward—they work hand in hand to enhance one another.

If you make the commitment to run and use play-action passes from the shotgun, your offense can be very explosive. To use play action from the shotgun, you simply need to apply the play-action passes that have already been installed for the I formation. If you employ one of the boots to each side of the formation and then use a couple of the sprint-draw actions, you can have a fantastic shotgun, play-action attack.

344 Bench

The first shotgun play action that is examined is the 344 Bench play from the Panther Gun formation. On the 344 Bench, the blocking assignments stay the same for everyone. The fullback attacks the defensive end, while the offensive line employs the same 344 pass-blocking scheme that was discussed in the chapter on the I formation play-action passing package. The routes stay the same as well, with bench routes by X and Z and a choice route by Y.

The biggest difference in the 344 Bench play is the quarterback is now five yards deep in the shotgun. On the play, the tailback takes a lateral shuffle step. The tailback then takes a fake from the quarterback and fakes 44, and then spots up at six-yards deep over the tightside guard. The quarterback makes the fake with the ball and then drops one step and drills the Bench route if it is open. If the Bench route is not open, the quarterback continues his drop for steps 2 and 3 and then sets up and looks to hit the choice route (Refer to Figure 26.1).

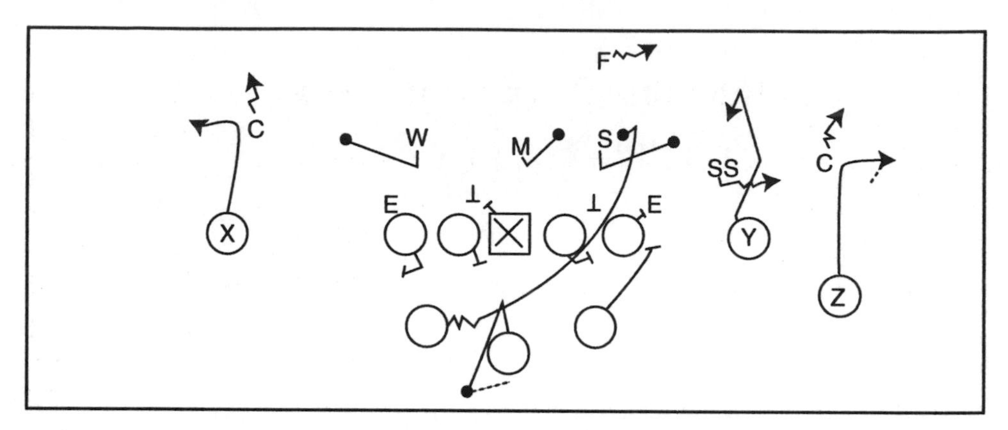

Figure 26.1—344 Bench from a Panther Gun formation.

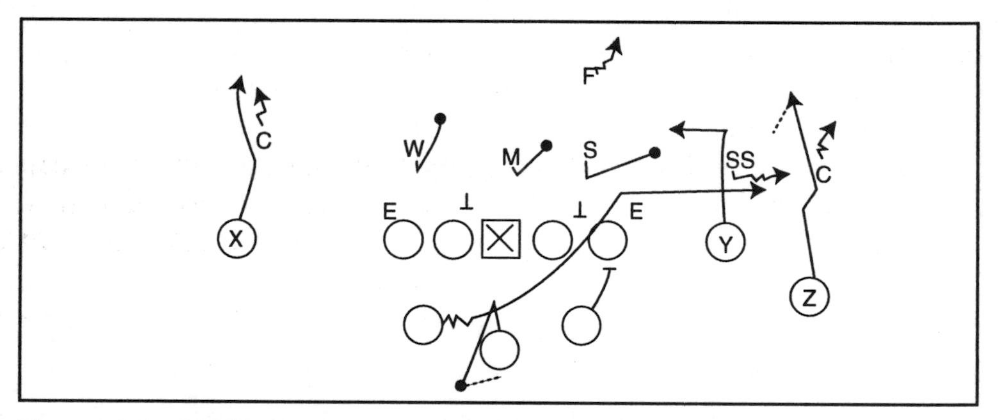

Figure 26.2—344 Dip Z post from a Panther Gun formation.

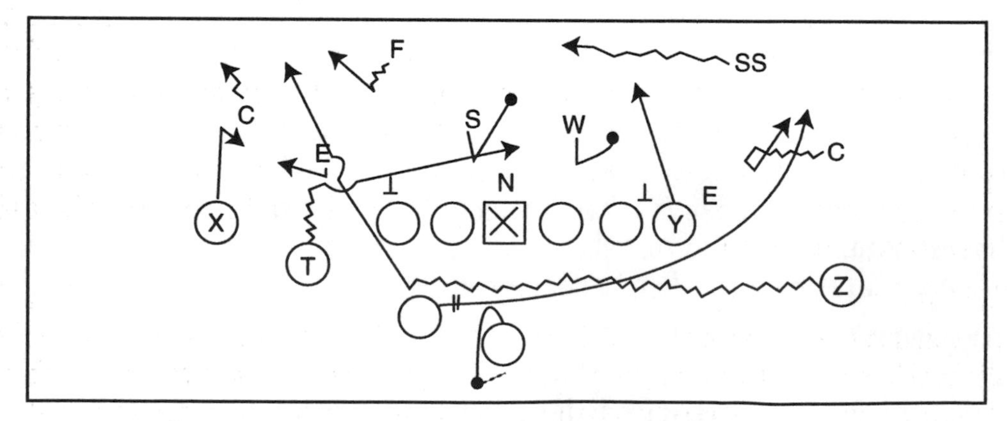

Figure 26-3. A Pop pass from the Pistol Zoom formation.

344 Dip Z Post

Another play action that can be installed from the shotgun is the 344 Dip Z post. This play is run just like the 344 Dip from the I formation, with the exception of Z who runs a post. The shotgun 344 action is exactly the same as it was on 344 Bench from the gun. The blocking scheme is also the same. The quarterback looks for the free safety to either backpedal or squat on the play. Most defensive coordinators have the free safety key the second inside receiver against a 3-wide receiver look. This play takes advantage of that key. The Y receiver runs a 10-yard dip route. If the safety jumps this route, the quarterback goes over the top of him to Z on the post. On the other hand, if the safety continues to drop, the quarterback hits Y with the ball in the first window he comes through in the zone coverage. FSU has used this play many times over the years for big plays. Because the play involves only one simple read, it is an easy play to adapt to the high school level (Refer to Figure 26.2).

Pop Pass

An effective shotgun goal line pass is a variation of the old "Pop" pass that so many high school teams run. This play is run from the Pistol formation, and Z is sent in motion across the formation to cause some confusion. This is one of those plays that you make sure that the other team has not seen on film before you use it. In all likelihood, they will blow the coverage if they haven't seen it because so little Z motion is used in the offense.

To run the Pop pass, you should line up in a Pistol formation and send Z in a Zoom (across the formation) motion. This action puts a trips-type look on the other side of the field. As a result, the secondary will begin making a trips rotation. Then, at the snap, the quarterback catches the ball and places it in the running back's belly, who is lined up on the quickside. The running back then sprints and fakes that he has the ball, just like the counter to the strongside. The quarterback then pulls the ball out, pivots to a quick set up, and looks to hit the tight end on a quick release straight up the field. If the corner jumps the tight end, the running back should carry out the fake around the end and then turn up the field and run straight down the rail.

The backside routes can be run in a variety of ways. In turn, a number of viable steps can be undertaken on the high school level. X can run a Smash route to five yards. Z, who comes in motion, can rub pads with the linebacker who is covering T and then proceed to run a corner route. As he comes directly across the field under the linebackers, T, who gets a rub on his man from Z, will come into the quarterback's vision as a #3 receiver on the play. Keep in mind that the quarter-

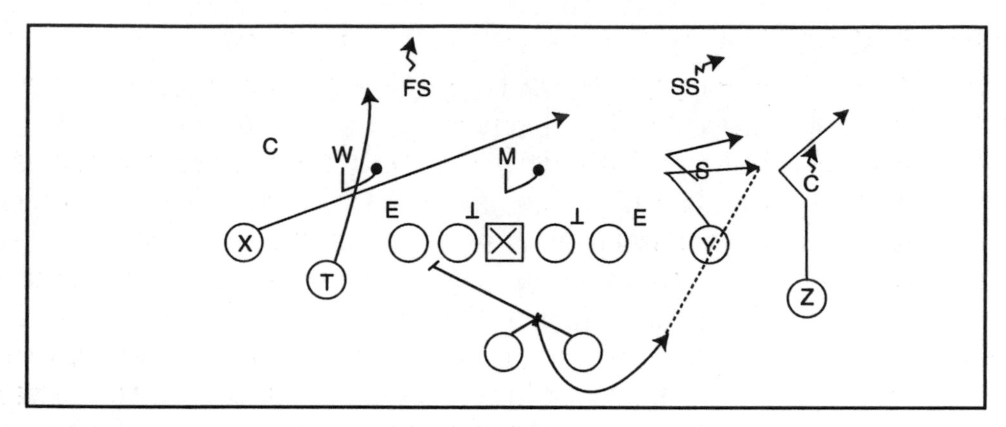

Figure 26.4—43 Dash from a Rifle formation.

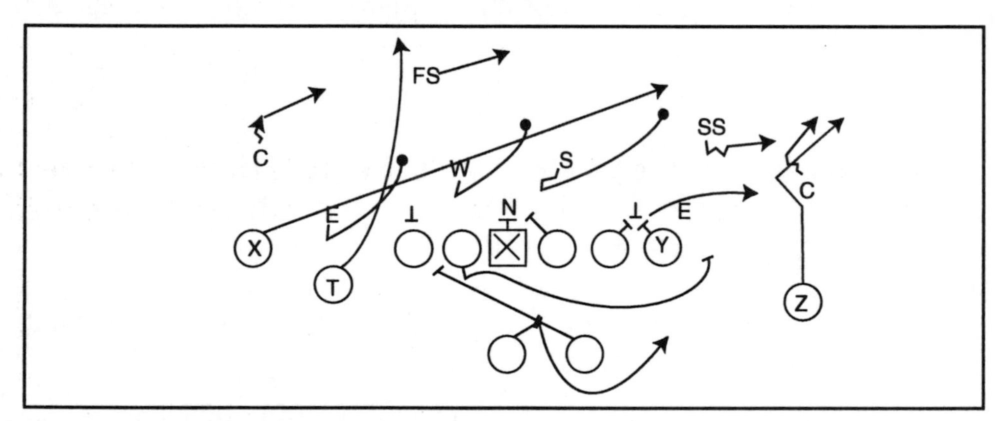

Figure 26.5—43 Dash from a Pistol formation.

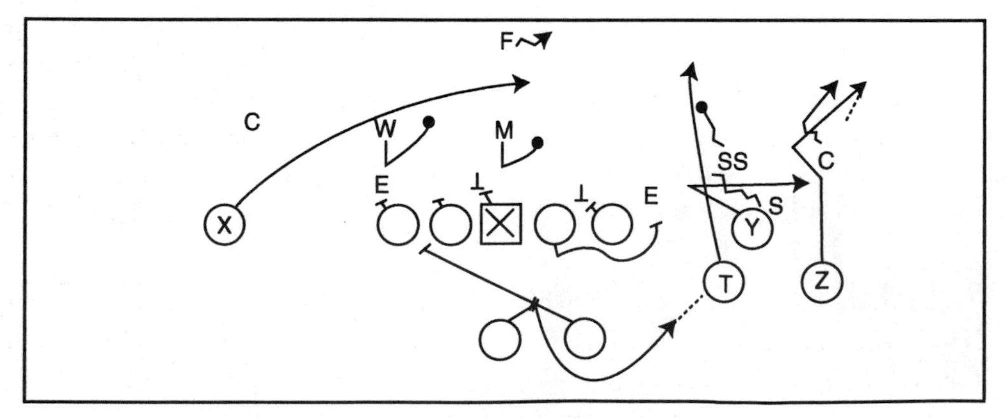

Figure 26.6—43 Dash from a Near formation.

back should read this play like a Pop pass to begin with and then proceed to the #2 and #3 receivers. FSU scored a touchdown on this play against UNC in its 1996 victory over the Tar Heels (Refer to Figure 26.3).

43 Dash can also be run from the a variety of other formations, including the shotgun. I like it best from the Rifle. In the shotgun, the blocking for the offensive line stays the same as in the I formation 43 Dash. This is one of the few plays that we ran from the shotgun before FSU used it. We added it to our offensive package prior to the 1993 season. FSU didn't use it until late in the '93 or early in the '94 season. In fact, this is the play that Danny Kannell scored on to bring the 'Noles to within 31-24 of Florida in the famous 31-31 game to wrap up the 1994 regular season. As such, this play conclusively demonstrates the threat of a running quarterback.

The pass blocking for the 43 dash from the shotgun was covered in Chapter 12 (refer to the information on the I formation on play-action passing and review the section for 43 Dash). The only change for offensive linemen from shotgun and I formation play actions is that the linemen use a two-point stance on all shotgun plays. With regard to routes, X still runs the 18-yard angle route. Y still runs the pigtail or arrow route, and Z runs a post corner. If the play is being run from a Rifle, Near, or Pistol, T should be sent straight at the free safety.

The quarterback makes the fake in the belly of the running back, who then runs toward the quickside B gap as if he is carrying the ball. The quarterback then gains ground to seven yards and attacks back downhill looking from Y to Z to X. He also has the option to run the ball (Refer to Figures 26.4—26.6).

The final play action that is examined from the shotgun is the bootleg off the strongside counter play. 48 boot, as it was called from the I formation, is run exactly the same from the shotgun. We prefer to employ this play from either Base shotgun or Panther shotgun. On this play action, X runs a takeoff route. Y runs a 10-yard drag across the field. Z has the post route from the backside of the play. Aligned in the shotgun, the fullback is positioned away from the side to which he needs to go. We cheat him into the guard-tackle gap and have him sprint to the lower flats on the opposite side as soon as the snap gets to the quarterback.

The quarterback catches the snap and fakes to the tailback, who carries out the fake of the shotgun counter and then blocks the backside contain player. The quarterback gains depth and breaks contain, following the block of the pulling guard. The read is the same as from the I formation—fullback first, Y second, and a run option third (Refer to Figures 26.7 and 26.8).

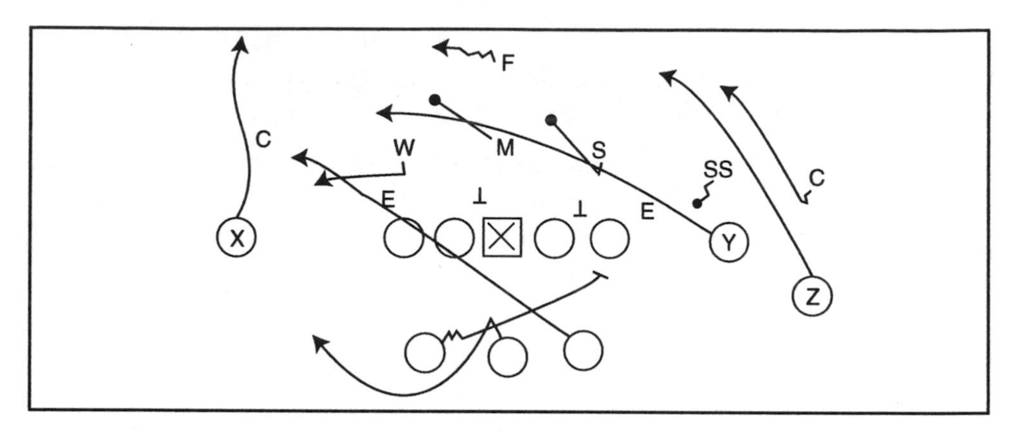

Figure 26.7—48 boot from the Panther Gun.

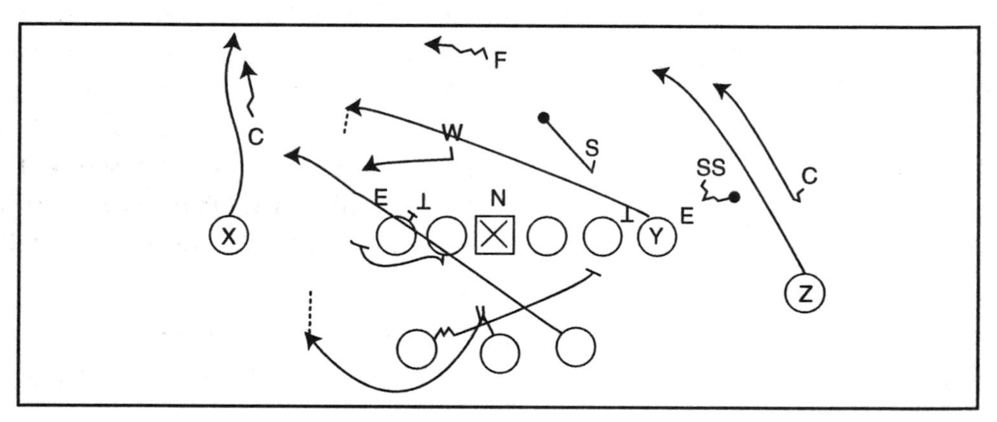

Figure 26.8—48 boot from the Base Gun.

COACHING POINT: A play-action pass is only as good as the effort that a player puts into the fake. Accordingly, an effective fake needs to be a focus of pride in practice to get the most out of play-action passes in the game. As such, you should stress the importance of making good fakes by both the running backs and the quarterbacks.

CHAPTER 27

Florida State Passing Attack: Screen Passes

Every offense needs screen passes, but none more than a pass-oriented offense. Not surprisingly, Florida State is also one of the best screen passing teams in the country. FSU's offense has at least three basic screen passes that can easily be adapted to high school football—each of which can enhance your passing attack. The first screen (344 Tulsa) is run off of the 344 play-action fake. While it can be thrown to the fullback or the tailback, we prefer throwing this screen to the tailback. The play is diagrammed in Figure 27.1. The positions and each position's assignments on this play are as follows:

PLAY:	**344 TULSA**
X & Z	Run a takeoff route.
Y	Release on a takeoff; block the safety when the ball is thrown.
ST	Block the man on or inside.
SG	Block the first man inside, pull lateral to quick- side to block support.
C	Block quickside A gap; pull to block support.
QG	Block quickside B gap; pull to block support.
QT	Block quickside C gap; invite him five yards up the field.
FB	Block the strongside defensive end.
TB	Make a bad 44 fake; set four yards behind LOS & hold for two counts; then sprint to a point four yards outside tackle and four yards behind LOS; catch the ball on the move.
QB	Make a bad 344 fake and a quick drop; pause one second on the balls of your feet; give ground delivering the ball firmly with a high release.

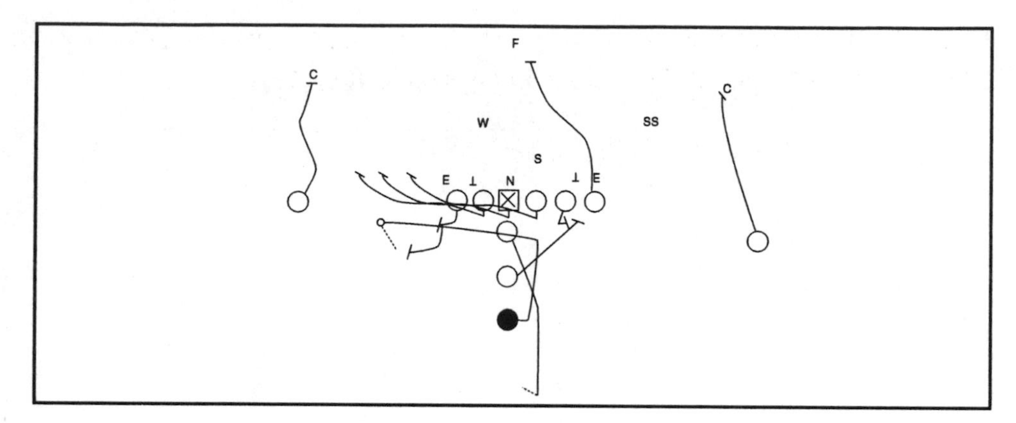

Figure 27.1—344 Tulsa from a Base formation.

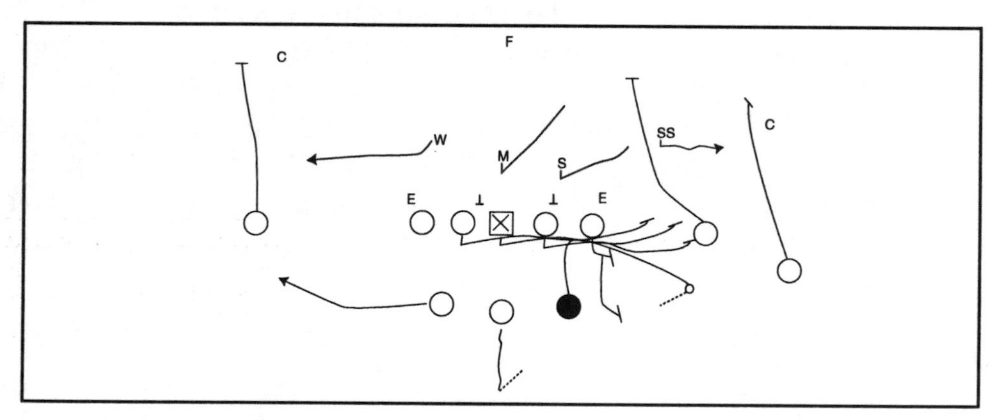

Figure 27.2—Fort Worth (fullback screen).

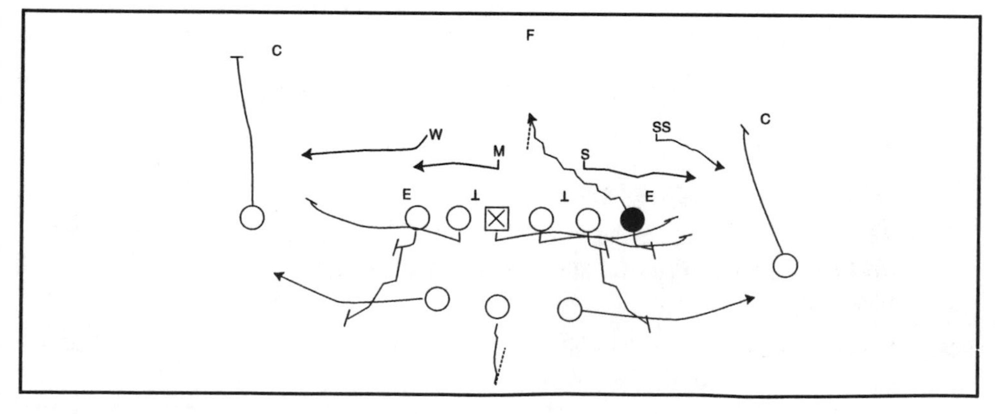

Figure 27-3. Gator screen.

The next screen is the shotgun screen to the fullback. The play is diagrammed in Figure 27.2. The assignments by position are as follows:

PLAY:	FORT WORTH (FULLBACK SCREEN)
X & Z	Run a takeoff route.
Y	Release on takeoff; block the safety.
ST	Set pass on man; sink five yards.
SG	Pass set, punch, and release to support.
C	Pass set, punch, and release to support.
QG	Pass set, punch, and release to support.
QT	Pass set; protect man on outside.
FB	Step up like checking the strongside linebacker, set at four yards behind LOS. Delay two counts and then sneak to point 4&4 behind LOS; catch the ball on the move.
TB	Check the weakside linebacker; run straight; release at three-yards deep if the linebacker drops.
QB	Shotgun; three-step drop; pause one second; give ground while zipping the ball with a high release to the fullback.

The final screen covered is the old Gator screen that was the biggest play for Auburn in their 1994 upset of #1 ranked Florida. Originally used at FSU, the play was even utilized in the National Championship game by the Seminoles against Nebraska. The play is designed to take advantage of linebackers who read screen passes well. The play is illustrated in Figure 27.3. By position, the assignments are as follows:

PLAY:	GATOR SCREEN
X & Z	Run a takeoff.
Y	Set up to pass block until the center crosses your face and then release straight up field.
ST	Pass set on man on or outside.
SG	Pass set on man; release to support.
C	Pass set on man; release to support on the strongside.
QG	Pass set on man; release to support on the quickside.
QT	Pass set on man.
FB	Swing route.
TB	Swing route.
QB	Shotgun; drop three steps; pump the ball to the fullback; keep dropping and hit the tight end on your fifth step.

**Make sure pulling linemen stay behind the LOS.

CHAPTER 28

Florida State Offense: Trick Plays

Florida State's offense cannot be discussed in depth without mentioning trick plays. To a point, Bobby Bowden and trick plays have almost become synonymous. Trick plays are normally employed early in a game, just in case they backfire. Keep in mind that they can backfire—even when one of the best teams in the country is using them. For example, in the 1990 game between Auburn and FSU, the fumble-rooskie backfired and led to a fumble that the Tigers recovered. Eventually, that turnover helped Auburn win a game in which they were outplayed in for 31/2 quarters.

However, trick plays can also ignite an offense and can help spark momentum—a factor that can be very crucial in football. A review of some of the trick plays that the Seminoles have unleashed over the years indicates why every coach needs a few of these plays in his team's offensive package. The point to keep in mind is that if you are going to adapt the FSU offense into your offensive scheme, then you've got to have some trick plays as well. The chapter reviews ten of FSU's most successful trick plays.

TRICK PLAY #1: 46 reverse. This is a play that FSU has used numerous times over the years. On this play, the quickside guard and the quickside tackle scoop down two gaps, and then pull out to lead for Z. The quarterback must make the key block on the contain player (Refer to Figure 28.1).

TRICK PLAY #2: 46 sucker. The play involves a fake reverse off the toss sweep (Refer to Figure 28.2).

TRICK PLAY #3: 43X reverse. On this play, you fake the weakside sprint draw and then give the ball to X who is coming from the shortside of the field. You have the option of pulling out the offensive line to lead the play. The Seminoles employed this play to open the game against BYU in 1991 (Refer to Figure 28.3).

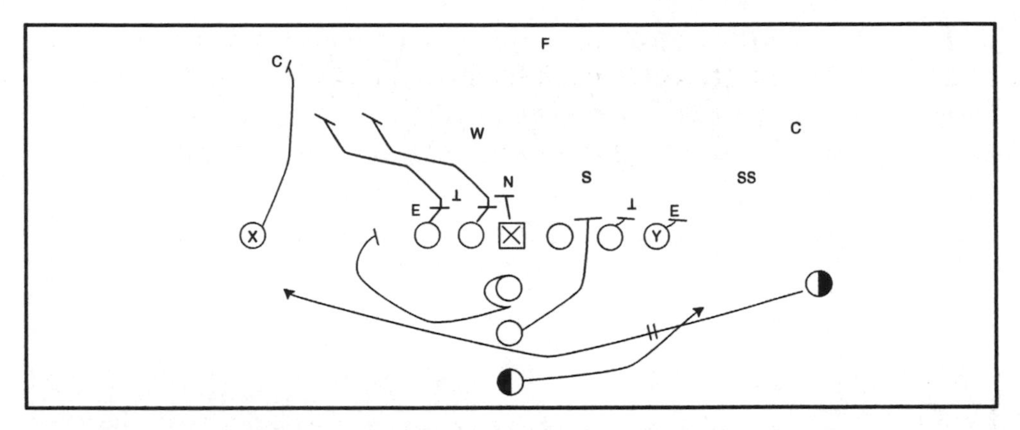

Figure 28.1—46 reverse.

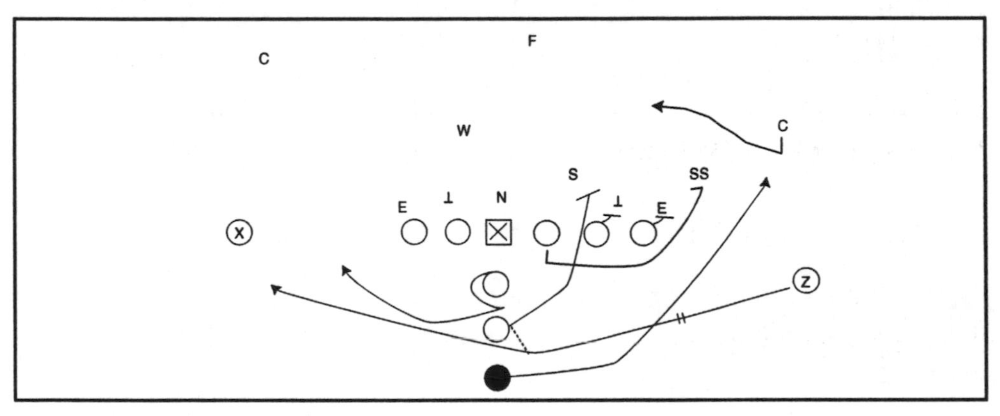

Figure 28.2—46 sucker.

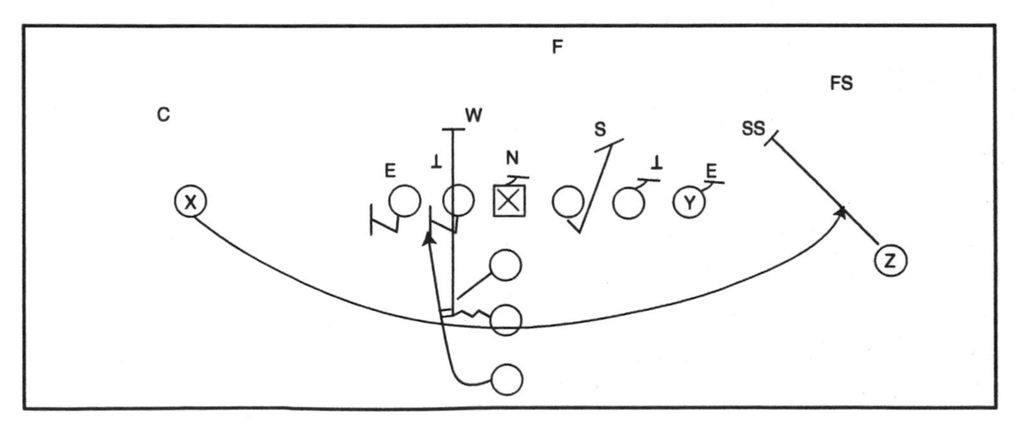

Figure 28.3—43 X reverse.

TRICK PLAY #4: 43 X reverse pass. On this play, you fake the 43 reverse and then hit Z on a deep post route. X continues to run to the sideline as a safety valve if Z is covered. The key is for the quarterback to sell the reverse by freezing and showing an empty palm. FSU's Danny Kanell was exceptionally skilled at this play (Refer to Figure 28.4).

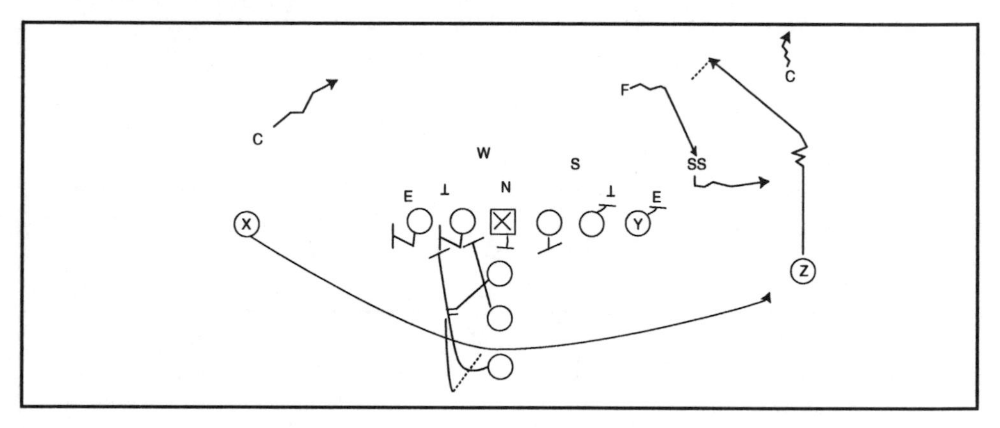

Figure 28.4—43 X reverse pass.

TRICK PLAY #5: 46 halfback pass. Almost every team has this play off the sweep. On this play, the tailback must act as if the play is a run before throwing (Refer to Figure 28.5).

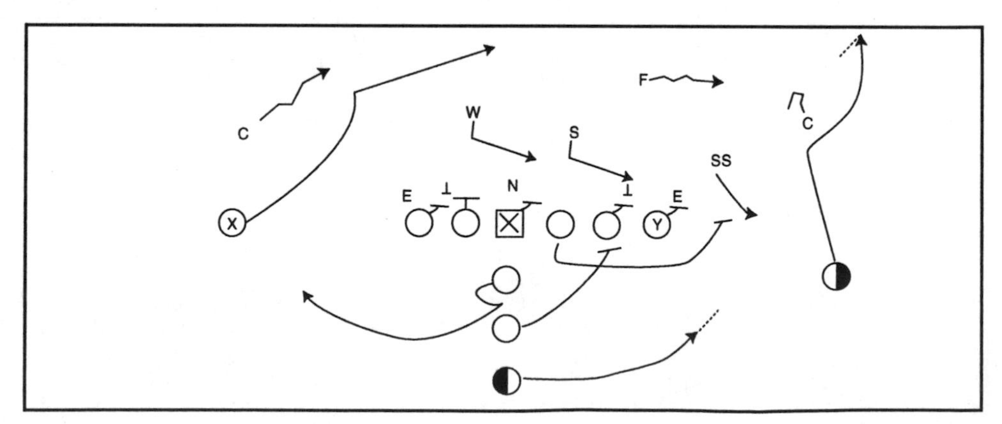

Figure 28.5—46 halfback pass.

TRICK PLAY #6: 46 tailback to quarterback. This play involves a fake sweep and then a throwback to the quarterback. You have the option of having the quickside guard and the quickside tackle could scoop two gaps and then lead the quarterback (Refer to Figure 28.6).

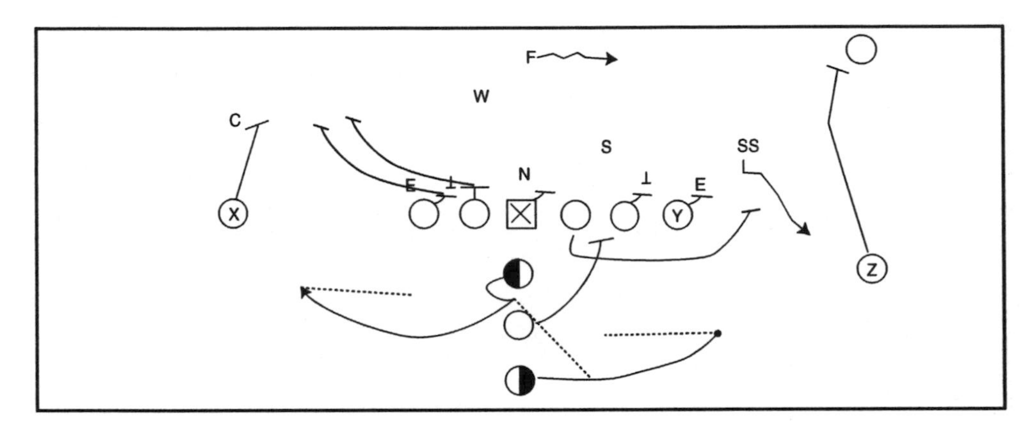

Figure 28.6—46 tailback to quarterback.

TRICK PLAY #7: Crocodile pass. This play involves a double pass back to the quarterback. This play helped the Seminoles to a victory over Michigan in 1991 (Refer to Figure 28.7).

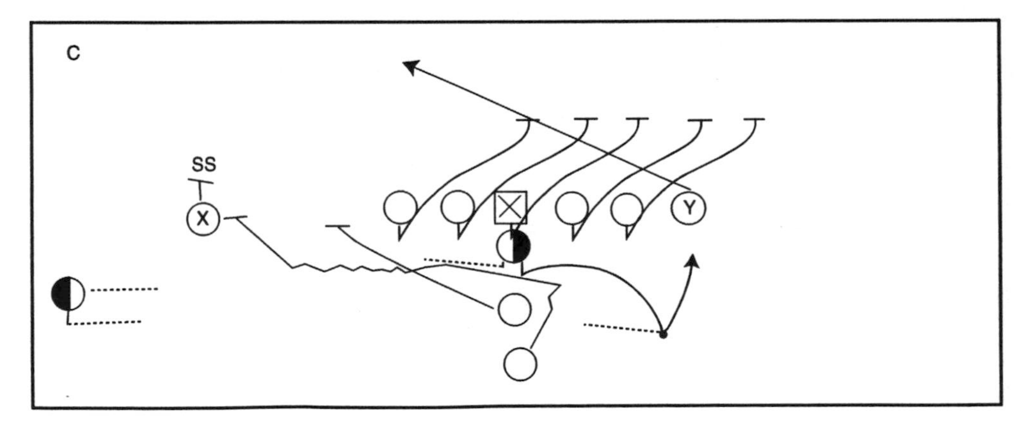

Figure 28.7—Crocodile Pass.

TRICK PLAY #8: 560 double pass. On this play, the empty back goes in motion. The quarterback then throws a pass out to him. The empty back then passes to Z on the post route. Other routes are optional. FSU ran this play against Florida in the Sugar Bowl in 1995 (Refer to Figure 28.8).

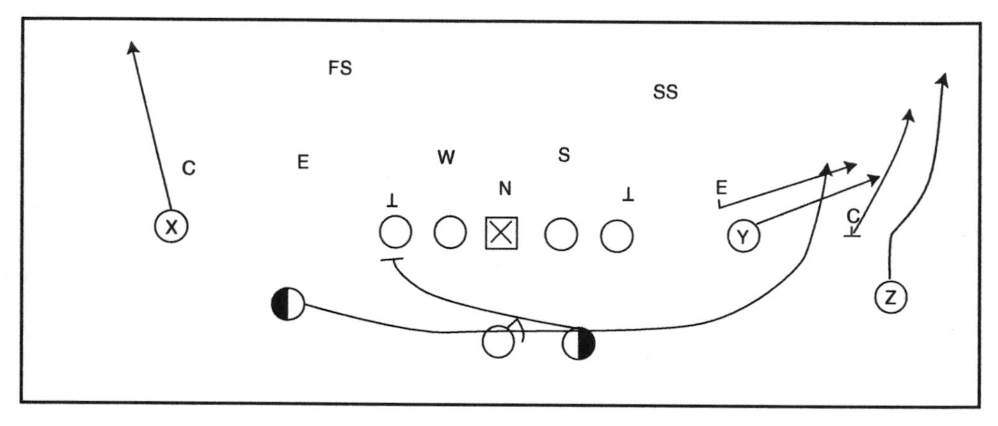

Figure 28.9—35 T reverse.

TRICK PLAY #9: 35 T reverse. On this play, you fake the sweep to the running back and then give the ball to the T receiver who is coming around. At the high school level, I recommend pulling the backside guard and letting the running back fill for him (Refer to Figure 28.9).

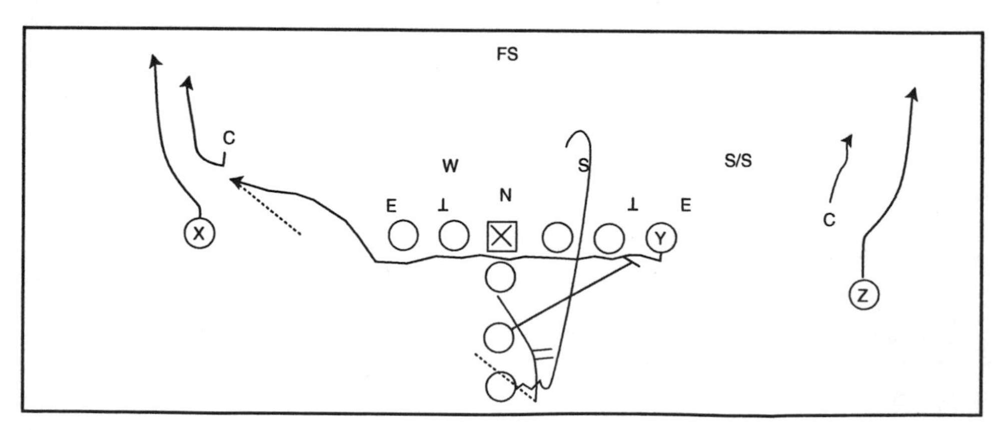

Figure 28.10—344 Y hide.

TRICK PLAY #10: 344 Y hide. On this play, you fake 44 with the running backs. 344 protection is utilized. Y sneaks along behind the line of scrimmage and then eases up the field into an open area for the quarterback to get him the ball. The quarterback should give a good look off to the strongside. FSU used this play during their first victory of the year over LSU in 1989 after an 0-2 start (Refer to Figure 28.10).

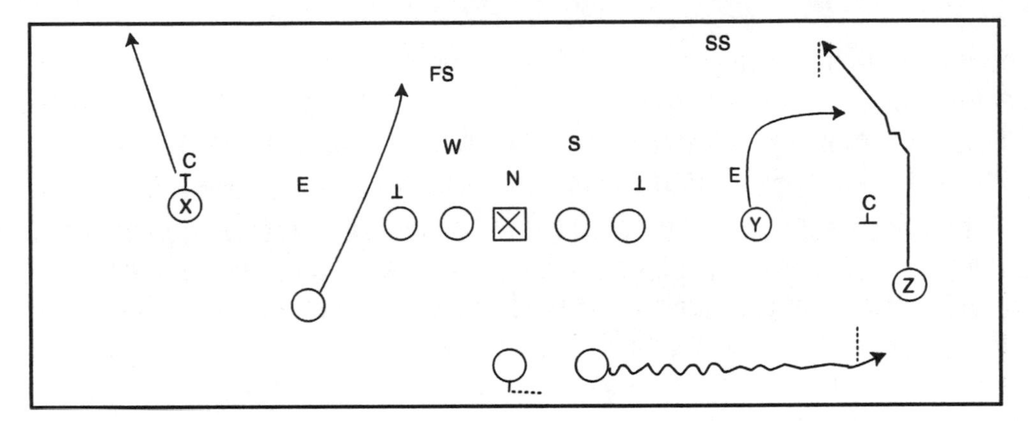

Figure 28.8—560 double pass.

You should also remember that there were several trick plays off of Smoke that were covered in Chapter 25 (shotgun rollout passes). When deciding on a trick play for your game plan, you should carefully consider those plays as well as the ten trick plays discussed in this chapter.

CHAPTER 29

Fast Break Offense: The No Huddle in High School

A no huddle offense can be employed in a number of ways, for example, some coaches only get it out and dust it off during the last few minutes of a ball game. In fact, many coaches feel the no huddle offense is simply too complicated to run at the high school level. Such an assumption, however, is not true.

The most important factor about the no huddle is effective communication. Just as in a normal offense, players have to know what the play is in the no huddle. Accordingly, a reliable system must be developed to get the play communicated to the players. If you are concerned with another team being able to pick up on your communication terms and signals, you should have two ways to call the most used plays in your offense.

COMMUNICATION FACTORS

The primary focus of this chapter is to take some of the offense that has been discussed in previous chapters and show you one way to use it with the no huddle. The initial step is to review the five elements that need to be communicated in the no huddle offense.

- Formation
- Run/pass play
- Protection or blocking scheme
- Route or dummy call
- Cadence (snap count)

Formation. This factor is easy to handle. If you are in the no huddle, you should always have the quarterback line up the offense on the strongside of the field and on the quickside to the boundary. If a sweep is run to the left, the quarterback should immediately yell, "Right, right, right," when the play ends. The offensive line eases toward the ball and rests as they stand at the LOS waiting for the next play call. The personnel you send in determines the formation you want. If you were in Base on the previous play, and you want to go to Panther on the next play, you say "Panther." In response, a wide receiver goes in for the tight end, all the while yelling for the Panther formation. On the other hand, what if you wanted to run the sprint draw. At that point, you would need to address the second factor—run/pass/play.

Run/pass play. The quarterback has already set the formation as right, and the wide receiver has come into the game yelling for Panther. You then signal to the quarterback to run the strong sprint draw, 44. You need to make a call that lets the offensive line know that the next play will be a run. You can call one of three colors, each with an "R" in them that indicate run to the offensive line. The color choices would be Red, Green, or Brown. The offensive line hears the quarterback yell "RED, RED." At this point, they now know the play is a run; they then listen to see which running play.

Protection or blocking scheme. For instance, if you have a name for 44 such as "Clyde", guess what the name would be for 43. That's right, "Bonnie". As a result, the call "Right Red Clyde" would mean that the formation is right, the personnel are in the Panther set, and the play is run 44. Since 43 and 44 are used frequently, you might want an additional way to call those plays. I recommend using a dummy number, such as 7, in front of the actual number of the running play. For example, if the quarterback says, "Right, Red, 744," the offensive line would know that the play is a run, and it is 44.

Route or dummy call. The fourth thing you must do is to let the receivers know if they should run a route or block. Most of the time they can't hear a call like "Red." As a result, you need some way to let them know if the route hand signal you give is live. There are lots of ways to do that. One way is to have the offensive tackles point their thumbs up in their stance if the play is a pass. If they don't, the receiver knows he should stalk block the corner. Obviously, however, your options for communicating with your receivers are only limited by your imagination.

Cadence (snap count). Handling the cadence is relatively easy. We always go on "1" from the I or on the center's go call from the gun, unless a "FREEZE" call is made. If the defense is anticipating the count, you might call "Blue Frosty," because blue is a cool color, and Frosty was made of snow. I often tell my players that snowmen don't really move, so they better not either if we call this play. In this regard, the play call means don't move.

You should keep in mind that all of the aforementioned points are just suggestions for you to employ or to help stimulate ideas of your own. While the no huddle is a really exciting offensive alignment, it takes thought and patience to come up with a solid scheme.

NO-HUDDLE PLAYS

Starting with runs and then covering passes, this section lists several of the plays that have been discussed to this point in the book and offers suggestions for employing them in a no-huddle scheme, using the previously cited examples.

Run Plays	Code Name	Dummy #
43	Bonnie	743
44	Clyde	744
45	Michael (Jordan's baseball #)	745
48	Jordan (opposite of Michael)	748
46	Tarzan (T for toss)	746
34	Ricky (Texas #34)	734
33	Williams (opposite)	733
31 trap	Mickey (catch a mouse with trap)	731

For play-action passes, you could call "Pink" or "Purple" for play-action protection. You should then call the name of the run play that is being faked. Hand signals should be given to the receivers on each play to communicate the route they should run. In the no huddle, the number, "3," is called on all play actions.

Play-action Plays	Run Fake	# call
344 package	Clyde	344 signal route!
344 Dash	Armour All (cleans the "Dash")	344 Dash
46 boot	Tom	346
48 boot	Jordan	348
344 screen	Tulsa	344 Tulsa

On drop-back passes with a 500 protection, you could make a "Daytona" call (i.e., 500). On drop-back passes with 400 protection, you could make a "TY" call (i.e., hit .400).

Pass Plays	Protection	Signal	# call
560 vert	Daytona	Thumbs up	560 vert
560 smash	Daytona	Fist in hand	560 smash
560 bench	Daytona	Hand on hip	560 Bench
561 Z cross	Daytona	Three fingers	561 Z
562 Y cross	Daytona	Two fingers	562 Y
561 X cross	Daytona	One finger	561 X
562 T cross	Daytona	Four fingers	562 T

For the backside routes in the no huddle, I recommend that you always use 561 with the outside crosses and 562 with the inside crosses. While you can adjust your system as you go, this is a good starting point. For screens in the no huddle, you should just call them by their play name, for example, Fort Worth or Gator.

This section has presented a basic outline of a few of the plays that FSU has used in their famed Fast Break Offense. Keep in mind that while you can certainly get more complicated than the approach that I suggested, the decision is yours to make. On the other hand, you might also be able to identify a more simple way to run the no huddle. When we first went to the no huddle, I employed many of the same ideas used by FSU and other no huddle teams, including the Buffalo Bills and the Cincinnati Bengals

WRISTBANDS

Some coaches have their entire team wear wristbands. I have tried that tactic myself. Frankly, the practice is very costly. (Note: At $10.50-$18.00 each, the practice can get expensive over the entire season). Furthermore, as a rule, wristbands are not very durable over an entire season of practice and games. If you reach a decision to have your players wear wristbands, keep in mind that they must wear them in practice to be successful with them in a game. At the minimum, one practical suggestion is to at least have your quarterback wear a wristband. That step would enable you to signal the play call to him.

CHAPTER 30

Florida State Punt Block: Creating Momentum for the Offense

Over time, all coaches periodically experience one of those games when their offense just seems sluggish. Occasionally, speeding up the tempo of the game with the no huddle can help. Other times, you need a big defensive play. However, perhaps the biggest momentum changer in football is a blocked punt. A blocked punt can breath fresh air into an offense, thereby giving it the positive momentum that it might be missing.

Florida State has one of the best punt-block schemes in America. While blocking punts is not really considered to be part of a team's offensive package, it can certainly help create offense—which is why the topic has been accorded its own chapter. The game-changing potential of a blocked punt is demonstrated by the fact that the Seminoles blocked 51 punts, caused 30 shanked punts, and trapped the punter eight times during one recent 8-year span. Those numbers have increased dramatically since then. In fact, during the 1983, 1985, and 1987 seasons, every kick that FSU blocked led to a score. In otherwords, blocked kicks can create offense and help win games.

The scheme for blocking punts is very simple. You overload, or outnumber, the punt protection by one man. You must be sure to disguise your punt rushing alignment by jumping around or scrambling right up until the snap. You should have 10 men at the LOS and have two of them drop back to play the fake. You should make sure to put pressure on all kicks, because you simply never know when a bad snap might occur—a point when we all wish we had the block on. If you don't get the block, your return man should run the kick back to the opposite side of the block set because the only wall that can be set will be away from the block set.

PRACTICING THE PUNT BLOCK

To practice the punt block, you should have your rushers alternate rushing a spot and have the punter pooch kick the ball as the rushers practice laying out to block the kick. To promote an aggressive layout, you should position several tackling dummies on the ground adjacent to the punter for the block man to land on after his lay-out in order to help build up his confidence. The FSU punt-block scheme is illustrated in Figure 30.1.

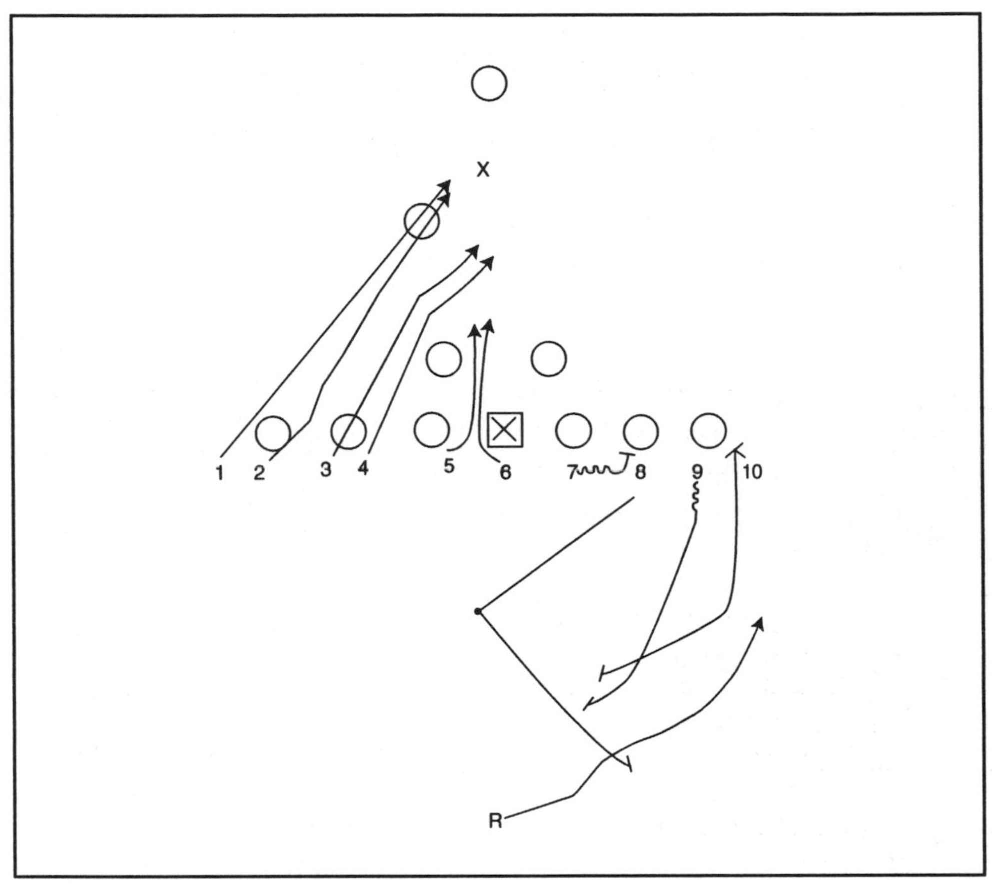

Figure 30.1—The FSU punt-block scheme.

FSU PUNT BLOCK BREAKDOWN

RUSHER #	
1, 2, 3, & 4	Rush to an assigned point with low pads.
3, 4, 5, & 6	Come underneath your personal punt protector blocker to clear for 1 and 2.
6	Move quickly around the center, accelerating through the gap.
7-	Jump from a 2-technique to a 4-technique when 8 and 9 drop.
8 & 9	Pull out to 8-12 yards deep, playing the fake; become a blocker once the ball is kicked.
10-	Jam the end, make sure of the kick, force the end inside; form a wall with 8 and 9.
Return man	Return the kick to the side opposite of the block set.

EPILOGUE

I hope that you have found this book to be informative. The years I have spent studying film after film on FSU's offense, as well as running it, have been one of my greatest joys. Keep in mind that I am not suggesting that every coach should install the entire FSU style of offense and scrap what they have done for years. Because there are many concepts within the offense that can be adapted to everything from the Wing-T to a split back veer offense, I hope that you can find something in the different aspects of the FSU offense to supplement your offensive package.

I also hope that those of you who implement all or parts of the FSU offense will look at your own personnel and utilize the plays that best fit your players' abilities. FSU's offense is an offense that can be modified in many ways. I have even seen teams who were copying the FSU shotgun offense successfully add an option from the shotgun. Accordingly, you shouldn't be afraid to tinker with your own ideas within the basis of the FSU-style offense. You might identify something that can really be effective.

Without question, the FSU offense is a product of Bobby Bowden. The man has proven conclusively that an old-school offense can evolve without giving up its basic foundation. Too many coaches either go through offenses that are quick fixes or hold on to an offense without adjusting until it has cost them a job. Not Coach Bowden. I applaud Coach Bowden and his staff for adjusting FSU's offense, without selling out on the basics of the offense.

While the time capsule on Coach Bowden's career will no doubt close up in a few years, his legacy and his offense will continue for many years. Coaches, like his sons and his present offensive coordinator at FSU, will carry it on. I hope that by reading this book, some of you can and will help carry it on as well.

It is important to note that this book has been published with Coach Bowden's blessing. As such, myself included, no coach or fan can ever hear the "WAR CHANT" and not think of what he has done for both FSU and the game of football. While I will continue to spend my coaching career studying films and adjusting the offense as I see necessary, I will always employ a foundation built from what I learned from the FSU system.

Someone once said "The more things change, the more things stay the same." That certainly is true about football. We have to make adjustments to different trends, but it's the same factor—the love of the game—that brings players and coaches together to play this exceptional sport called football.

ABOUT THE AUTHOR

Wayne Wilkes has been coaching high school football in Alabama for the last eight seasons. During that time he has served as either a head coach or offensive coordinator and quarterback coach each season. He considers himself to be a serious student of the game, spending tremendous hours at coaching clinics, reading football books, and watching game films from both the high school and college level.

During his coaching career, he has turned out All-State quarterbacks, receivers, running backs, and a tight end on the offensive side of the football, and a cornerback on the defensive side of the ball. He is highly respected for his knowledge of the passing game and innovative offensive ideas. He has coached teams that averaged over 30 points per game, rushed for over 3,000 yards, passed for over 2,500 yards, and won area championships at schools that had struggled in the past. Often, his offenses will attack with the no-huddle offense.

He and his wife, Gena, who serves as the "head coach" of the Wilkes house during football season, have two sons, Cory and Blake, and a daughter, Haley. Coach Wilkes enjoys spending as much of his spare time as possible being "Dad" to his family at the Wilkes home in Jasper, Alabama.